Dedicated to the many who perish so that a
few may be rich.

To the forty-seven victims from Lac-Mégantic,
its twenty-seven orphans, and those who were
too devastated to survive.

We're resilient, not halfwits.

—ROBERT BELLEFLEUR
resident of Lac-Mégantic

FOREWORD

ON JULY 1, 2013, CANADIAN PACIFIC RAILWAY SUBMITTED AN invoice for $496,527 to World Fuel Services Corp. for the conveyance of 14.8 million pounds of shale oil from New Town, North Dakota, to the Irving Oil Refinery in Saint John, New Brunswick. World Fuel was acting as a wholesaler, buying and reselling oil extracted by several producers. This invoice, which is reproduced on page 129 of this book, shows that a long train would travel first on a CP line and then on a track owned by Montreal, Maine and Atlantic Railway (MMA). The MMA portion of the route offered a substantial financial advantage, for it led directly from Montréal to Saint John. But it also had the disadvantage of being the riskiest way.

Anne-Marie Saint-Cerny reminds us that MMA had, at the time, the worst accident record in North America, "a fact known to all the carriers (including CP, obviously) and to all the departments and agencies responsible for transportation safety in Canada and the United States." The reputation of the MMA's president, Edward Burkhardt, preceded him. On March 4, 1996, when Burkhardt was president of the Wisconsin Central railway, one of their trains hauling liquefied crude oil and propane ran down the gradient leading to the town centre of Weyauwega, Wisconsin. The train derailed on a broken, neglected section of track, and its tank cars piled up and caught fire. The two thousand inhabitants of the town were evacuated under a state of emergency. It took sixteen days to bring the fire under control. The ensuing reports showed that, for greater efficiency, the company was operating its trains with a single crew member and had been doing so without informing the Federal Railroad Administration (FRA), the official U.S. regulatory body.

In June 2012, MMA began using unit trains* to transport crude oil from Montréal to Saint John. A month later, without informing

---

* A unit train carries a single type of cargo from its point of departure to its destination, avoiding delays for unloading or adding cars along the way.

Transport Canada, MMA began to run its trains with a one-person crew. It failed to fulfill its undertaking to improve the condition of its track so that its trains could be allowed to travel faster. It failed to evaluate the risk of parking its trains unattended at the top of a significant grade on the main line between Nantes and Lac-Mégantic in the Estrie region of Québec, also known as the Eastern Townships. Economizing on safety and working conditions allowed MMA to offer competitive rates for the transportation of crude oil coming from the shale formations of Bakken, North Dakota.

MMA's aged railway track, which had once belonged to CP but which the latter had sold, was originally constructed to transport inert materials such as lumber. (There is every reason to think that Burkhardt had a contractual agreement with CP to transport goods along its old stretch of track, but this is one of the many pieces of information journalists have not yet been able to obtain.) Much more sensible options were available for the transportation of extremely volatile petroleum. From Montréal, it would have been possible to entrust the train to Canadian National (CN), which reaches Saint John by way of the Bas-Saint-Laurent region. CN was far from having an impeccable safety record, but its locomotives and track were much better maintained than MMA's, and its trains were not operated by one-person crews. But this route would have been longer and more expensive. Furthermore, CP might not have liked giving up part of its transportation contract to its major competitor.

A company is not relieved of its responsibility when it entrusts part of its work to a subcontractor. Let us imagine that a large company is awarded a contract worth $100 million for the construction of a bridge. It pockets a handsome profit by entrusting the work to a small subcontractor with a poor reputation, which does the work for $50 million. One year after completion, the bridge collapses, causing ten deaths; the larger company, which subcontracted the work, remains responsible for it. The Québec Civil Code is perfectly clear about this: "Every person has a duty to abide by the rules of conduct ... so as not to cause injury to another," and is also bound to "make reparation for injury caused to another by the act *or fault of another person* or by the act of things in [their] custody" (section 1457, my emphasis). It continues: "Every person has a duty to honour [their] contractual

undertakings; neither he nor the other party may in such a case avoid the rules governing contractual liability by opting for rules that would be more favourable to them" (section 1458).

The federal Railway Safety Act, though very accommodating, makes it clear from the outset that one of its objectives is to "recognize the responsibility of companies to demonstrate, by using safety management systems and other means at their disposal, that they continuously manage risks related to safety matters" (section 3c). The law further stipulates that "where a corporation commits an offence under this Act, any officer, director, or agent of the corporation who directed, authorized, assented to, acquiesced in *or participated* in the commission of the offence is a party to and guilty of the offence, and is liable on conviction to the punishment provided for the offence, whether or not the corporation has been prosecuted or convicted" (section 43, my emphasis). In 2003, the Canadian government amended the Criminal Code to provide a more precise definition of the legal responsibility of organizations. Section 217.1 of the Code added the words: "Every one who undertakes, or has the authority, to direct how another person does work or performs a task is under a legal duty to take reasonable steps to prevent bodily harm to that person, or any other person, arising from that work or task." In short, the responsibility for negligence does not reside exclusively with those who actually perform the work.

The question therefore arises: Who made the subcontract with MMA? And who was therefore answerable for the disaster of a train whose runaway trip resulted in the deaths of forty-seven individuals on July 6, 2013? As unbelievable as it may seem, several years after the tragedy we still do not know. Was the subcontract granted by CP, World Fuel, Irving Oil, or by the three companies jointly? We simply don't know. The Transportation Safety Board's report is silent on the subject.

We do not know because no public inquiry has been held into this disaster, one of the worst railway accidents in Canadian history. And that, too, is difficult to believe.

Since 1980 there have been Royal Commissions and Commissions of Inquiry to investigate a host of files involving war criminals, the use of performance-enhancing drugs, the pharmaceutical industry, the failure

of the Canadian Commercial Bank, unemployment insurance, the *Ocean Ranger* disaster, Canadian troops' treatment of prisoners in Afghanistan, the future of daily newspapers, the tainted blood scandal, the deployment of Canadian forces in Somalia, the financing of political parties, Air India Flight 182, the seal hunt, the crash of a plane near Dryden, Ontario, transactions between Karlheinz Schreiber and Brian Mulroney, allegations concerning Sinclair M. Stevens, the sponsorship scandal, and so on. Not long ago, one was held to investigate the decline of sockeye salmon in the Fraser River. In 1986 a commission of inquiry held forty-eight days of public hearings on a train accident responsible for twenty-three fatalities in Hinton, Alberta. A few years earlier, another commission of inquiry investigated the derailment of a train hauling hazardous goods which caused the evacuation of inhabitants of Mississauga, in Ontario, but did not cause any fatalities.

So what about the disaster in Lac-Mégantic? Nothing. Not even an inquest by the public coroner. To repeat: forty-seven fatalities. A town centre devastated. Costs amounting to $1 billion. Irreversible environmental damage. Yet trains loaded with volatile petroleum continue to criss-cross Québec, passing through numerous towns on the way. On July 6, 2013, the night was lit up by balls of fire hurled out by the explosion. One might have thought that they would have opened our eyes. But when day dawned, the smoke had obscured the skies. The government was busy hiding the truth under a thick layer of ash.

Anne-Marie Saint-Cerny pulled on her boots, took out her notebook, and spent five long years searching through that ash. Having myself searched through much less tragic ashes, first as a journalist for *La Presse*, then at the Charbonneau Commission inquiring into the awarding of contracts in the construction industry, I am well aware how many obstacles are strewn in the path of "muckrakers" – and the sort of persistence their quests require.

In this book, Saint-Cerny returns to the origins of the tragedy, examining especially the responsibility of the avaricious, immoral capitalists who saw the fortunes that could be made by conveying highly explosive shale oil – crooks with enough power to induce the Canadian government to deregulate indiscriminately.

This is not the first time that the railway industry has made the weight of its political influence felt. The industry has exerted considerable sway

over the Canadian government ever since the early days of Confederation. It has been too readily forgotten that CP was at the centre of the country's first great scandal. In 1873, Sir John A. Macdonald's Conservative government was accused of accepting funding from Hugh Allan, the head of CP Rail, in return for the contract to build a railway all the way to British Columbia. The government had to resign, and a commission of inquiry was established. The disclosure of a telegram from Macdonald to Allan's legal adviser provoked quite a scandal: "I must have another ten thousand; will be the last time of calling; do not fail me; answer today." CP's owners had provided substantial funding to other eminent politicians, such as Premier George-Étienne Cartier – an exploit which was not included on the plinth of his huge statue at the entrance to Mont-Royal Park in Montréal.

Almost one hundred and fifty years later it may well be thought that the railway industry lobby played a part not only in manufacturing the bombs that terrorized and wounded the population of Lac-Mégantic, but also in the government's incomprehensible refusal to initiate a public commission of inquiry.

The investigation conducted by the Transportation Safety Board (TSB) did identify numerous causes of the accident. But the TSB failed to fully cast a light on the underlying causes of the tragedy. Moreover, its report let everyone off the hook. By doing so, it left it possible for the railway and petroleum industries and the government to continue denying any responsibility. When Wendy Tadros, the chair of the TSB, presented the Board's report to the press, she allowed herself to apportion blame more severely than her own report had done, probably because it was her final public appearance before leaving the Board and so she had no need to fear dismissal, as had happened to other senior public servants in similar circumstances. "Who was the guardian of public safety?" asked Tadros. "That is the role of government. To provide checks and balances – oversight. And yet this booming industry, where unit trains were shipping more and more oil across Canada and across the border, ran largely unchecked."*

---

*   Andy Blatchford, "Lac-Megantic: TSB Blames Railway for Safety Issues, Ottawa for Poor Oversight," CP24, August 19, 2014, www.cp24.com/news/lac -megantic-tsb-blames-railway-for-safety-issues-ottawa-for-poor-oversight -1.1965653.

Once more: thousands of potential bombs began to criss-cross Canada, travelling through towns and villages without any genuine oversight by the Canadian government, which was too busy making life easier for the railway and petroleum lobbies. Was it right that only the driver of the locomotive and two other MMA employees ended in the dock? The day after their acquittal, the Québec National Assembly unanimously adopted a resolution requesting the federal government to establish a Commission of Inquiry. Marc Garneau, the federal minister of transport, rejected it out of hand, saying that it would serve no useful purpose. Yet an independent inquiry is essential to bring all the information into the public arena and oblige those ultimately responsible for the tragedy to answer for their actions. It is scandalous to see such a crime – for a major crime was indeed committed – go unpunished. Without the pressure that a commission of inquiry would bring to bear, Transport Canada has not even been obliged to follow all the recommendations of the Transportation Safety Board.

"As *ad hoc* bodies, commissions of inquiry are free of many of the institutional impediments which at times constrain the operation of the various branches of government," noted the Supreme Court of Canada in its judgment on the Commission of Inquiry into the Tainted Blood Scandal. "One of the primary functions of public inquiries is fact-finding," added the Court. "A public inquiry before an impartial and independent commissioner which investigates the cause of tragedy and makes recommendations for change can help to prevent a recurrence of such tragedies in the future, and to restore public confidence in the industry or process being reviewed."

Readers of this book will lose whatever confidence they may still have in government's ability to ensure the safety of rail transportation. This loss of confidence should not lead to cynicism, but rather to action and mobilization. We must demand accountability. It is everyone's duty.

—ANDRÉ NOËL
May 2018

PROLOGUE

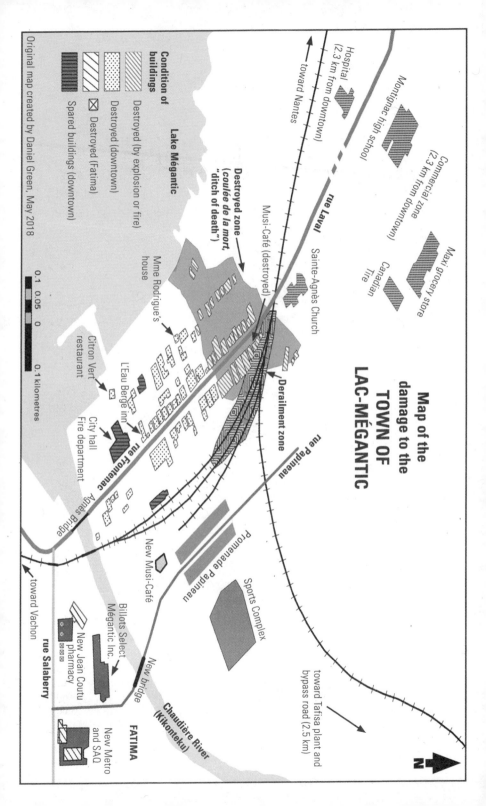

Map of the damage to the TOWN OF LAC-MÉGANTIC

N

Lake Mégantic

Condition of buildings

- Destroyed (by explosion or fire)
- Destroyed (downtown)
- Destroyed (Fatima)
- Spared buildings (downtown)

Original map created by Daniel Green, May 2018

0.1 0.05 0
0.1 kilometres

toward Nantes

Hospital (2.3 km from downtown)

Montignac high school

Commercial zone (2.3 km from downtown)

Maxi grocery store

Canadian Tire

rue Laval

Sainte-Agnès Church

Musi-Café (destroyed)

Destroyed zone (*coulée de la mort*, "ditch of death")

Mme Rodrigue's house

Citron Vert restaurant

L'Eau Berge Inn

City hall

Fire department

rue Frontenac

Agnès Bridge

Deraillment zone

rue Papineau

New Musi-Café

Promenade Papineau

Sports Complex

toward Vachon

rue Salaberry

Billots Select Mégantic Inc.

New bridge

New Jean Coutu pharmacy

New Metro and SAQ

FATIMA

Chaudière River (Kikonteku)

toward Tafisa plant and bypass road (2.5 km)

JULY 6, 2013, 1:14 A.M. A RUNAWAY TRAIN PULLING SEVENTY- two tank cars of petroleum – each of them a virtual bomb – demolished the town centre of Lac-Mégantic. Forty-seven victims perished on the spot, consumed by fire and terror.

Three employees, including the train's engineer, would be accused of criminal negligence by the justice system. Five years later, a jury of twelve men and women brought down its verdict: "Not guilty."

Was the jury mistaken? Or had it simply concluded that the three accused were not the real criminals? Who had allowed a single-person crew to operate a train hauling $8 million worth of volatile petroleum through a mountainous area? Who were the true criminals in this tragedy? What were its causes?

Troubling questions also remain about the aftermath of the disaster. Who would take control of the cleanup of the devastated site? Who would rebuild the destroyed town centre? And for whose benefit? Who would pay for it all?

In the devastated area where there had once been a lively, bustling main street, the people of Mégantic,* received no answers to these questions – or else they did not believe the answers they got. And in Mégantic, like elsewhere, everyone wondered if such a tragedy could reoccur.

One thing is certain: at the time of writing, in Mégantic, trains carrying gas and petroleum products still travel through. "I have a business to operate. I transport what is profitable. That's what I'm

---

* The town's official name is "Lac-Mégantic" (after the nearby lake whose name comes from a lost Abenaki word meaning "at the salmon trout camp"). For the sake of simplicity and to reflect common usage, it will often be referred to simply as "Mégantic," with no distinction implied. The town occupies land covered by the Nionwentsïo (1670 Murray Treaty), and is the Traditional Territory of the Abenaki, Huron-Wendat, Nanrantsouak, and part of the Wabanaki Confederacy.

paid to do," says John Giles, the new CEO of Central Maine Quebec Railroad (CMQR),[1] which took over from the ill-famed MMA.*

The real causes of the tragedy remain intact. They are discussed and decided in the plush offices of ministers and lobbyists. Only real answers can provide protection – but to do so they must be known.

This is the story of a tragedy waiting to happen.

✕ ✕ ✕

In the years preceding the disaster in Mégantic, a plethora of reports on railway safety were published – a long list of studies, inquiries, accusations, and admonitions dating back over a decade. Each of these reports contained a warning for elected representatives and senior public servants about the dangers represented by trains, crude petroleum, CP, MMA, etc.

The reports dealing with the Mégantic disaster itself focused on negligence involving the brakes, tracks, locomotives, wagons, public policy, Safety Management Systems (SMS), existing laws, and regulations. The Transportation Safety Board, whose final report was altered by some as yet unidentified authorities, listed eighteen causes of the accident.

Despite all this, there remains a feeling of being left in the dark. Railway tracks, brakes, and regulations don't exist independently. Behind them stand people of flesh and blood who have developed laws and security measures which they have enacted and enforced. Others own and manage the mammoths of steel and the bombs that travel along the railway tracks.

In the hours following the tragedy, every politician imaginable visited – and revisited – Mégantic. Each promised in turn a "series of measures" to deal with the "identifiable causes" and to make railway safety a "higher priority." Yet at the time of writing, it is still permissible to park a train unattended on a main line, on a gradient,

---

* Following the disaster in Mégantic, MMA was placed under bankruptcy protection before being taken over by CMQR (which was sold to Chinese investors in 2017). According to recent reports, CMQR is currently in the process of being bought by CP.

where no derail device exists – even though these two factors were recognized by the TSB report as crucial factors in the disaster.

In the spring of 2018, the necessary bypass line around Mégantic was finally announced by the politicians – an announcement which, while it solved the problem of the devastated little town, did nothing to resolve the issue of railway safety in general.

✕ ✕ ✕

> It's in the hyena's nature to try to eat domestic animals, and however much the world may change it will never become vegetarian or give up its hyena nature to allow the herders to relax. In a capitalist system, companies are hyenas too – mechanisms with only one purpose: making money. To do so, they work openly to influence and corrupt those who can enrich them further.[2]
>
> —Boucar Diouf

Mégantic is the perfect story of modern capitalism, almost caricatural in its depiction of distant predators, Wall Street investors, cowboy producers of cheap, dirty Dakota crude, and the headquarters of huge international conglomerates. What those people did was facilitated and enabled by the very people who are responsible for our safety, the elected representatives who have succeeded one another at the Ministry of Transport.

For the people of Mégantic, the disaster did not end with the initial impact on July 6, 2013.

This was because the town's population subsequently fell into the hands of various Québec developers, of some of the most influential financial interests in the province, as well as of various predators of lesser stature but whose influence on the town's elected representatives – also in a state of shock – would undermine the confidence and resistance of the townspeople, their faith in a possible rebirth. The massive expropriations and demolitions which took place in 2014 and 2015 provide a troubling example of the workings of the economist Milton Friedman's "shock doctrine," denounced by Naomi Klein in her book of that name.[3] Here again we find a perfect story of capitalism.

In this saga, one thing is as certain and predictable as a Hollywood screenplay: 132 days after the tragedy, trains were running through the town centre again, hauling explosive tank cars, rending the night – and the sleep of the terrified inhabitants of the disaster-stricken town.

✕ ✕ ✕

I arrived in Mégantic five days after Night Zero. Daniel Green* and I noticed a few suspicious disparities between the official data supplied by the authorities and the empirical information that could sometimes be discovered by a simple internet search. It was therefore decided to take samples of the contamination in order to establish some reliable facts that might be of use to the victims of the disaster.

Before I had spent barely an hour in Mégantic, I realized that I would not abandon the town before coming to understand the true causes of its unimaginable tragedy – before I'd probed as deeply as I could to discover which mechanisms and failures were to blame.

I did not understand this initially, but my quest became clearer as my investigation progressed: the victims of the Mégantic disaster stood for all the victims of pollution for whom I had never been able to do anything. Deaths caused by asbestos, for example, which are still covered up and denied by the authorities; victims of mining disasters; the people of Shannon, Québec, contaminated with TCE (trichlorethylene) by National Defence and the private interests that have now become SNC-Lavalin, also left unacknowledged by the authorities and the justice system.

All these deaths, including those in Mégantic, share the same narrative: a tale of predators whose activities are facilitated and encouraged by our own elected representatives, those to whom we have entrusted the public good but who abdicate that responsibility for the benefit of the powerful. Such politicians (and, sometimes, senior public servants) betray us by pandering to the interests of the wealthy with their almost unlimited resources, leaving it entirely up to victims and ordinary citizens, who often lack the necessary resources, to prove and denounce enduring abuses.

---

* Daniel is a toxicology expert with the Société pour vaincre la pollution (SVP), of which I am also a member.

In this context, the story of Mégantic possesses a tragic but invaluable advantage. While the deaths due to asbestos and those that occurred in Shannon continued to be systematically overlooked by the justice system, and sometimes even by those responsible for public health, it is impossible to cover up the forty-seven deaths that occurred in Mégantic. They remain the indelible proof of a system that serves the interests of big money and the powerful – and disregards our safety in doing so.

I believe that – thanks to the activism of those I have met in Mégantic over recent years, and to all those fighting with admirable persistence in other places – the truth about Mégantic will eventually emerge. This is, I hope, a truth that will serve to rectify the deficiencies of the Canadian railway system, call our elected representatives to account, and exert pressure on the leadership and shareholders of companies, a truth that will make the restoration of safety an absolute priority, this time in a tangible way, and a truth that will shake up a system which too often serves people poorly. For transparency – truth placed in the hands of citizens – is a powerful weapon. We just need to use it – and allow nothing to pass.

PRESS RELEASE

Train Derailment – Cars of Crude in Flames

Québec City, July 6, 2013 – The regional office of the environmental control centre for Estrie and Montérégie has announced the derailment of a goods train close to the downtown area of Lac-Mégantic. A fire has broken out among the tank cars containing crude oil. The TAGA [Trace Atmospheric Gas Analyzer] mobile laboratory of the ministry has been alerted to intervene if required.

Urgence-Environnement has been informed of this event and an emergency responder has been dispatched to the location.

The necessary measures to ensure the safety of the population and protection of the environment have been taken by the Ministère du Développement durable, de l'Environnement, de la Faune et des Parcs and its partners.[4]

× × ×

At approximately 1:14 a.m., the aforesaid train derailed at the rue Frontenac road crossing in Lac-Mégantic and crashed into the downtown core and business centre of the town, incinerating and killing nearly fifty (50) people.

—Fourth amended motion authorizing a
class action suit, February 12, 2014[5]

NIGHT ZERO

OF COURSE, WE NEVER KNOW IN ADVANCE THAT OUR LIFE IS going to be permanently disrupted, nor when the moment will suddenly arrive when it becomes impossible to restore things to the way they were before. The insignificant details that precede this flashpoint seem so banal that we see them, yet fail to pay attention to them. We tell ourselves later that even so, there had been signs from time to time. But really we noticed nothing, or almost nothing.

That evening, it was something about his taxi's windshield that set André Turcotte to wondering.

Wednesday, June 5, 2013, 11:30 p.m.
One Hundred and Three Minutes before Impact

Tom Harding's stocky figure emerges from the darkness and is caught in the taxi's headlights. The engineer's silhouette is indistinct through the windshield, which is covered with droplets, as if a heavy November drizzle is falling on the high plateau between Nantes and Mégantic. Yet this is the first Friday of agreeably warm, almost sticky, weather, when at last it is becoming possible to hope that summer has arrived. From his taxi stand in Mégantic's town centre, Turcotte can see people strolling along the main street, almost lethargic in the warm air, and disappearing into the bar called L'Enjeu or the little inn named L'Eau Berge,* but mostly lingering on the terrace of the Musi-Café.

For Turcotte it is not unusual to be called out to a country road at midnight in order to pick up a train engineer. There is no address for these spots, no street corners like there are in town. When the railway company's controller calls him from Farnham, Turcotte sets out along Route 161 and peers into the night to spot the lead locomotive, the head of a snake that stretches along the curving main line which for

---

* The name was a pun on the French word *auberge*, "inn," combining the words *eau*, "water," and *berge*, "bank, shore."

the past ten years has been owned by the Montreal, Maine and Atlantic Railway – MMA for short. Its track has been part of the landscape for more than 150 years; people know it well, and for a long time it was a friend, conveying lumber across the nearby Canada–U.S. border. The train provided work for everyone in Mégantic who worked in the sawmills or in the particleboard factory.

It is true, however, that some people in the town, especially the fire brigade, have begun to feel uneasy about the railway. Over the past year the trains have been getting longer and heavier. There is something new: instead of lumber, the four or five locomotives heading the new trains are hauling interminable lines of black tank cars filled with crude oil – a rather lugubrious sight when the wagons emerge from the early morning mist that sometimes hangs over Mégantic, especially when their shrill sirens wail at every crossing. And since there are twelve such crossings, the train is far from passing unnoticed before it reaches the far side of the little town.

As a taxi driver, Turcotte is familiar with the crews of the MMA trains, whether they are coming from Farnham or Maine. At night, he picks up the crew from Maine at Vachon, eight kilometres east of Mégantic, where they park their trains, returning from the United States mostly empty. These are "the Americans," as folk call them in Mégantic. The others, like Harding this evening, come from the west, by way of Montréal and Sherbrooke, hauling tank cars filled to the brim. They leave their trains at Nantes, about thirteen kilometres northwest of Mégantic. The trains parked at either Vachon or Nantes leave their engines running all night on the high plateaus surrounding Mégantic: trains abandoned to fate, unattended, stationed on either side of the depression at the bottom of which the little town nestles – a perfect target, as people will discover only too late.

In fact, for the past two years or so the trains have not been carrying quite as many crew members as usual. Now there is only a single-person crew on MMA trains to operate their four or five locomotives and the eighty to one hundred cars they are hauling. Since MMA introduced "single-person train operation," the locomotive engineer has borne sole responsibility for operating their train, checking the track and the level crossings, applying the handbrakes, and shunting – in short, everything. Always alone, engineers must

perform the handbrake effectiveness test for the night – meaning that they must put the train in gear to make sure that nothing can or will move until the next day. After all, a train like this evening's weighs over ten thousand tons and is more than a kilometre and a half long, as would be learned two years later, when official reports about the tragedy begin to appear. It is a train much heavier than the company (officially) allows to travel on this track, which is in very poor condition. But the company's American bosses are headquartered far away and can do whatever they please.

So the trains left at Nantes spend the night on the main line, engines running, ready to get going again first thing the next morning, when "the American" takes over the controls for the trip through Maine. In fact, there is a parallel subsidiary track just alongside the main line which should be used to park unattended trains, especially ones whose engines are left running. Furthermore, this second line is equipped with a derail device which would have made a runaway train immediately pitch into the trees instead of speeding down the steep grade leading down to Mégantic. This would clearly have been a wise precaution, and it is precisely the reason why, many years ago, the railway's owners at the time installed the secondary track. After all, the gradient leading down to Mégantic is one of the steepest in any inhabited area in North America. But the good sense originally responsible for its construction was abandoned when MMA arrived on the scene. And, for as long as people can remember, the secondary track has never been used to park unattended trains. Instead, it is always blocked, being used as a shunting track and parking place for train cars left standing idle. The outlines of the containers parked there, motionless and covered in graffiti, stand out against the dark forest, giving it a post-industrial look. The useless secondary track also forms part of the usual scene, so much so that nobody notices it, or even thinks about it very much anymore.

11:35 p.m. Ninety-Eight Minutes before Impact

Harding takes a while to emerge from the cabin. Turcotte can see him speaking on his phone, silhouetted against the only patch of light that penetrates the darkness. It is a long conversation, longer than usual

when the men are simply informing the control centre in Farnham that the train is parked and that they are setting off for their hotel, in Mégantic.

Harding is talking calmly – he always gives the impression of being in control – but he seems to be explaining something, for he occasionally raises an arm toward the locomotive's exhaust, as if the person at the other end can see him. Finally he climbs down from the cabin, turns around a last time to ensure that he has removed the reverser (used to restart the train quickly) and places it on the driver's seat along with the train's paperwork, in plain view for the American locomotive engineer who will take over the train.

Harding closes the door behind him. MMA's standards dictate that the door should never be locked, even if the lead locomotive is left running all night. Leaving the locomotive running saves money for the company because U.S. regulations requires an air brake test if the engine has been turned off for four hours or longer. (Canadian regulations are more lax: we allow a locomotive to be turned off for twenty-four hours before the brakes must be retested.)

From time to time, like a pulse, the headlights of a car driven fast along Route 161 sweep the dark tank cars, the unusual black-and-white smoke escaping from the exhaust of the lead locomotive, and the gleaming equipment number on its side, identifying it as locomotive MMA 5017.

Turcotte, a former policeman, is good at noticing anomalies and likes to know their explanation. He wants to ask the engineer about that strange smoke. But Harding, whom he knows, is not usually very talkative. Except this evening, when Turcotte senses that something is troubling him.

Polite, methodical, a well-respected engine driver from a railway family, Harding is a rather reserved individual. He is not the sort you would find at the bar of L'Eau Berge in the evening, complaining as the other engine drivers do about MMA, which is cutting back on everything: wages, working conditions, the upkeep of the tracks and the rolling stock, and, above all, complaining about single-person crews, which, according to the drivers, are outright dangerous – and utterly exhausting.

When Harding gets into the taxi, a strong smell fills the vehicle.

Harding, as Turcotte recognizes, is spattered by droplets of oil. And as he drives off, the taxi driver needs to use his wipers because of all the oil on the windscreen. Turcotte picks up on this highly unusual detail.

✕ ✕ ✕

André Turcotte's Statement to the Sûreté du Québec Twenty-Four Hours after the Disaster

Conversation in the taxi:

TURCOTTE: What's that smoke?

HARDING: An engine wasn't working properly. One of the locomotives was labouring on the way. I've been telling the company about it all the way from Farnham, but they told me to carry on to Nantes just the same. This evening the company told me to leave it running and it'll stop when the oil gets low.

TURCOTTE: And what about the environment in all that?

HARDING: The boss in Farnham is family with the environmental people and they never have the locomotives checked.

TURCOTTE: (pause)

HARDING: I'd really like to call the American side. They're stricter, and maybe they'll tell me to shut down the engine.

11:38 p.m. Ninety-Five Minutes before Impact

Along the dark country road, the taxi meets a car coming in the other direction. Barely two minutes later its driver, who remains anonymous, makes the first official phone call of the disaster.

911: What's your emergency?

MOTORIST: I'm between Nantes and Lac-Mégantic, and there's a train on fire.

911: A train? Is it still moving?

M: Yes, a train. No, the train's parked but the engine's still running. The flames are reaching the top, so it's pretty scary.

911: Do you know what it's carrying?

M: I dunno, it looks like tank cars behind.

911: Something dangerous?

M: I've no idea. It's dark but there are tank cars behind. No way am I getting any closer.

At the moment the call is made, the taxi is still less than three kilometres from the locomotive. If its two occupants had simply turned their heads, they could have seen the glow of the flames in the darkness. Fifteen minutes later, Harding, learning about the fire, will ask permission to go back and check his train. Permission will be refused. "There's no need," is the answer he gets from Richard Labrie, the rail traffic controller – an answer that will turn his life upside down.

✕ ✕ ✕

The 911 call ends. Turcotte's taxi, carrying Harding, crosses the railway line between Nantes and Mégantic and navigates the roundabout halfway up the hill before turning onto Mégantic's main street, which draws a straight line through the entire town; it passes the bars, restaurants, and shops on rue Frontenac and reaches its destination, the hotel where Harding stays, a downhill trip of five kilometres.

As they pass the hospital, whose routine is about to be thrown into chaos, the two men catch magical glimpses of the large lake, streaked at this late hour by dark reflections as if of black steel, and of the pretty little town nestled in the bottom of the valley, the pulse of its lights expressing the animation of this warm summer night.

Harding, thanks to the irony of fate, is one of the last people able to admire a view that a few minutes later will be erased from the face of the planet – he is one of the last to drive through the town, and one of the last to witness its final moments of life.

✕ ✕ ✕

A few steps from the imposing Sainte-Agnès Church, which overlooks the business centre from its height, Louis-Serge Parent and his wife are sound asleep. Their apartment is not far from the Musi-Café, and

they find the sounds of partying coming from it that evening almost comforting.

Kathy Clusiault, who lives just beside them, should have also been partying that evening. It's what you might expect of a happy-go-lucky twenty-four-year-old. But at last she has a new home, an apartment of her own, in the heart of the "golden kilometre" opposite the Musi-Café, which is the centre of action for Mégantic and its nearby residents. Kathy only needs to look out through her window and the world lies at her feet – its vastness, a whole planet waiting to be explored, and also a more familiar world, one that this evening spreads its carefree atmosphere over the terrace of the Musi-Café and all the way to the sidewalk below her window. Anyway, she'll have all that remains of the summer, of the year – of years – to take a nightcap at the Musi-Café or somewhere else. And she's also expecting her sister, who is coming to spend the night at her place, which is fantastic.

Mégantic, which might almost be a World Heritage Site for its starry skies, is simultaneously dark and twinkling with light. There are the town's lights of course, which proclaim the small businesses: the lingerie store and the shoe store. But at the same time the town is discreet, with muted lighting that never points skyward, ensuring perfect darkness for the multitude of stars that adorn its ceiling.

In the apartment above the Musi-Café, Yannick Bouchard is also asleep. People say he's shy. Now he has a brand-new degree in his pocket. With it maybe one day he'll be able to afford something a little less modest to call home. Because, along rue Frontenac, the living quarters are indeed modest, sometimes extremely modest. But everyone knows everyone else. There's a warmth that envelops everyone, even the very shy.

As for Jean-Pierre Roy and Lucie Vadnais, they have just arrived at the Musi-Café – late because they live a little distance away. Despite this, they'd been tempted to join their friends, including Gilles Fluet, for a beer. That evening the partying is especially lively, with lots of drinking and dancing, for there are several celebrations: three birthdays, someone moving away, and the arrival of a new baby. The Lafontaines are there, the brothers, sisters-in-law, and their employees; they are fêting Josée, even though she has gone home. Even Raymond,

the father, looked in earlier. The Lafontaines are well known: Raymond has built a good part of Mégantic, and now his sons Christian and Pascal are taking their turns working in the company, which is based just a few steps away.

Stéphane Bolduc's birthday party is very lively, and the members of the group are taking photos of one another. Later, Isabelle Hallé's dress will be spattered with Kronenbourg 1664, though she only drinks margaritas. The spilled beer will make a puddle in the middle of the dance floor – yet its smell won't be enough to mask the aroma of the bar's famous home-cooked sweet-potato fries, which always wafts in from the kitchen. The musicians on the stage are playing Pink Floyd but are ready for a cigarette break – Yvon Ricard is, at least.

Rémi Tremblay, the sensitive journalist and columnist from *L'Écho de Frontenac*, isn't at the Musi-Café, especially not so late at night. It's not his style. Besides, he left a final email that Friday evening saying, ironically: "On holiday. Don't call unless there's a derailment."

Perhaps it's because the border is so near, but several natives of Mégantic have chosen to embrace the world passionately. There was of course Nelly Arcan,[*] the winner of many prestigious literary prizes, the mountaineer Gabriel Filippi, the only Québécois to conquer Everest from both sides, and the popular novelist André Mathieu. And at the back of the Musi-Café this evening is David Lacroix-Beaudoin, about to return to Switzerland, where he now lives with his Swiss wife. The guys from the hockey team he played with when he was younger, along with their coach, have naturally come for a few farewell drinks. In any case, one of them, Maxime Dubois, is soon to be a father, which provides another excuse to celebrate. David's father was with them, but by this time he has left.

At her age, Talitha Bégnoche should also be out partying. But her daughters Bianka, age four, and Alyssa, nine, have already been asleep for some time, and will be up early. In fact, in the modest homes, and even in the more upscale ones, most folk are sound asleep. After all, it's late.

---

[*] Nelly Arcan won international recognition as the author of fictionalized autobiographies. She won many literary prizes in Québec, Canada, and abroad, including the very prestigious International Dublin Literary Award. Tragically, in 2009 she died by suicide at the age of thirty-six.

On boulevard des Vétérans, the street of handsome Victorian houses along the lake, Madame Parenteau-Boulanger has gone up to bed. This lady is herself almost Victorian, for she is well into her ninety-fourth year. She has just spoken to her son and is feeling reassured. Her neighbours Geneviève and Miroslav (Miro for short) are out of town and their home on rue Kelly is empty. Their kids were to have been looked after at home, but there has been a last-minute change of plan.

Yannick Gagné, the owner of the Musi-Café, is supervising the evening together with his pregnant wife, who is in charge of the cash register by the door. The bar has been completely renovated, as has the terrace, and it looks great. This evening is something of a house-warming, for the work was completed barely three weeks ago. The evening is going well; the regular musicians, Yvon and his buddy Guy Bolduc, are going crazy, that's just the way they are. The servers, Maude Verreault and Andrée-Anne Sévigny, have the situation well in hand, and even the new one, Élodie Turcotte, just eighteen, is managing well. Her boyfriend, Miguel Rouillard, turned up on the terrace but then left to fetch his wallet from home. He'll be back. Jean-Pierre Roy is ordering a few beers, and offers one for the road to Gilles Fluet, a regular who lives a little higher up. Gilles declines the offer: it's getting too late, he says.

Gilles Dor is spending the evening at home, nearby. His little girl is asleep; his girlfriend is spending the night. In the street, Luc, who has been sprayed by a skunk while on his way to the Musi-Café, is pedalling homeward, cursing the stench. Jean Paradis and Marie-Claude Lessard are strolling toward the lake not far from the municipal garage, a large yellow building.

The main street is particularly busy this evening. Karine, who finished her day's work as a waitress at the Musi-Café at nine o'clock, can't find a parking spot to go and treat herself to a nightcap. Across from the bar, René Simard has just finished parking his brand-new Mini Cooper.

Gilles Fluet loiters for a moment on the terrace. "Sure you won't have one more beer, Gilles?"

The new summer, like the new Mini Cooper, is going to be splendid.

After crossing the town, passing in front of the Musi-Café's terrace and the little buildings where everyone is asleep, Harding's taxi reaches the end of rue Frontenac, just before the river. It pulls up at L'Eau Berge, which offers the finest view: the lake, on the right, with the big concrete dock and the marina, and opposite, the outlet where the lake drains into the discharge chute of the little dam and gives birth to the long Chaudière River, which flows all the way down to Québec City. At one corner is the famous Citron Vert, a restaurant with its terrace perched directly over the lake. People travel to it by boat from the nearby villages, Piopolis and Marston, and tie up in the marina – where, that very afternoon, with great pomp and several splendid speeches, the mayor, Madame Colette Roy-Laroche, inaugurated a new cruise boat for expected tourists. The air is mild, and the shrouds of the sailboats are knocking gently, including those on Jacques Gagnon's pretty old wooden one.

Harding enters L'Eau Berge through the bar; at this late hour the reception is closed. There are people around, and he is covered in oil. Discreetly, he takes the key to his room, number five, and goes upstairs to clean up. From his window, from the other side of rue Frontenac, he can see the station and the track he should be travelling on in less than six hours, at the controls of the train from Vachon that he is to drive back to Farnham. It's a quarter past midnight, and a glorious night. Fifty minutes hence, disaster will strike. Some will survive, others not.

✖ ✖ ✖

The fate of the dead and of the survivors has already been decided hundreds or even thousands of kilometres away from Mégantic, by people who have never even heard the town's name.

On July 5, 2013, a few minutes before the impact, there really remained only two unknown variables in this inevitable tragedy: first, the precise moment when it would occur, when everything that

could go wrong would do so, when the final mechanism would come into play. It was a moment chosen at random, dependent on chance.

Chance would also provide the second unknown variable: the number of deaths. Would there be thirty, fifty, or two hundred? That would depend entirely on the number of people present in the downtown at that precise moment.

PREPARATIONS

Downtown Lac-Mégantic in 2012, a year before the disaster
Photo: Photo Hélico / Yves Tremblay

The same area after the disaster
Photo: The Canadian Press / Ryan Remiorz

RECIPE FOR A BOMB

If that's a culture of fear, they better get ready to
deal with fear.

—Hunter Harrison
  CEO of CP Rail, May 22, 2013, forty-
  five days before the disaster

This death could have been avoided.

—Statement repeated in each of the
  forty-seven coroner's reports on
  the Lac-Mégantic disaster

DURING THE PRELIMINARY HEARINGS FOR THE TRIALS THAT
took place in 2017, four years after the disaster, Tom Harding's defence
lawyer remarked that what occurred in Mégantic should be called a
crime. The lawyer representing the Transportation Safety Board of
Canada replied that on the contrary, only the words "incident" or
"accident" provide an appropriate characterization of this unfortunate
event. The TSB lawyer did agree that the word "incident" was perhaps
a little inadequate, considering the number of fatalities. However, the
matter would not be resolved during that session. And on that day
no one brought it to the attention of the respectable members of the
Bar that in Mégantic itself "tragedy" was the only word used by the
survivors.

"Tragedy": a word that is barely adequate to render the reality of
anyone who was immersed in the stench of charred flesh, oil, and
wreckage during the early hours of the "incident/accident." We can
also speak of "tragedies" – in the plural – to include what would follow
over the next few years.

But beyond the choice of words lies a reality. Here, the reality was
that a crime took place. A crime took place because, as the coroner
declared, the lives of perfectly innocent people had been stolen from

them. *Who? How? Why?* Such is the formula any good detective story relies upon in solving a crime.

So, like any crime, the one that took place at Mégantic was committed using a weapon. That weapon was developed and used by someone – and that person, or persons, had a motive for what they did. The weapon used in the crime of Mégantic was a train operated by CP and MMA.

The ammunition used was an explosive type of crude petroleum originating in North Dakota and belonging to World Fuel Services and Irving Oil. This lethal weapon was wielded by financiers like William Ackman and the all-powerful rail lobby,* of which Hunter Harrison was a member.

The motive: making a quick profit. The weapon was created and made available by powerful individuals and elected representatives, including John Baird, minister of transport from 2008 to 2010, other previous ministers, and a few senior public servants.

✗ ✗ ✗

In the aftermath of the Mégantic tragedy, CP continued to vehemently refuse all responsibility and categorically reject any suggestion that it compensate the victims. Apart from the obvious fact that the deadly train was chartered and travelled almost entirely on CP tracks, it was the direct actions of CP's shareholders and management that transformed a simple goods train into a lethal weapon.

A fierce battle for the control of CP, beginning in June 2011 and ending in April 2012, initiated the process of making conveyance by rail potentially lethal and enabled the implementation of one of the first major components of the mechanism which, two years later, sent a deadly runaway train racing toward a peaceful little country town.

---

* The Railway Association of Canada. (Attempts to obtain comments from representatives of the lobby were unsuccessful; repeated requests to some, including Gérald Gauthier, vice-president of the Association, remained unanswered.)

WILLIAM ACKMAN, A WINNER

We do have a plan ...

—William Ackman, email to John
Cleghorn, January 3, 2012

I'm not emotional about investments. Investing is something where you have to be purely rational, and not let emotion affect your decision making – just the facts.

—William Ackman[6]

Prelude: A Dinner (June 2011)

"Who the hell cares if the train is on time or not, my shares are worth damn-all. Who cares if there *is* even a train! Just bring CP's profits into the twenty-first century!" a Canadian Pacific shareholder hollered one evening in June 2011.

Oak panelling and paintings of the Basque coast decorate the private room in the very chic Benoit Bistro in New York, which hosts the upper-crust guests of the celebrated chef Alain Ducasse. Here, only members of the elite are to be found – the elite of beauty, art, show business, sport – and money, mind-boggling amounts of money. And yet, between the bouillabaisse and the *quenelles de brochet,* this dinner was descending into hostility.

Seated around the table were managers of large portfolios with investments in transportation companies eager for "new investment opportunities." But one of these magnates of the stock exchange could no longer stomach the chronic underperformance of CP. As a shareholder in the company who was upset to discover that he was simply not pocketing any returns, he had been motivated to organize this dinner party. The hidden objective was to induce William Ackman, the owner of Pershing Square, a hedge fund that provides spectacular returns, to rectify the intolerable situation. Ackman

was not present at the dinner party, but Paul Hilal, his long-term associate, was among the guests.

"For six years now, CP has been declining to microscopic returns. Some of its competitors are showing returns of over 50 percent, while CP can never do better than three or four ridiculous crumbs of percentage points! And that's when it's not squarely in the red. CP is run by a bunch of incompetents!" The anger and frustration were becoming too much for the shareholders present to digest – especially given the additional spice of jealousy.

Viewed from Wall Street, the financial crisis of 2008 did indeed create losers, though not ones of any importance: just a host of families rendered homeless, wandering the streets without housing or employment. And in the world of money and finance, those financiers who had taken a tumble were considered "losers" – pension funds drained by managers lacking in vision and out of their depth, incompetents indeed, products of outdated financial establishments like CP, who lacked any understanding of the modern world.

But in the eyes of the dinner guests at Benoit that evening in 2011, the crash of 2008 had above all created extremely wealthy winners, great Gatsbys, objects of secret envy. The 2008 crisis had indeed propelled some financial megastars to spectacular instant fortunes. While billions of dollars vanished into thin air, these happy few were able to record the most enormous successful wagers in history, sometimes in the space of a few hours. Ackman, the man courted by these CP shareholders, was among them.

Like a select number of financiers, Ackman was indeed quicker than others to grasp the extent to which one of the hidden faces of modern capitalism had changed, and to succeed in using this understanding to his advantage. Henceforth, the capital supplied to companies by private shareholders would no longer be used to "invest" in the expansion or improvement of a factory or assembly line, the economy, or the related employment, but would instead be expected to produce quick – very quick – profits for a few privileged individuals. This was precisely what the shareholders present at Benoit that evening wanted: an immediate upward spike in CP's profit curve. For them, it was an obsession.

Of course, everything always depends on your point of view. Some

people's obsessions are often met with the indifference, or obliviousness, of others – for instance, the obliviousness toward those made homeless by the crisis of 2008, unwitting victims of the extremely wealthy traders who have turned them out onto the street.

In Mégantic too, people were oblivious. CP's miserable yields, which preoccupied the crayfish eaters at Benoit that evening, could not have been farther from the preoccupations of the little town's inhabitants. Who in Mégantic, for instance, on that same evening in June 2011, between the barbecue, cold beer, and hopes of catching a few trout, shared this preoccupation with a company's profits? Who in Mégantic was as obsessed as the guests at Benoit with the desire to see an immediate increase in a company's returns? No one. For the people of Mégantic, these luxury-loving traders were at most photos on the glossy covers of the magazines displayed at grocery checkouts – a world very far from their reality.

But such is life. The consequences of certain actions are not distributed equitably between the decision makers on one hand and the bit players on the other. Some make decisions, while others suffer the consequences. On that evening in June 2011, their fates were linked. For some, the decisions would mean good fortune; for others, tragedy.

✗ ✗ ✗

The future would prove the diners in the Benoit Bistro absolutely correct. An incredible concentration of wealth in the hands of the very rich would indeed occur in the few months following that dinner. While in 2013 the poorest half of the world population shared between 0.7 percent of the planet's net wealth, in 2016 the poorest half would possess an even more meagre 0.2 percent. By then, eight billionaires alone would share between them more wealth than half the world's population.[7] Without dreaming of becoming one of these eight mega-rich, our diners were at least hoping to have a place in that marvellous constellation.

However, the new doctrine of ultra-rapid and stratospheric returns rested on a new premise: in 2011, for Ackman and his associates, a company's efficiency no longer provided a meaningful reason to

invest, nor anything to be proud of. In other words: the correct, efficient delivery of a good, service, or product was no longer a relevant consideration, nor even, in the eyes of a company's shareholders, a secondary objective worth maintaining. For instance, that a pair of shoes made in a factory should be delivered to a customer complete with two heels or just one, or whether a train ran on a well-maintained track, were now matters of secondary importance, or perhaps even undesirable, since providing two heels or the proper maintenance of a railway line involved an increase in costs, and therefore a reduction in profits, which was to be deplored.

In this, our diners and other shareholders were in the process of becoming fervent Marxists. They were (no doubt unwittingly) applying Karl Marx's equation which states that the profits earned depend directly on the cost of production of the merchandise, with the addition of its "surplus value" (in other words, the amount of productive work that costs employers less, or nothing).

Complicated? Not really. Let's say, to simplify things, that the less it costs to produce a good – when you avoid buying new track to replace what is worn out, for instance – and the more labour you can obtain from your workers above and beyond what they are paid for (the famous "surplus value"), the greater the shareholder's profit. The surplus value can be increased, for instance, if several workers are replaced by a machine such as an automatic remote control instead of a locomotive engineer. Likewise, requiring a single train inspector to do the work of four is a perfect way to put into practice what Marx termed the "capitalist mode of production."

Roughly speaking, the higher the production costs, the lower the return to shareholders. Of course, Marx hoped to reverse the equation to the benefit of the workers and the little people ... but that's another story.

✕ ✕ ✕

For the investors attending that dinner at Benoit, the time had come for a changing of the guard at the head of CP. The company, they thought, had potential – the proof being that its competitors were amassing a pretty pile – and they asked Hilal to spark Ackman's

interest. It was essential that Ackman take control of CP and get rid of the existing management.

But why Ackman? To take control of CP, a so-called activist financier was needed, the kind who can take brutal control of a company and carry out a clean sweep of its board of directors, structure, and employees – in short, someone able to use an axe to chop away the excess fat and increase returns dramatically. To carry off such a coup, nerve, high-handedness, self-assurance, and considerable gall are required. But none of the diners in the bistro that night was up to the job.

By coffee time it was all settled. Later, Paul Hilal would speak to Bill Ackman.

When the diners finally emerged into the nighttime warmth of 55th Street, the adrenaline, car horns, and carbon dioxide dominated everything. For the CP shareholders, it was mission accomplished: the days of the establishment figures at the head of the railway company were numbered.

It would have taken little for our overjoyed diners to chant the very same slogan that had been resounding for the previous few months of 2011 in some equally noisy streets, but tens of thousands of kilometres away from the Big Apple – a slogan that was to become symbolic. "Enough!" they were shouting in Cairo, Tunis, and Tripoli, in that hope-filled Arab Spring. "Enough!" was also the shareholders' cry to those in charge of CP – a demand that would be flung in their faces scarcely three months later, in New York itself, expressed by the demonstrators of the Occupy Wall Street movement who, in their turn, would shout "Enough!" to the Ackmans, shareholders, and other wealthy individuals of this world.

It was an irony of history. At that very moment, in the summer of 2011, the CP shareholders, the demonstrators in the Arab world, and the rebels of Occupy Wall Street shared an objective and a hope: that wiping the slate clean would help to build a better world. The difference between them can be summarized in a simple question: For whom? A better world for whom? Sometimes the devil is in the details. And, along the same lines, one may wonder who among those demanding change across the world would actually achieve it over the coming months.

The answer may be painful.

✕ ✕ ✕

"It has been a while since I've seen a movie any more entertaining than the show that New York investor Bill Ackman put on yesterday in Toronto."[8] Clearly, Fred Frailey, the witty columnist of *Trains*, a magazine devoted to the North American railway industry, savoured the penultimate phase of the epic battle for control of CP. The entertaining event he referred to had taken place the previous evening, February 6, 2012, at the Hilton Toronto (barely seven months after the dinner at Benoit), in the presence of three hundred invitees, with another two hundred watching the simulcast – a record attendance if one remembers that the "show" was merely a dry financial pitch presented by Ackman. His objective was to convince the shareholders to throw out CP's sitting board of directors and appoint a new CEO to head the company.

The size of the attendance demonstrated that he had already won his case. What's more, Ackman had announced his expectation of victory in a January 4 email to John Cleghorn, the then chair of CP's board of directors: "In the proxy contest as a first step we will take the largest public hall available in Toronto and we will make a presentation to the shareholders and the public ... about management and board failures over the last ten years at CP ... We will win the election by a landslide vote."[9]

This battle, which would delight financial media from Bloomberg to CNN, would become known as the "proxy fight," an extreme sport in the U.S. that in 2011 major Canadian companies had not yet begun to practise as spectacularly. "For the first time," a witness says, "shareholders looked the immovable directors straight in the eye, told them they were useless, and appealed to them to quit. On Bay Street, where everyone frequents the same Canadian Club at the fashionable Royal York, nothing of the kind had ever been seen."[10] The battle was a confrontation between two protagonists who were almost caricatures in their respective roles.

Playing the part of the venerable establishment man was John Cleghorn, seventy-nine, the chair of CP's board of directors, a respectable Bay Street financier, a retired banker, and an Officer of the Order of

Canada, who had been elected to the Canadian Business Hall of Fame in 2008. A serious gentleman in every respect, he was the epitome of stability and moderation, of discussions behind the closed doors of oak-panelled rooms, and of business meetings at the aforementioned Royal York Hotel in Toronto – a hotel originally developed and owned by CP and once considered the largest and most prestigious in the British Empire. Cleghorn, a history buff, is known for frugal habits such as taking the subway and flying in economy class. As CEO of the Bank of Montreal, he had denied his directors the use of a limousine and a private jet.

Facing him was the flamboyant William "Bill" Ackman, forty-five, invariably described as "silver-haired," the owner of a private jet, and of a property in the upscale Hamptons, on Long Island. Passionate about tennis, he's played with greats such as Pete Sampras and André Agassi and has boasted of beating them. His smile often graces the New York Social Diary, a gossip website for the social elite; he rubs shoulders at parties where stars like Baryshnikov come to live it up, and where diamonds sparkle, both real and fake. His name also appears on the list of the fifty most generous philanthropists in the U.S., dispensing (or lending – there is cause for controversy) tens of millions to charity. He is omnipresent, as is his wife Karen Herskovitz, who sits on the board of Human Rights Watch, an organization to which Ackman, through Pershing Square, is said to have donated $10 million, as a believer in "strategic interventions to combat the roots of poverty and repression."[11] (However, in early 2017 it would be learned that Ackman and his wife were involved in a difficult divorce, endangering their $90 million penthouse – one of the priciest in New York – the family condominium with its view over Central Park, valued at $35 million, and their $23 million property in the Hamptons).

Early in his life, Ackman received a cheque from his millionaire father that enabled him to launch his first hedge fund. Since then, he has become omnipresent on television, in magazines, on the web, on the front page of *Forbes*, and in the pages of *Vanity Fair*. With his flair for the visual and for spectacle, he has turned up on the sets of the most highly rated TV talk shows, such as that of the prominent journalist Charlie Rose, whose star was recently extinguished following revelations unearthed during the Me Too movement. In 2016, after

starring in a documentary, Ackman would walk the red carpet at the prestigious Tribeca Film Festival.

So Ackman was a complete, modern-day hero – a hero, that is, to investors, to would-be shareholders, and to the artistic and media elites. He was undeniably one of a new sort of financial star that the masses have come to worship – and elect to office. He personified opulence. People eagerly swallowed his every pronouncement and envied his life. His own role model was the great financial guru Warren Buffet, who stirred his competitive spirit as much as his admiration. Glowing with pride, Ackman was able to boast that in 2011, while Berkshire Hathaway, Buffet's holding company, had achieved a return of 22 percent, his Pershing Square had registered 24 percent.

After several initial setbacks, Ackman made his first billion as one of the big winners of the 2008 crisis when, having discovered the vulnerability of the collateralized debt obligations (CDOs) it had issued, he bet against MBIA, a company that insured mortgages and bonds and which enjoyed an AAA credit rating. His bet would succeed if MBIA collapsed on the stock exchange, an outcome he was able to provoke by launching a ferocious press campaign denigrating the company and exposing its vulnerabilities. His profits amounted to 1.3 billion in 2009, while MBIA collapsed, throwing mortgage and bond holders into a crisis.

To be sure, Ackman was one of the rare individuals able to spot and profit from the stock exchange failures and phony financial derivatives[12] which caused the collapse of the real-estate market in 2008, plunging the United States into their greatest recession since 1929. Paradoxically, but perhaps characteristically, Ackman appeared in the film *Inside Job*, with Matt Damon as narrator, which described precisely and even denounced the behaviour of the strategists of the crash, and which won an Oscar for Best Documentary.

Moreover, Ackman was considered a workaholic. After learning to profit from a few stock-exchange failures, he refined his approach. Henceforth, based on a minimal number of shares, he would take control of the boards of directors of the company he was targeting, push out the existing management, and put his own people in charge. The latter would be at his beck and call as he tried to satisfy his thirst for profit.

One of his first coups of this nature was an investment in JCPenney, a large U.S. chain of retail stores. After taking control of it in 2010, he abruptly replaced the CEO with one of his own people, Ron Johnson, formerly senior vice-president of retail operations at Apple, where he had pioneered the concept of the Apple retail stores. Following this takeover, JCPenney was at death's door for two years. Ackman finally sold his shares, swallowing a loss of $400 million, though not without first letting go nineteen thousand employees, who were accused of various misdemeanours. Ackman left JCPenney on its last legs.

He would renew the exploit in 2015 and 2016, this time garnering the jewel of the Canadian and Québec stock market, Valeant, a pharmaceutical company situated in Laval, Québec, which collapsed, immersed in a miasma of fraud and the price manipulation of essential medicines. On March 2, 2016, in a single hour, Ackman, the controlling shareholder of Valeant, is said to have lost two billion dollars.[13] The fall of Valeant affected just about all the major share portfolios in Québec, notably the pension funds.*

So a confrontation took place between the flamboyant, risk-taking Ackman and the pragmatic, steady Cleghorn: two diametric opposites, two different worlds, two conceptions of finance, two ways of making money. Cleghorn's way was slow and sure, Ackman's fast and brutal. It can be said in Cleghorn's defence that he ran the railway company in the traditional way, with many employees (too many, Ackman would say) and programs to ensure proper maintenance of the tracks and the inspection of rolling stock.

At stake in the Cleghorn–Ackman battle was one of the largest Class 1 railway networks in North America, offering direct links to eight important ports, including Montréal and Vancouver, and providing its North American clients with access to major markets in every corner of the globe. CP also had the advantage of links to a host of small local networks such as the Montreal, Maine and Atlantic Railway (MMA). And, as we shall see later, it occupied a strategic position in North Dakota.

---

* Valeant became Bausch Health Company in 2018. In 2020, Ackman would make an enormous profit betting on the COVID-19 global pandemic, a profit business media would uncritically laud as "the single best trade of all time."

As Ackman would discover while poring over the figures after the dinner at Benoit, CP was a gem of a company – a largely underexploited gem.

✖ ✖ ✖

All this gives an impression of high surrealism, even of conspiracy theory in relating the manoeuvres of glitzy transcontinental billionaires to the fate of an obscure, very "ordinary" little town – in linking the flamboyant existence of Bill Ackman to that of quiet young Kathy Clusiault.

Yet it's impossible to explain in any other way the runaway trip of a defective train laden with crude oil one beautiful summer night in Québec; it was the direct, predictable, and logical consequence of certain distant events that occurred during the months preceding the tragedy.

✖ ✖ ✖

"It is estimated that a thousand photos were taken during the weekend! A wild success!" wrote the journalist Rémi Tremblay in *L'Écho de Frontenac*, in 2011. "Far surpassing our wildest hopes! Astonishment on arriving, delight on visiting the sports facilities, and a feeling of pride as one left! Skating and swimming were open to all and free during the three days, so the arena and pool were crowded. The festive atmosphere was sustained by the presence of buskers, the magician Sébastien Louis-Seize, and inflatable games for the children."

While the struggle for control of CP was going on, the thing that aroused the strongest passions and even divided the little town of Mégantic had been the construction (where, how, for whom, with whom, by whom?) of a sports complex complete with skating rink and swimming pool. The conflict finally resolved, Mégantic's new sports complex had just been opened. It was soon to serve as a refuge for a decimated, stunned community.

War Is War (September 2011 to May 2012)

The battle for the control of CP[14] would be ferocious, at least according to the ethereal criteria of financiers sitting snugly in their leather armchairs. But it would also be zany, a sort of vaudeville involving greedy wheeler-dealers.

The first shot was fired on September 23, 2011, when Ackman, acting through his Pershing Square hedge fund, quietly purchased his first shares in CP, on the very day when CP's shares happened to reach their lowest point on the Toronto Stock Exchange. After six years of mediocre returns, CP had announced a decline of 25 percent in profits over nine months. But above all, and unforgivably, over the past five years CP had provided its shareholders with a total return of just 19.4 percent, while its competitors recorded returns of between 56 and 117 percent.

On October 28, 2011, when Ackman's investment, valued at $1.4 billion, finally became public knowledge, CP's shares rose by 7 percent, as if hope and life had suddenly been breathed into the company. Cleghorn and his allies should have seen this as a sign that the hunt was on. But they saw nothing, or didn't want to see anything, and during the coming months would spend $33 million in their attempts to frustrate Ackman.[15] But Ackman only needed to win the support of three or four major shareholders to win the day. Moreover, most of the large shareholders came from the United States and were already in favour of maximizing quick profits.

The first meeting between Cleghorn and Ackman took place in a hangar at a small airport in Montréal on October 29, 2011. The members of the CP Board of Directors had travelled halfway across Canada by train, while the trip took Ackman only an hour in his private jet. Arriving at the airport hangar at 6 a.m. on that chilly, damp, unpleasant morning, the anxious CP board members, accompanied by their lawyer, William Orr, waited in a room while Cleghorn and Fred Green, the CEO of CP met Ackman and Hilal in the adjoining room.

Cleghorn affably presented the American financier with an attractive book about the American Civil War. Ackman, who already owned 14 percent of the company's shares, instead showed him his figures and plans for CP – in a word, his demands. For the first time, the

name of Hunter Harrison, the former head of Canadian National, was mentioned by Ackman as the next CEO of CP. According to Ackman, it was essential that Green, the CEO from the inner circle of CP, be replaced by Harrison without delay. Green, apparently, did not particularly appreciate this brutal announcement that firing him was part of the program. In addition, Ackman claimed two seats on the Board of Directors for himself and Hilal.

After a meeting lasting barely an hour, Ackman was preparing to leave Montréal feeling sure that the matter would be settled in no time, for CP would quickly throw in the towel – especially since Cleghorn left his directors high and dry, rushing out onto the tarmac on foot, without Green, and stopping Ackman's plane to give him his personal reassurance in private: "It will all go well," he is said to have told him. "We'll talk again."

✗ ✗ ✗

On December 11, 2011, Ackman and Hilal flew to Calgary, having been summoned to a meeting of the CP board at which Ackman was convinced his action plan would be approved, along with the two seats he was asking for.

It was a complete humiliation. Ackman left the meeting in a rage. Not only had the board turned down his plan and refused to fire Green – a contemptuous slap in the face for Ackman – it had also refused to grant him a second seat on the board for Hilal, his friend and right-hand man. Worse, the board took the odious step of refusing Hilal admission to the boardroom, leaving him to chafe in a side room.

Ackman prepared his counterattack during the 2011 holiday season. On January 4, 2012, he sent Cleghorn a lengthy email. "WAR AND PEACE" was written in uppercase at the top of the message. Cleghorn was furious. The email in question would be described as "infamous" (by CP, naturally, but by the media too). In it, Ackman issued a warning to Cleghorn: "Let's avoid having a border skirmish turn into a nuclear winter."

Despite this, it became a nuclear wipeout. In February 2012, as Ackman had promised, he rented the largest meeting room in the Toronto Hilton. Accompanied by Paul Hilal and Hunter Harrison, and

in front of a considerable crowd, he presented a critique of Green's six years at the head of CP. The exposé was "brutal, and frankly devastating," wrote Fred Frailey in *Trains*.

On Harrison's advice, Hilal pointed out that CP was conveying only 70 percent of the amount of freight handled by CN. Yet CP employed the equivalent of 90 percent as many locomotives and was even planning the purchase of ninety-one new ones, which made no sense. The average speed of CP's trains was 20 percent slower than those of CN, and its employees were 20 percent less productive.

Ackman concluded by asking the large investors who they would pick: him or Cleghorn? Fred Green, the present CEO, or Hunter Harrison, the man who had driven CN's returns to their present heights? Who did they think was the best man to help this company fulfill its full potential?[16]

The outcome of the war would finally be decided on May 17, 2012, with the unconditional surrender of Cleghorn's team. The Canada Pension Plan (CPP), a major institutional investor whose mission statement is to "invest the assets of the CPP Fund with a view to achieving a maximum rate of return without undue risk of loss,"[17] supported Ackman, and at 9 a.m., a few moments before the Annual General Meeting at which the new members of the board were to be elected, Green and five other board members resigned. The AGM would not take place. Ackman had won.

CP's shares immediately spiked and would not fall again for several years. When Ackman began to sell his shares barely a year later, on June 3, 2013, he had tripled his original investment of a billion dollars, pocketing $3.25 billion.[18] Ackman was "swimming in profits," read the *Globe and Mail*'s headline.

The new board of CP and its CEO, Hunter Harrison, had a single mission: to fulfill shareholder demands. In a way, the decision-making flowchart had been turned on its head, since management would henceforth prioritize the interests of major shareholders rather than do what was necessary for the company to function properly.

This reversal is important, and it would have repercussions on every decision affecting the safety of the company's commercial activities, which normally represents a major expense for any transportation company.

Many Canadians, through their contributions to the Canada Pension Plan, with its nineteen million subscribers, were collectively implicated in this reversal as institutional shareholders in CP. As indirect shareholders in CP, many working Canadians therefore profited not only from the maximal returns and increases in CP's share price but also benefited from the firings, the reduced maintenance budgets, and the "collateral damage" – the destruction and the creation of victims, for which we fail to recognize our responsibility.

× × ×

Beginning on May 17, 2012, CP's mission called for a rapid, stratospheric spike in its share value rather than for the cautious (safe) operation of a railway company.

The takeover of CP was the starting point of the tragedy in Mégantic, at the heart of which lies the whole process of deregulation and the abandonment by state authorities of the oversight of North American and Canadian railway safety to private industry.

HUNTER HARRISON, RAILWAYMAN SUPREME

> Criminal negligence: demonstrating a rash and immoderate indifference to the lives of others.
>
> —Judge Gaétan Dumas's direction to the jury in the trial of Thomas Harding, Richard Labrie, and Jean Demaître

ALL THINGS CONSIDERED, IN JUNE 2012 IT BECAME RATHER boring to watch video after video showing Ackman, the major shareholder, and Harrison, the new CEO of CP, as they deluged our TV screens, in our magazines and other media, continually reiterating their "new" vision of how a railway company should be managed.

Artful speakers, equipped with the air of profundity and maturity typical of people "in the know," the two men repeated their business mantra ad nauseam to an audience of admiring journalists. Their mantra consisted of five guiding principles for good business management, according to Harrison: offer good service, operate safely, optimize assets, reduce costs, and improve the quality of the employees.

It was an upbeat official statement but one that merely repeated a banal recipe valid for any kind of business, whether a railway or a pastry shop. It is a safe bet that Cleghorn's team believed in the same business principles.

Still, it has to be admitted that the two men obtained radically different results in the returns they provided to shareholders.

✗ ✗ ✗

With his well-worn cowboy looks, shiny striped suits, and Southern drawl, Hunter Harrison was something of a wag, a combination of popular hero and villain – the sort of person you love to detest. Born

in Memphis, Tennessee, the son of a policeman who had once been a pastor, Harrison began as a carman-oiler with the St. Louis–San Francisco Railway (called familiarly "the Frisco") and, embodying the American myth of the self-made man, rose steadily through the ranks of several railway companies before ending as CEO of Canadian National Railway in 2003.

Harrison was adored by financiers seduced by the dazzling results he achieved while at the controls of CN Rail – it was he who had transformed CN into the most generous provider of shareholders' returns in North America. Among his employees, however, he left much more bitter, not to say outraged, feelings in his wake. Many spoke of a bloodletting, of a climate of fear within the company.

Strangely, dissatisfaction also prevailed among his largest customers, the grain producers of Western Canada. In 2014, Wade Sobkowich, executive director of the Western Grain Elevator Association, was reported as feeling that "the cost-cutting push resulted in poorer service and, more broadly, a transfer of wealth to CP's investors from the shipper."[19]

When Ackman invited Harrison to lunch at the New York Museum of Modern Art in August 2011, two months after the dinner at Benoit, Harrison was enjoying his properties in Connecticut and Florida after his retirement from CN, well provided for by a little farewell handshake worth $40 million.* On his magnificent property, named Double H Farm – the source of dream images on Pinterest – Harrison bred and trained horses of Olympic calibre. (HH Rebozo, one of his stallions, would star at the London Olympics in 2012.) To pass the time, Harrison had been playing at being a financial backer, chairman, or special representative of any prestigious association in the world of horse breeding and show jumping, whether in North America or abroad. Concerned about the environment, he proudly proclaimed that his Connecticut ranch ran on geothermal power.

But by 2011 Hunter Harrison was starting to feel bored; when Ackman contacted him, he willingly agreed to put his famous implacability into use as the head of CP. Harrison had already diagnosed

---

* This would later be suspended by CN in the aftermath of the controversy and civil suit that followed Harrison's move to CP, which compensated Harrison for the loss.

PREPARATIONS

CP's problem, as summed up by Ackman in February 2012: the trains were too short and too slow, there was too much rolling stock and too many employees. Harrison ended his diagnosis by setting up a single target, a magic figure which needed to be attained and which would become an obsession for him. This was 60 percent – a benchmark representing the cost/profit ratio of a railway company and, consequently, its profitability.

In 2012, when Harrison took over at CP, this ratio stood at over 80 percent. Harrison would hit 59.8 percent by the end of 2014, in barely twenty-four months: desperate times call for desperate measures. How would Harrison achieve such a spectacular result? Simply by following the "plan," adhering to a logic as unanswerable as it was implacable: reduce costs and brutally pursue higher profits. Harrison was a "mover and shaker."

✗ ✗ ✗

One of the advantages enjoyed by Ackman and Harrison was their frequent presence on media platforms. They would assume an affable or arrogant air, depending on the circumstances, but were always extremely self-assured. This was especially true of Harrison, who in the months following his arrival at CP in 2012 appeared constantly on Bloomberg, MSNBC, CNN Money (now called CNN Business), and elsewhere, in order to update viewers on the progress of his four-point plan aimed at remedying the excesses at CP.

The first problem – slow trains – was solved within a few months. As early as 2013, with a self-satisfied grin, Harrison could publicly confirm that his trains were now running 15 percent faster than before.

✗ ✗ ✗

Of course, ordinary mortals may well wonder why, if all this was so straightforward, the former management of CP hadn't thought of it.

However, we do know that the permissible speed on a railway track depends on its condition, on its classification according to five categories. The more a track has deteriorated, the lower the permissible speed.

In November 2016, three years after the disaster, Marc Garneau, the federal minister of transport, visited Mégantic to reassure the townspeople. Yet he failed to dispel their concerns, especially because, shortly before, a resident named Robert Bellefleur had published a number of photographs showing the poor condition of the track on the gradient that descends toward the town – just as bad as it had been in 2013, even though in the meantime trains had recommenced hauling explosive and toxic materials.

"If a railway complies, according to the criteria, we must respect the norms, we have no choice. Even when a track is worn down to the limit, but is still within the limits, there's no other choice than to allow the company to run its trains on it," Garneau explained to a journalist who was alarmed to note the visible wear and cracks in the line.

"So you can live with the maximum allowable wear and tear of a track behind a hospital?" the journalist pursued.

"I have to live with the technical reality that if a track is in conformity with the standards, and if the norms are reasonable ones ... The experts at Transport Canada think that the standards are reasonable."[20]

Who is to decide how much wear and tear is acceptable? Why, the railway company itself. And who inspects the track to determine its condition and decide, accordingly, what speed is permissible? Who determines the type of cargo, dangerous or not, that may be transported on it? Who decides on the maximum weight of the trains that the track in question can bear? The company, always the company. Not exactly reassuring!

It is true that Transport Canada supervises all this – in theory. We will return to this later.

Only the CP employees directly concerned in the maintenance of the track can explain to us how Harrison managed to increase the speed of his trains without replacing some excessively worn track – for he simply didn't have time to do so in the few months that followed his arrival at CP.

Nevertheless, he did increase the trains' speed – while at the same time increasing their weight.

"We have no choice," admitted the minister (the person entrusted with the specific mandate of ensuring our safety). "We've no choice but to allow companies to act however they want ..."[21] But who

PREPARATIONS

deprived him of that choice? Who tied his hands? Not "we the people," for when we elected him we were conferring on him for four years the power to change whatever was unacceptable. So who was it then? Who had that choice, that power, which the minister claims was taken out of his hands?

✕ ✕ ✕

The second item on Harrison's agenda was to make the trains longer. He soon took care of that as well.

During the triumphant interview that he gave after being named "Railroader of the Year" for the second time in 2015, Harrison explained proudly that his trains, which previously had weighed only four thousand tons, now weighed as much as twenty thousand tons. To achieve this, he increased the length of the trains, which grew to as long as two kilometres by 2015 and three kilometres by 2020.

Harrison had quintupled the weight of his trains in less than thirty months. This represented a real revolution in the mode of operation, something quite remarkable in a company with thousands of employees and hauling thousands of tons of freight. To manage such an outcome, Harrison turned to an idea that had previously been of only minor importance – the concept of the unit train, those interminable processions of lugubrious tank cars, mostly DOT-111s, that are nowadays seen everywhere on our railways.

Unfortunately, these are the same outdated DOT-111s that have been denounced by all the safety agencies in both the United States and Canada, and whose withdrawal from service those agencies have been demanding since at least 2004.[22] They are the same DOT-111s which, after more than twenty-five inquiries into accidents occurring over the years, the TSB has targeted as extremely dangerous.

It is always easier to add tank cars than to remove them, it seems. The industry seems extraordinarily inept when it comes to taking unsafe tank cars out of circulation. Indeed, it was not until 2016, three years after the Mégantic tragedy, that the railway companies – and Transport Canada – finally announced that they planned to withdraw DOT-111s from the transportation of explosive, toxic, and dangerous materials – a withdrawal that would, however, extend into 2025!

× × ×

The third item on Harrison's agenda was the rolling stock (the locomotives, cars, and other vehicles used on the railway) and the tracks.
More cuts!

When we take time to think about it, we realize that the feat of
engineering that allows steel mammoths weighing thousands of tons
to travel safely around curves and down gradients on slender, mush-
room-shaped strips of steel, the whole thing supported by simple
wooden ties, is a product of the purest human genius. The delicate
balance of the different forces at work, the various laws of physics,
the nature of the materials and their durability, centrifugal force,
and gravity, all subtly calculated to the nearest millimetre, result in a
structure of Herculean strength that allows it to carry colossal loads
at considerable speeds. But this incredible strength also rests on an
extreme fragility, an almost microscopic minutia of details, of all the
various parameters. A few millimetres here or there, and the train
with its load inexorably departs from its intended direction of travel,
unleashing as it does so an incredible destructive power.

In 2006, the Transportation Safety Board, the federal agency that
acts as a watchdog for safety in Canada, considered the possibility of
a link between accidents – CP's accidents – and the deterioration of
the tracks. It concluded that:

> [a] statistically significant relationship was established
> between the incidence of rail defects and the level of
> bulk traffic. Where rail weight is less than 130 pounds,
> increased bulk unit train tonnage significantly increases
> rail defects, resulting in a higher risk of broken rail
> derailments. This safety issues investigation report iden-
> tifies risks related to the problems in balancing track
> maintenance and degradation to the comprehensiveness
> of the Railway Track Safety Rules and to deficiencies in
> rail inspection capabilities and maintenance practices.[23]

Bureaucratic jargon perhaps, but not entirely incomprehensible: the

heavier the trains travelling on inadequate tracks, the more damage to the tracks is caused. And the greater the damage, the more likely – and the more severe – the derailments. It is a truism that anyone living near a railway line could have visually confirmed over the past few years.

Unfortunately then, those heavier, faster trains of which Hunter Harrison was so proud were now running on the same old tracks that had been built in an era of hauling timber and lighter cargoes. The trains of that time, numbering barely forty cars, would conveniently stop in each village to deliver foodstuff and necessary workers' supplies. But the old tracks were not durable enough for today's unit trains. It turns out that such trains, travelling at speed on rails that are too weak, run an increased risk of accidents.

Harrison actually admitted that if the new cargoes of crude oil and potash were taken into consideration, certain levels of maintenance were inadequate. "We're operating up there with one-hundred-pound, jointed rail, 1950s vintage," he said. But, he explained, that was no reason to repair the track. The market, especially for oil, was too uncertain. "We have to build infrastructures that will last forty or forty-five years when we don't know what the market will be like in five or six years." [24] Nevertheless, the CEO, obsessed by his thirst for increased returns, would reduce the company's investment in the upkeep and improvement of its trains and tracks.

It was indeed precisely a weak, deteriorating track that caused the derailment of the train in Mégantic. The TSB explained in its report on the disaster that the rails concerned had a weight of 115 pounds (having been manufactured between 1966 and 1971), before going on to say: "Previously at this location, work had been performed to improve the geometry conditions recorded in 2012. However, without the use of mechanized equipment, the improvements were temporary; therefore, similar geometry conditions were likely present the day of the accident." [25]

In fact, much of the track that runs through our communities today weighs 115 pounds per yard – fifteen pounds per yard less than was considered unsafe in the 2006 TSB study. And they now carry present-day loads weighing twenty thousand tons.

In Mégantic in the spring of 2017, Robert Bellefleur took some

photographs at the precise spot in the town centre where the train had derailed, a few metres from where the devastated Musi-Café once stood. The 2017 pictures show that the rails undulated, as if sinking into the ground, which was possibly insufficiently compacted and rendered very unstable by the spring thaw. A few days later, Bellefleur filmed a train of some forty tank cars carrying sulphuric acid, propane, and more travelling on those same rails.

Bellefleur immediately alerted Transport Canada, who referred him to the new owner of the track, CMQR (MMA's successor). Bellefleur showed his alarming photographs and demanded an inspection.

After long weeks of waiting, he eventually received the responses of the company and Transport Canada on the state of the tracks, with the verdict: "Nothing to report. Everything in order." [26]

✕ ✕ ✕

The same sort of pinchpenny economies applied in the case of rolling stock, including the DOT-111 tank cars. Alain Richer, a Transport Canada inspector, reported that when he examined the first trains entering the CP triage station in Montréal on their way from Bakken, he found the tank cars in such deplorable condition that he alerted Transport Canada in Ottawa and his colleagues in the United States at the Federal Railroad Administration (FRA). Yet that did not prevent him from allowing the trains to proceed on their journey. It was also Richer who, on July 5, 2013, twelve hours before the Mégantic disaster, carried out the inspection of the lethal train – only the fourth train originating in Bakken that he had had the opportunity to examine. On that occasion he declared himself "delighted" with the improvements in the CP/MMA train.

Be that as it may, for Harrison the dangerous condition of the equipment, its wear and tear, weakness, or fractures, did not necessarily dictate its repair or replacement.

The priority was its cost effectiveness – meaning its efficacy where profits and the returns provided to shareholders were concerned. The oil market was uncertain? No point in investing then. Just leave things the way they are.

The fourth item on Harrison's agenda: too many employees. The superfluous ones must be eliminated.

It is certainly a common tactic among business leaders to reduce the number of their employees, a tactic that invariably results in an immediate uptick in the share price. For shareholders, it is a question of doing more with less, of better returns with fewer employees. That is Marx's surplus value at work, and it is also, curiously, a byword among politicians, who often rely on a promise to "shrink government" in order to win elections – but that's another story.

Harrison therefore reduced his wages bill. It took him six months to cut almost 4,500 jobs in CP. Within three years of the beginning of his tenure, a total of six thousand employees had been cut. His method of managing human resources was draconian, as he explained to the media: "You've got to find the meanest son of a bitch and whip his ass – you get a lot of attention," he said. "If you're in a rail yard, where a big bully has always got his way, you take care of the big bully and a lot of things come together."[27] Obviously, in several cases, including at CP, the "big bully" turned out to be the unions, which protested the massive firings.

The unions were indeed becoming alarmed. They warned that the budget cuts at CP were directly affecting public safety. In May 2013, two months before the tragedy in Mégantic, the union spoke publicly about its fears that major accidents were to be expected. "In some cases, our guys are not allowed [to inspect the rail cars] because they just want to get them out fast, and if you take too long, you're sent home," explained Tom Murphy, the president of Canadian Auto Workers (CAW) Local 101, adding that disciplinary action could range from a five-day suspension to outright dismissal.[28]

Employees spoke of a "culture of fear" among CP's employees, as a result of which public safety was being endangered.[29] But Harrison replied sharply to the union and workers through the media: "If they don't follow the rules and instructions, and [don't] do what they're supposed to do, they ain't gonna like the consequences," he added. "Now if that's a culture of fear, they better get ready to deal with fear."[30]

That CP's employees spoke of a culture of fear hardly came as a surprise. In 2008, when CN was under Harrison's leadership, the Standing Committee on Transport, Infrastructure, and Communities, alarmed by the public safety concerns raised by CN employees, launched a study that specifically targeted CN under Harrison's direction. The report concluded:

> The Committee heard that railway workers are reluctant to report safety violations for fear of reprisal by the employer. The problem appears to be particularly acute at CN, where railway workers say they work in a climate of fear ... The fear of reprisals strongly discourages reporting of violations of safety instructions. Union representatives told us that the establishment of a non-punitive reporting system was one of the best guarantors of the ... effectiveness of accident reduction.[31]

"We agree," concluded the Committee. Employees, it maintained in its report, should not have to risk reprisals (possibly involving dismissal) if they reported failures to comply with safety rules and regulations.

But the Committee had no power to impose a different approach on companies, for, according to the law, companies remained the arbiters of safety on their own tracks. The report therefore joined the others on a table already overloaded with alarming reports which, if only attention had been paid to them, could have prevented the disaster in Mégantic. But there was no reaction from the government, from Transport Canada, or from the minister at the time, Lawrence Cannon, and especially not from John Baird, the minister who replaced Cannon and immediately took matters in hand, to whom we shall return later. Such a silence is difficult to explain.

Yet starting in 2012, the scenario of increasing numbers of accidents would continue in the CP where Harrison had undertaken his major "rationalization." According to CP's 2014 Annual Report, in 2013 there was a 7 percent increase in the number of rail accidents.

Not very many, you may think. Except that in October 2014 the TSB announced that in 2013 alone sixty accidents had been left officially unreported by CP. Of those, thirty-four accidents or incidents – fifteen

of them unreported – involved hazardous materials. Worse, a thorough investigation by the CBC would show that CP had failed to report more than 150 accidents to the TSB. This was a cause for concern for TSB Chief Operating Officer Jean Laporte, who confirmed those numbers. CP objected (as did CN and MMA, who also failed to report accidents) that according to the regulations in effect – which, incidentally, had been developed by the industry itself, as we will see later – the company was not required to report these accidents.

Nevertheless, reported or not, the accidents did indeed occur, inflating the figure of 7 percent cited by CP.[32]

In the six months preceding the Mégantic tragedy, the number of accidents was increasing, and they now involved longer trains hauling crude petroleum. The townspeople had already escaped a few potential tragedies. For instance, on June 10, 2013, a month before the Mégantic disaster, a train derailed in the village of Frontenac, just at the top of the descending gradient east of Mégantic, and, as on July 6, a malfunctioning locomotive was involved.

On June 27, 2013, the Bonnybrook bridge in Calgary, which belongs to CP, collapsed under the weight of a 102-wagon train, leaving six cars of oil hanging over the swollen current of the Bow River and threatening several sources of drinking water. Calgary was in crisis at the time, dealing with unprecedented flooding. The city's mayor, Naheed Nenshi, wondered how it could be possible that the City had no authority over the CP when city employees were risking their lives working above the flood as they tried to repair the damage. Then he added: "I'll be very blunt. I'll probably get in trouble for saying this. We've seen a lot of people lose their jobs at CP over the last year. How many bridge inspectors did they fire?"[33]

✖ ✖ ✖

But never mind the controversy: in the spring of 2013, shortly before the Mégantic tragedy, Hunter Harrison fulfilled his commitments to the shareholders. There were fewer crews, fewer employees, and fewer locomotives, but many more tank cars and much more freight in these new trains travelling at higher speeds.

People had not yet become concerned, and the shareholders

were jubilant. Less than a year after coming on the scene and two months before the tragedy, CP announced the largest profits in its 132-year history. Of the twenty-five largest companies listed in Canada, CP recorded the highest return to shareholders: 26 percent in the space of ten months.

Harrison was crowned with glory and, like Ackman before him, was considered a hero of the business world. In 2015, two years after the Mégantic disaster, he would be named "Railroader of the Year" for the second time. In 2007, the *Globe and Mail* had already awarded him the title "CEO of the Year."

A few feeble voices were raised to suggest that there might be more to running a railway company than increasing the return to shareholders, but they were drowned out by the cheers. The *Windsor Star* wrote, for instance, that "U.S. magazine *Railway Age* made a poor choice in recently selecting CP CEO Hunter Harrison as its 2014 Railroader of the Year. That choice seems based purely on stock price and Wall Street interest and not upon any larger questions." But the *Windsor Star* was swimming against the tide.[34]

In 2016, Harrison would be Canada's highest-paid CEO. CP explained that, with Harrison at the helm, its net profit had increased by 69 percent in 2015. In an email quoted by the *Calgary Herald*, CP spokesperson Martin Cej justified the situation by recalling that Harrison had created more than $14 billion in shareholder value since his arrival at the company in 2012, adding that CP's share price had outperformed the S&P/TSX Composite Index by 120 percent through the end of 2015.[35]

✕ ✕ ✕

Hunter Harrison died in December 2017 while at the head of CSX, a leader in rail freight transportation in the United States. Yet however considerable his influence, his departure did not solve the basic problem. Hunter Harrison – at CN, CP, and elsewhere – had never been anything but the spearhead (obviously visible, but nevertheless merely a simple representative) of all those shareholders hidden in the background, thrilled at the magnificent returns on their investments.

Other CEOs – more or less colourful individuals – have replaced

Hunter Harrison as the heads of the railway companies he used to lead, and these CEOs continue to act in the interests of the shareholders, regardless of the consequences.

In the face of its rather miserable financial results for 2018, and the accordingly disappointing returns to shareholders, Ghislain Houle, CN's chief financial officer, announced that the company would start investing again: in new locomotives, new employees, and so on. Was this for safety reasons? Not at all. It was because the demand for oil trains was growing, and CN, which had reduced the company's resources too much, was missing out on new business opportunities and new customers. Houle promised shareholders that he would restore their returns to a more generous level.[36] Promise kept – CN increased its dividend to shareholders by 18 percent in 2018 and forecast an even more profitable year for them in 2019.[37]

In Canada and the U.S., the latest catchword is "Precision Scheduled Railroading" – whatever that means. "It has nothing to do with precision anything," John Previsich, president of the Transportation Division of the International Association of Sheet Metal, Air, Rail, and Transportation Workers, testified before the U.S. House Transportation Committee in 2019, when lawmakers challenged Federal Railroad Administration head Ronald L. Batory regarding three-mile-long trains, and about his decision to withdraw a proposed rule that would have mandated two-member crews on most trains. "What it is, is hedge-fund investors moving into an industry that was well operated, well funded, and well maintained, and harvesting money," added Previsich.

Class 1 railroad earnings topped $16 billion in the first half of 2018. House Committee on Transportation and Infrastructure chairman Peter A. DeFazio concluded that the nation's railway system had fallen into the hands of "the jackals on Wall Street," accusing federal regulators of colluding with them.[38]

NORTH DAKOTA, THE POT OF GOLD

That is a terrific way to make money.

—*Bloomberg Business*, June 29, 2012

SINCE THE EARLY TWENTIETH CENTURY, PETROLEUM – AS WELL as its transportation – has been a fabulous source of fast money, a major geopolitical strength, a foundation of colossal fortunes, and a promise of great wealth for the Western empire-states. These states shared control of the major oil-producing regions of the world; they launched major colonial conflicts and took advantage of the two world wars to arbitrarily draw the borders of countries like Iraq and Niger, to name only two, enabling them to get their hands on those countries' reserves of black gold.[39]

Billions from Fracking

Oil has also been a source of wealth, in the past as in the present, for individuals well placed to take advantage of the opportunity. John D. Rockefeller's fortune came in part from trains hauling the oil owned by his company, the huge Standard Oil. Nowadays Warren Buffet follows his example – both in fortune and in methods. Recognizing the promise of the region, Buffet acquired the Burlington Northern Santa Fe, LLC, one of two major rail networks serving North Dakota, for $26.5 billion in 2010 (yes, $26.5 *billion*!). [40] North Dakota had recently become the new Eldorado of oil.

A cherished region of the American Dream, the legendary realm of the magnificent horsemen of the Mandan First Nation – now called the MHA Nation (Miiti Naamni [Mandan], Awadi Aguraawi [Hidatsa], and ačitaanu' taWIt [Arikara]) – North Dakota, under its velvety prairie, has become the domain of the Bakken geological

formation's fabulous reserves of shale oil, the black gold produced by fracking.

We must forget the pictures of chemists in white lab coats or drillers in coveralls and helmets. North Dakota became a land of "wildcatters," cowboys and ranchers made absurdly rich just because they happened to be in the right place at the right time. It is the homeland of men like JR Ewing, the celebrated tycoon from the cult soap opera *Dallas*, one of whose sayings became highly popular on social media: "A conscience is like a boat or a car. If you need one, rent it!"

Oil is dirty by nature. But when it is obtained by hydraulic fracturing, or "fracking," its extraction is beyond toxic. It releases deadly hydrogen sulphide and turns fertile soil into a chemical desert. With the rise of fracking, North Dakota has become a lunar landscape, bristling with thousands of chimneys, a land of fire that is clearly visible from space.[41] The mythical prairie is now covered with wells that spew poisons, while honest, hard-working oil workers sleep in their vehicles and try to garner some of the manna. For the Mandan Nation whose territory it is, the curse of the black gold has only increased the legacy of poverty and misery bequeathed them by colonialism, along with the legacy of drugs and crime that accompanies an excessive influx of money.

We owe the invention of hydraulic fracking to a certain George P. Mitchell, the immigrant son of a Greek shepherd. A trained engineer, he made his first million by finding oil in previously unexplored areas of Texas, allowing him to quickly make his way onto the Fortune 500 list. Mitchell was obsessed with the idea of exploiting difficult-to-reach oil by extracting it from the very deep layers of rock in which it was held captive. All that wealth close at hand and yet inaccessible – how tantalizing!

In 1990, after $6 million worth of research and ten years of experiments, Mitchell finally succeeded in developing a method of extraction by fracturing rock. He has more than ten thousand boreholes in Texas to his credit, but in another historical paradox, he has also become a major advocate for, and funder of, sustainable development. Loaded with billions, but concerned about the fate of the environment, Mitchell became one of the earliest environmentalists – certainly in Texas at least – to campaign publicly for sustainable development. He has

been a strong supporter of the Club of Rome* and of the idea of limited growth and has spent over $400 million on various environmental causes.

The fracking technique developed by Mitchell is quite simple. It consists of boring a well straight down into the earth, often almost three kilometres deep, and then extending horizontal probes outward to form a sort of octopus around the main axis. Sand and hundreds of chemicals are then injected under very strong water pressure in order to break – fracture – the rock. This frees the pockets of gas and oil trapped in the rock and allows them to rise to the surface, along with the water contaminated by the salts naturally present in the depths of the earth and by the added chemicals. It is simple and efficient.

Interestingly, fracking also gives rise to an odd sort of dyspepsia, or gastritis of the earth. Indeed, one of the most hazardous aspects of fracking is capturing the water that returns naturally to the surface and re-injecting it into the earth, down abandoned wells. Why? Simply because the quantity of water and its toxicity are such that it is preferable to put everything out of sight, and beneath the surface of our planet. This re-injection of contaminated water comes, however, with a price. In September 2016, for instance, the people living on the territory of the Pawnee Nation / Chatiks si chatiks, in northern Oklahoma, were shaken by a magnitude 5.6 earthquake that caused heavy damage and many injuries. It seems that the Earth tries to reject these astronomical quantities of contaminated water that are injected into its bowels; as if affected by a bad fever, it starts to tremble ever more often and ever more powerfully – a reality that was highlighted in 2016 in a study by the very reputable Department of the Interior and Institute of Geological Studies of the United States: "The frequency of earthquakes has recently increased sharply in many sectors in the central and eastern United States, particularly since 2010, and some scientific studies have linked most of this increase with the injection of water into deep dump wells."[42] The report adds that many inhabitants were concerned about the increased number of earthquakes in

---

* The Club of Rome is a non-governmental organization (NGO) that functions as an international think tank on global issues. It was founded in Rome in 1968 by a group of European businesspeople and scientists.

populated areas, including the threat to their drinking water and the possibility of destruction and injury.

It is difficult to argue that these inhabitants are paranoid, but it is always possible to attempt to reassure them by telling them that the officials of the Texas government's energy and natural resources agency – curiously called the Railroad Commission of Texas – categorically rejects any connection between fracking and earthquakes. "A lot of nonsense," they say, basically. How reassuring. It should be noted, however, that this agency is also responsible for enabling and promoting the exploitation of oil.

In any case, thanks to Mitchell, a whole series of new JR Ewings emerged in North Dakota, instant multimillionaires created by hydraulic fracking. The most eloquent example is undoubtedly that of Harold Hamm, a fierce promoter of the region as a source of petroleum. Starting from nothing, like all legendary heroes, he began by renting plots of land from neighbouring farmers, at $200 per hectare, on which to bore his first wells. Becoming a vocal apologist for the exploitation of Bakken shale, Hamm made his sales pitch, reaped his profits, and exerted as much political pressure as possible to impose the philosophy of every black-gold producer: "Drill, baby, drill." In 2012 Hamm was a staunch supporter of Mitt Romney, the Republican candidate for the White House, but the *Wall Street Journal* asserted that at the time he had already become Donald Trump's personal adviser on oil issues. This was confirmed when, during the new President Trump's first official press conference, announcing an open season for oil drilling, the President declared that he relied on the advice of "his very, very great friend Harold Hamm."[43] Indeed Hamm, along with other multibillionaires, was standing directly behind the president at the swearing-in ceremony in January 2017.[44]

Hamm reaped staggering profits. For instance, in December 2016, after a meeting of the Organization of Petroleum Exporting Countries (OPEC) at which the Organization agreed to reduce its production of oil (resulting in increased prices), Hamm's wealth grew overnight by three billion U.S. dollars – an amount boosted, of course, by the election of Donald Trump. The influence of Hamm and his multi-billion-dollar oil companies on the Trump administration would

necessarily lead to a major expansion in the conveyance of oil by rail and pipeline.

Hamm, the Dakotan oil magnate, swore that more than twenty million barrels of oil were buried under the state's golden, level cornfields. Was this a good or a bad thing? Whichever it was, since 2009 the oil boom has been rampant in North Dakota, where, Hamm prophesied, tens of thousands of wells would most likely be drilled.

North Dakota became bedlam between 2010 and 2012. Thousands of workers flocked in from all sides, unaware of or unconcerned with the living conditions that awaited them. This was in the aftermath of the 2008 crisis, which was still wreaking havoc: an ailing economy, unemployment, families with no homes or on the verge of losing them, and so on. Attempting to support their families, workers chose mass exile in North Dakota. As a makeshift economy reigned, the oil workers slept wherever they could, in their cars or trucks, or in shabby motel rooms. Riskily, truckers would transport explosive charges along dusty roads. Small businesses mushroomed here and there: hairdressers, variety stores, mechanics. Life was very hard in North Dakota.

But not for everyone. For some it was an extraordinary business opportunity. "Ackman was smart," commented *Bloomberg Businessweek*. "When he bought his [CP] shares he knew that an aggressive management could take advantage of opportunities in the Bakken Shale. He probably was in before the value of the Bakken was reflected in the public stock price. That is a terrific way to make money." [45]

CP and the Winning Hand of Ackman and His Associates

Starting in the early 1900s, more than eight thousand kilometres of railway track were built in North Dakota to carry western grain to markets. But just two lines were available to serve the Bakken oil fields. One was the Burlington Northern Santa Fe line, which, as mentioned above, was acquired by Warren Buffet in 2010 for $26 billion. But Burlington Northern Santa Fe suffered from two disadvantages: it lacked a widespread network, and it did not operate in Canada.

The other line, the real gem, was CP's. It ran from Minneapolis in the south all the way across North Dakota and it was the only one that crossed the Canadian border northward into Saskatchewan,

where it linked up with CP's Canadian network. CP reached not only into North Dakota but also, with its Canadian lines, into the Canadian oil sands and shale oil-producing areas – for the Bakken geology extends across the border into Canada. It was therefore in a unique position to transport all that oil to ports in both western and eastern Canada, including Vancouver, Montréal, Halifax, Saint John, and also New York.

This route for the transportation of oil to major markets and seaports was worth its weight in gold for producers who found themselves landlocked in the centre of the continent. Held hostage by rail carriers, they were ready to pay the price. Why? It was a matter of profit, naturally.

If oil producers could manage to get their oil to ports from which it was possible to reach international markets, they could sell it at the benchmark "Brent crude" price. This price is determined by the international oil market and was considerably higher, certainly at the time of the Mégantic tragedy, than the benchmark domestic price for oil sold in the United States, known as the "WTI (West Texas Intermediate) price." In short: access to a port or a refinery close to a port means much higher profits for oil companies and their shareholders than if their product is confined to the U.S. market alone.

But, you may ask, is transportation by rail not costlier than by pipeline? Indeed it is, except that the pipelines, especially in Dakota, lead to the U.S. market in the middle of the continent, mainly to the refineries in Cushing, Oklahoma, and these were already struggling to keep pace with the volume of oil to be processed. This surplus was resulting in a lower price. It was therefore more profitable for a producer to pay for rail transportation to a port (between $7 and $10 per barrel in 2012, and between $15 and $18 in 2016, compared to $7 to $10 by pipeline before 2014),[46] provided, of course, that this cost remained reasonable – something Hunter Harrison at CP would ensure. Rail is also a more flexible means of conveyance, since tank cars can be removed or added as required and can also be directed to wherever required – for instance to other refineries less overburdened than those in Cushing. Given the congested pipelines, this flexibility was a valuable asset.

In this race for profits from oil by rail, the CP line had another

ace up its sleeve. In fact, the CP network was the only railway with a line leading directly to the very heart of the oil business in New Town, North Dakota. New Town, as the small town in the centre of the Williston Basin is now called, sits at the centre of the Bakken oilfield. Located in the Fort Berthold Reservation, New Town would experience a 90 percent increase in crime and tragedies due to the advent of new drugs, an unfortunate development that would wreak havoc on the population. But to the indifferent and the cynical this was merely collateral damage.

In short, CP was the only network able to deliver to New Town all the material and products needed for fracking, including astronomical amounts of sand, and then take the oil out and haul it to anywhere in North America as required. CP thus controlled both the incoming supplies and the outgoing product. John Anderson of Greenbriar Equity Group, quoted by Bloomberg in 2012, confirmed this: "If you have access to both the sources of supply and the destination, your advantage over your competitors is 100 percent, resulting in the maximization of profits."[47]

In 2012, CP held a winning hand, and was able to crush any competition.

However, in 2011 most investors remained unaware of this – most, but not all. When he decided to take control of CP that year, Ackman was fully aware of the value of this hidden gem. He and Hunter Harrison had done their homework. "Ackman was brilliant," New York analyst Tony Hatch told Bloomberg. When he bought his shares in CP, added John Anderson, the financial potential of the Bakken shale – and of the railway – was still unknown and still had to be reflected in the company's share price. In short, Ackman was able to acquire a splendid source of income at a discounted price.

For Ackman, this was indeed a "dream opportunity to make money," as Anderson had enthused. From five hundred tank cars in 2009, the transportation of petroleum products would rise to 140,000 tank cars in 2013, an increase of 28,000 percent. CP would double its revenues thanks to oil – as indeed was also the case for CN.[48]

× × ×

From the Canadian Pacific Railway website:

> We connect the Bakken Shale to refineries and other facilities throughout North America.
>
> If you're shipping to or from the Bakken Shale region, talk to us. We are the only rail carrier providing single-line haul service between the Bakken and major crude oil markets in the Northeastern United States. Our location in the heart of the Bakken region means easy access for shipping and receiving other oilfield-related products such as frack sand, steel pipe, oilfield tubular products, aggregates, chemicals, fuel condensate, construction materials, and dimensional cargo.
>
> We work with companies on both sides of the border, and with our access to ports and transload facilities and our connections to short line, regional and Class 1 carriers, we provide unparalleled access to the Bakken Shale region and the U.S. Gulf Coast, U.S. Midwest, U.S. Northeast, and Canadian markets.
>
> We also provide rail access to other crude oil markets in Alberta and Saskatchewan and the oil sands through Alberta's Industrial Heartland.
>
> For a quote or more information about shipping to the Bakken Shale [fill out] our online form or contact ...
>
> Our industrial development team will help find suitable locations and determine site-specific requirements for rail service.[49]

× × ×

The Unit Train, a Bomb on Rails

> These guys are up and running in one year while everyone
> is sitting around and waiting for pipeline construction to
> be allowed.
>
> —*Bloomberg Business News* [50]

Getting up and running within a single year was exactly the feat
Hunter Harrison accomplished in North Dakota. In July 2012, Harrison and Ackman were leaving nothing to chance as they prepared
"Operation Black Gold."

First, on Harrison's arrival in office, CP announced the signing of
an agreement with U.S. Silica, the second-largest producer of sand for
hydraulic fracking in the United States. In 2013 it was anticipated in
well-informed circles that CP would haul a million metric tonnes of
sand from Sparta, Wisconsin. [51] This marked the start of CP's twofold
involvement in the Bakken market, conveying merchandise both into
and out of the area.

Second, Harrison was looking for new customers, assisted by
World Fuel, his major business partner. He found a buyer in the Irving refinery in Saint John, New Brunswick, owned by the well-known
family of the same name. The company held a special place in the
heart of then Canadian Prime Minister Stephen Harper. Irving owned
an Atlantic port, the outlet to the international market so coveted by
producers. An initial test trainload of Bakken oil was sent there. The
refinery's management was delighted: the Bakken oil was light and
easy to refine, a treat to work with.

In November 2012, just five months after Harrison took over at CP,
shipments began arriving at Irving's refinery in Saint John. A total of
3,830 tank cars of crude would travel through Mégantic in the months
preceding the disaster.

Third, Harrison the visionary enthusiastically embraced the
unit train revolution. [52] Finally, he could realize his dream of ultraprofitable transportation by rail using longer, heavier, faster trains.

In the photos of the ruins of Mégantic after the tragedy, it was the blackened carcasses of a unit train's tank cars that we would see. It is also a unit train that you may notice passing close to where you live: a long convoy of tank cars as much as two kilometres long. The black ones are used for hauling petroleum products, but they can also transport other dangerous goods.

A unit train can complete a trip as much as 28 percent faster than a regular train, travelling directly from its starting point to its destination without having to constantly stop along the way to load or deliver cargoes for various customers. This eliminates lengthy manoeuvres in marshalling yards that can unduly prolong the length of a trip and create a need for numerous employees – hence the potential for layoffs. For anyone who has ever travelled by train, the unit train is the difference between an express and the interminable "milk runs": passengers can save hours by taking the express. In the same way, unit trains spare the railway company – and the buyer – significant time and costs.

But for the unit train to be truly profitable, those hundred tanks all need to be filled in record time. To achieve that, a modern, well-equipped transloading centre of enormous capacity is required.

Harrison had thought of that. Fourth, therefore, on March 15, 2013, Harrison and CP announced the establishment of a partnership with Dakota Plains Holdings, owners of transloading centres, and World Fuel Services, a Florida oil consortium extremely active in Dakota, to expand the transloading centre in New Town, in the very heart of the Bakken Formation.

CP already enjoyed a monopoly on the use of the New Town transloading centre, but the Pioneer project announced that day would allow it to increase its capacity, according to the press release, from thirty thousand to eighty thousand barrels per day, with a storage capacity of 270,000 barrels. No wonder Craig McKenzie, CEO of Dakota Plains, was on cloud nine: "2013 will be another great year for Dakota Plains shareholders as we anticipate a significant increase in the size of our business."[53]

CP executive vice-president Jane O'Hagan was also pleased, asserting that CP would be able to provide cheaper access to Bakken's productive sectors, and describing CP as a low-cost supplier.

CP would achieve its goal of hauling 140,000 tank cars in 2014.[54]

Result: in four operations, and after having already taken the first step (a drastic reduction in CP's operating costs) Harrison could turn to the second part of his challenge – transforming the previously untapped potential of the CP line to Bakken into a major money-maker.

"Mr. Harrison," wrote the magazine *Les Affaires*, "carried out a restructuring operation that has reduced the productivity gap between CP and CN. Many analysts have admitted their surprise at how quickly the results have improved. Since May 1, 2012, the share price has climbed by 92 percent."[55]

✕ ✕ ✕

On March 15, 2013, optimism reigned at the announcement of the Pioneer expansion project at the New Town transloading facility. The press conference was in full swing, and the cocktail sausages were disappearing fast. All the guests were taking a last look at the current facility, which was soon to see its capacity triple. In the meantime, business continued to boom.

Front stage at the press conference were the proud, happy representatives of three of the main actors in the Mégantic disaster: Dakota Plains, the source of the highly volatile oil; CP, the carrier; and World Fuel, a legendary giant of the Fortune 100 list and the owner of the oil that would catch fire at Mégantic, whose powerful hand would intervene discreetly at the highest levels in the wake of the tragedy.

In the room where the press conference was held, feeling proud of his employer, World Fuel, and of Dakota Plains, was someone whose name would later crop up in connection with the Mégantic tragedy. Eli Jasso was a family man, a fishing enthusiast and, apparently, a bon vivant; he was also involved in running the transloading facility.

Nearby, stage left, sat some DOT-111s, the unsafe tank cars, awaiting their next departure. It was precisely from this transloading facility, on the following June 30, that the ill-fated train set off for Mégantic.

Making the official photo of those ultimately responsible for the tragedy of Mégantic incomplete, representatives of MMA were missing from the Dakota Plains festivities in New Town that day. A few Canadians were also absent, including members of the government, such as

the ministers Baird and Denis Lebel (federal minister of transport in the Harper government) and a few senior public servants, and, of course, the railway industry's lobbyists, Michael Bourque and his associates.

✗ ✗ ✗

However, to ensure the delivery of oil at a low cost, a price had to be paid. That price was risk. Trains weighing more than ten thousand tons travelling on "100 lb. jointed rails dating back to the 1950s" was a risk that Harrison, the celebrated 2002 Railroader of the Year, was ready to take in order to reduce his running costs.

He was also chartering the old DOT-111 tank cars, despite their fragility and poor condition – and choosing the railway company with the worst safety record in North America as a subcontractor.

MMA, THE MISSING LINK

> The MMA network ... was the shortest and most direct link
> between Saint John and Montréal.
>
> —TSB report on the Mégantic tragedy [56]

IN THE EARLY FALL OF 2012, LESS THAN TEN MONTHS BEFORE
the disaster in Mégantic, Harrison and Ackman were pleased: not only
had they configured their Bakken market, they now had the ability to
move oil all across North America. Moreover, along with World Fuel,
they had just signed their lucrative contract with Irving, selling the
company more than seventy-three unit trains of oil.

But there was a slight hitch: CP was missing a few hundred
kilometres of track between Farnham, Québec, and New Brunswick –
a short stretch of line and a small gap in the CP network, but one of
major importance where the contract with Irving was concerned.

But this, too, had been foreseen. Harrison, the man on the ground,
was very familiar with the North American railway system. CP's network spread out like a huge hand with tentacular fingers comprising
dozens of small networks reaching into some of the most remote
corners of the North American continent.

These were small, independent carriers, often with limited resources, not very scrupulous, and not very reliable. But above all, they
were inexpensive. One of them, the Montreal, Maine and Atlantic
Railway (MMA), had the great advantage of offering the shortest route
between the sudden end of the CP network and the customer, Irving
Oil – a simple, practical, and inexpensive solution.

The other option for World Fuel was to use a port in New England
to convey the oil to New Brunswick by ship – a long, complicated,
expensive process. Or they could use the CN line via the lower Saint
Lawrence. But CP, the "low-cost provider," had a better idea. The
shorter the route the faster it is, and consequently the more profitable.

For World Fuel (the seller), CP (the carrier), and Irving (the

customer), MMA was the most profitable solution. The oil delivered by CP would therefore travel on the MMA line, the most direct. Of the seventy-three trainloads sold to Irving in 2012, sixty-seven would have time to reach the refinery before the disaster in Mégantic, meaning that some 3,830 tank cars purchased by Irving would by then have passed through the town on the MMA track.

MMA was the railway company with the worst accident record in North America. This fact was known to all the carriers (including CP) and to all the departments and agencies responsible for transportation safety in Canada and the United States.

✖ ✖ ✖

In the early morning of a late-winter day, a train hauling liquefied petroleum and propane was travelling too fast down the gradient leading to the centre of a small town. It reached a damaged section of track which the company that owned it had never thought fit to repair, and went off the rails. At high speed, the crushed tank cars piled up and caught fire. By the time firefighters arrived, five minutes later, the fire was raging, and fireballs were exploding one hundred metres into the air, visible for more than a twenty-five-kilometre radius. An hour after the accident, the railway informed the firefighters that the tanks would not last more than ninety minutes before exploding, given the apocalyptic intensity of the heat: it was possible that the explosion might obliterate the downtown area completely. Two thousand inhabitants were evacuated urgently, so urgently, indeed, that the firefighters' hoses were even left lying where they had been dropped. The fire would destroy the entire infrastructure of the town, burning for sixteen days, during which the evacuation order would remain in place.

This accident is considered one of the worst ever in U.S. railway history, and the authorities agreed it was a sheer miracle that there had been no casualties. Subsequent reports would show that "to improve efficiency" the company was running its trains with a single-person crew and doing so without notifying the Federal Railroad Administration (FRA), the official regulatory body. Major problems in the maintenance and training of employees would later come in for severe criticism.[57]

Place: Weyauwega, Wisconsin, USA.

Date: March 4, 1996.

Railway company: Wisconsin Central.

Its president: Edward Burkhardt.

× × ×

In 1999, three years after the Weyauwega disaster, the above-mentioned Ed Burkhardt was awarded the title of "Railroader of the Year." Four years after that, he bought Montreal, Maine and Atlantic Railway.

The Weyauwega derailment provided an almost perfect preview of what would happen seventeen years later in Mégantic, on the MMA line. The same can be said of the 2010 accident at Brownville Junction in Maine, not far from Mégantic, when an unattended MMA train ran out of control down a gradient and crashed in the village, resulting in injuries and pollution.[58]

No Canadian or American authority has been able to put a stop to this deadly series of similar, eminently predictable accidents. Burkhardt was merely allowed to acquire additional weapons by being entrusted with large explosive trainloads. And this was despite everyone being fully aware of the facts.

For those who witnessed his arrival in the shocked community of Mégantic five days after the disaster, there could be no doubt that Burkhardt, the president of MMA, was an utterly obnoxious individual, displaying no compassion whatsoever and eager to blame his lone locomotive engineer, Thomas Harding.

It would, however, be quite wrong to think Burkhardt was merely a greedy clodpoll of limited intelligence. On the contrary, for almost thirty years he has been showing his scowling face along the world's railway lines with amazing – or maybe we should say appalling – success.

As the head of Rail World Inc., his personal holding company, he possesses a wealthy portfolio of about fifteen companies that do business from the Netherlands to New Zealand, from Eastern Europe to Delaware and Colorado and Illinois. Burkhardt is one of those adventurous characters who has chosen railways as his field of activity, the way some people hunt for gold mines or rhinoceros horns.

He (and his trains) have travelled the world for decades, accumulating deals in a broad swathe of countries.

All Burkhardt's deals are similar. He is somehow able to persuade governments to grant him permission to privatize a state railway company. Then he takes control of the newly formed company as CEO, managing it with a parsimonious hand. For instance, in the late 1990s, he orchestrated the privatization of New Zealand Rail (now KiwiRail) and for six years headed the company, Tranz Rail Holdings, that was created as a result. Some people must certainly have emerged from this manoeuvre as winners, since the New Zealand government appointed him honorary New Zealand consul in Chicago.

In 2001, we find Burkhardt in Estonia where, once more, he was able to privatize the state railway and lead the resulting company as its CEO until 2007. But without doubt one of his greatest successes seems to have been Rail Polska, a company he founded in 2003 after acquiring two small regional railway lines in Poland. Based in Warsaw, Rail Polska was granted an unrestricted operating licence, allowing Burkhardt to immediately commence long-distance haulage of coal in that same year. Rail Polska soon played an important part in the newly deregulated market of the European Union.

In 2018, Burkhardt was as ubiquitous as ever. According to several sources, he even managed to get involved in a project that was viewed as a priority by the European Union: the improvement of rail links between Western and Eastern Europe, no less. While still chair of the Board at Rail Polska, he extended his reach by becoming chair of the Supervisory Committee of Baltic Rail AS, a company based in Tallinn, Estonia, one of the main ports offering access to the Baltic Sea. He also participated – the exact details remain unclear – in the development of Rail Baltica, a 950-kilometre project including a ferry and a tunnel, in addition to the track itself, with the objective of connecting Finland and Poland by way of Estonia, Latvia, and Lithuania.

Far from putting a stop to his activities, then, his dismal record and the tragedy of Mégantic seem to have actually aided his ascension in the business world, including in the United States, where he became chair of the Board of Directors of Wheeling and Lake Erie Railway, a short but strategically located railway line carrying large quantities of hazardous materials – a scenario very similar to that of MMA. In 2017,

a railway workers' union had to appeal to the Supreme Court in its attempts to halt the dangerous practice of the single-person crew, which Burkhardt was still attempting to introduce on that railway, for if Burkhardt had a signature, it was the notorious single-person crew. Often imposed without the knowledge of the authorities, on the pretext of increasing efficiency and integrating new technologies, this practice bears witness to Burkhardt's obsession with cutting costs to the bone – the devil take the consequences.

We don't know the accident record of his railways in other parts of the world, but in North America it is well documented and known to everyone in the field of rail transportation. This was true long before the Mégantic tragedy. In the United States, the Federal Railroad Administration has developed an index comparing carriers. Between 2003 and 2011, MMA had an average of 23.4 incidents per million miles and a total of fifty-six accidents, while the national average was around sixteen. Between 2010 and 2012, MMA reported twenty-three accidents, injuries and other incidents for less than one thousand kilometres of track. Also in 2012, when the company began shipping oil with unit trains, MMA was averaging 36.1 events per million miles travelled, compared to 14.6 for other carriers – more than double the average.

Was this normal? No. Burkhardt did everything required to produce accidents on his lines. He cut back on maintenance, employees, and training. Former employees at Farnham, who were often lower-paid CP retirees, even confided that he was skimping on toilet paper and Band-Aids!

It was in 2003 that Burkhardt purchased the 1,200 kilometres of track belonging to the Bangor and Aroostook Railroad in northern Maine and Vermont, and Quebec Southern Railway, a bankrupt company, which he merged under the name of the Montreal, Maine and Atlantic Railway (MMA).

Quebec Southern was just about on its last legs when Burkhardt bought it. Active throughout a good part of the twentieth century as a hauler of wood and pulp, Quebec Southern had created an economic link between the northeastern United States and Québec by way of Mégantic, giving birth to the town. The network (which for a long time had been owned by CP) had been reduced to a mere shadow of its former self: the logging sites were deserted, the mills were closing,

northern Maine had been bled dry, and the lumber industry was shrinking. Burkhardt was struggling.

Running out of cash, he found savings by ceasing proper maintenance on the track and rolling stock – an ugly practice he would continue even after business improved. Thus, it would later emerge that the lethal locomotive 5017, technically responsible for the tragedy of Mégantic, was ready for the breaker's yard, several repairs to its engine mounts having been made using polymers. "We had the engine held in place with epoxy and liquid plastic," Jacques Breton, public safety officer for the Mégantic tragedy, later told me. It would also emerge that the train had derailed while travelling on a track in poor condition that had undergone a "temporary" repair.

And, naturally, Burkhardt slashed wages, starting with a 40 percent cut. In addition, he "cut fat" from the workforce, provoking several waves of layoffs in 2006 and 2008. Starting in the United States, he initiated his signature move, which was to have trains operated by just a single crew member. The TSB would later establish that MMA employees suffered from chronic fatigue: they were being overworked, had to use faulty equipment, and endured excessively long shifts.

MMA's first substantial inflow of cash, with Burkhardt at the helm, occurred in 2010, when he managed to sell off 375 kilometres of track to the state of Maine itself for $20 million. To force decision-makers to act, he had threatened to abandon the network, which served sizable communities in the state.[59]

Burkhardt got a new infusion in 2012 when he signed a lucrative contract with CP to haul crude petroleum to the Irving refinery in New Brunswick. By the time of the derailment, as we saw earlier, almost seventy unit trains had already passed through Mégantic on their way to Irving's facilities.

2012 was, therefore, a pivotal year for Burkhardt, when he was thrilled with the radical cost reductions he had made, coupled with the lucrative oil contracts with CP, for he did not want anything to get in the way of his success. That year, exasperated by the bureaucratic hassles caused by some Transport Canada officials, he initiated the single-person crew on his Québec section without troubling to inform the relevant officials, bypassing them and going directly to the higher reaches of the ministry.

Looking at Burkhardt's career, one has to wonder how this man, wherever he goes in the world, can win such blind trust and avoid interference from governments which, as in Estonia and Poland, did not hesitate to entrust him with the future of essential railway lines – railways that supplied businesses and residents with their vital requirements for energy and heating, such as coal. We could say that those deals were happening in distant countries with perhaps less stringent laws and less cautious, if not downright corrupt, authorities. But surely not here in Canada?

Well, in that we would be quite mistaken. It was precisely here, in Canada, and in Québec in particular, that Burkhardt would carry off one of his most awe-inspiring coups. Here are several pieces of evidence.

First, Hunter Harrison would knowingly entrust CP's lucrative explosive-laden trains to Burkhardt's company, despite its catastrophic accident record.

Second, Burkhardt would be able to obtain $15 million from the Québec and Canadian governments. These funds came from a budget for joint infrastructure programs and another for shortline railways[60] ($6 million came from Ottawa, $4 million from Québec, and $5 million from the shortline railways program). After the Mégantic tragedy, according to Le Devoir, Pauline Marois, who was premier of Québec at the time, undertook to investigate rumours that the $15 million contributed by Canada and Québec had been invested in the United States. We are still waiting for an answer.

Third, the Québec government would be even more generous to Burkhardt. Despite his alarming record, the Caisse de dépôt et placement du Québec* would lend him an additional $14 million to allow him to buy MMA's severely degraded track in Québec – an investment that would hand Québec savers a $7 million loss.† In fact, in 2013, at the

---

* An institutional investor that manages several public and quasi-public pension plans and insurance schemes.

† The Caisse lost slightly more than $7 million that had been invested in the form of capital shares. See their "Communiqué: Montreal, Maine & Atlantic Railway Corporation," July 8, 2013, www.cdpq.com/fr/actualites /communiques/precisions-investissement-de-la-caisse-dans-montreal -maine-atlantic-railway.

time of the tragedy, the Caisse was still a minority shareholder in MMA, with 12.7 percent, which by then was worth almost nothing. Was the Caisse completely blind? Yet in 2003, one of its directors was on the board of MMA. This was Yves Bourdon, a former manager with CN, who must be credited with a certain degree of railway expertise. Clearly, however, the Caisse overlooked the company's cutbacks in manpower and maintenance, along with Burkhardt's terrible accident record.

But was this blindness or deliberate ignorance? (It is true that since 2003, the year when the Caisse invested in MMA, it was headed by the same Henri-Paul Rousseau who lost $40 billion for Québécois in the crisis of 2008.)

Final evidence of Burkhardt's ability to obtain money and favourable treatment from our governments is provided by the fact that, to help MMA and its CEO, the highest authorities of Transport Canada, answering to the ministers John Baird and later Denis Lebel, would put a stop to the hassling of MMA by certain officials who feared for public safety.

Who would intervene to ensure that MMA, despite its infractions, deficiencies, and degraded track, could be left to operate free of interference? Who would intervene to stifle the concerns expressed by some, including a handful of public servants, about the implementation of the single-person crew? Perhaps Burkhardt was merely a wretched risk taker. But that didn't prevent him from taking advantage of our blindness and becoming the fortunate recipient of considerable largesse right here in Canada and Québec.

Estonia and Poland have no reason to envy us.

✕ ✕ ✕

As a resident of Nantes, Québec, for fifty-five years, Jacques Breton has in his backyard, next to the town's propane tanks, the railway track from which the runaway train began to roll. At the time of the tragedy, he was responsible for public safety in Nantes, and it was Breton's firefighters who put out the fire in the locomotive a few minutes before the disaster. They were also the first responders to rush to deal with the inferno in downtown Mégantic.

As a neighbour of the town and its citizens, he plunged into the

fire and chaos to save his loved ones before participating in the first response, as public safety officer of the Granit Regional County Municipality. Finally, as mayor of Nantes, he received copies of the subsequent reports on the tragedy. Jacques Breton saw everything. He was a perfect witness to the crime, to the crime scene, and to the aftermath. He should have received and seen all the official responses, and so be fully informed. But he wasn't.

On July 6, 2013, after I activated the emergency communications and protocols, I had a bite at McDonald's a few hours after the derailment. Then I got a call from the Sûreté du Québec. They wanted to talk to me, right away. They came, and I got into their car. Then they asked: "How did you find out that MMA went from two people to one on their trains?" I explained to the police that people from MMA came to inform us that from now on there would be only be one person on the trains.

We thought right away it was a major safety issue. We wondered what would happen if the single driver fell ill, or had a heart attack? There'd be a safety device on the throttle, they said, and if the throttle wasn't moved for twenty seconds, the train would begin to slow down.

Slow down? That hardly inspires confidence. It'll decelerate, yes, but if it's going to hit something, it'll hit it anyway, we said. It'll keep slowing down until it stops, they answered.

We disagreed completely with this approach. It's not a practice that should exist on trains with the kind of loads they're carrying around here.

Oh, they tell us, it's been approved by the federal minister, and that's it.

Ouch!

Well, we don't understand it at all. They got the minister's go-ahead to keep on doing that? It makes no sense. It can't work like that.

So we called the federal Transportation Department.
They told us yes, in this case, that's the way it is, that's
the way it'll stay.

It makes no sense.

And just look at what came of it!

✕ ✕ ✕

The devastation of Mégantic was so cruel, its causes were so widely
dispersed and so technical, its underlying stories were so dense, that
you have to fear that you'll never be able to understand what happened. We always hope to find an answer – just one answer that's easy
to understand and can provide some reassurance.

The authorities and their reports do indeed supply answers to our
questions and those of the victims' families: "Brakes, DOT-111s, wear
on the tracks …" Very well, but …

Surely there must be more to it than that. Those are only technical
details. They're real all right, but they're not enough. The disaster was
too enormous to be explained by a failure to apply enough brakes.
What, then? There's at least one obvious question to which it would be
good to have an answer. How can those dreary trains of black tank cars
that stretch for miles be allowed to travel through our towns, valleys,
and mountains with a crew of just one? Who authorized that in the
first place? How could such a practice even be contemplated? How
could a single individual be given the responsibility for conveying
$8 million worth of explosive material? An answer is needed: a clear
and simple one. Will it provide the key to all the others? It seems,
intuitively, that that must have occurred to the Québec police who,
just a few hours after the fire, were already questioning Jacques Breton
on the matter.

Intuitively too, we feel that the answer will be obvious. In a world
cynical about governance, we expect to find someone – someone in
authority, perhaps even an elected official – who, one day, in exchange
for some favour, signed a document, a decree, a regulation, whatever,
authorizing the single-person crew.

On closer examination of the case, the first answers to emerge are
quite predictable. Burkhardt knows the world he operates in, and one

of the first things he did after creating MMA-Canada was, despite his shortage of funds, to hire one of the best lobbyists in Ottawa. In fact, less than three days after the accident, Gilles des Roberts, editor of the legal news media outlet *Droit-Inc.com*, wrote under the headline "Owner of Death Train Had Contacts in Ottawa" that:

> Between 2002 and 2008, Montreal, Maine and Atlantic Railway carried out no fewer than nine lobbying campaigns with elected officials and federal decision-makers, assisted by a lawyer from Gowlings! ... This was Henry S. Brown, a leading expert in railway law, who handled all these files. Maître Brown, who is also an exceptional advocate before the Supreme Court of Canada, worked in the office of the minister of justice and the minister of transport before joining the law firm. During this period, the company met dozens of times with officials from Environment Canada, Industry Canada, Transport Canada, and the Canadian Transportation Agency, as well as with MPs and senators. What were MMA's concerns? The environment, immigration, grant applications to various funds and programs, and of course the regulation of rail transportation.[61]

Brown had developed such a relationship with the Conservative government that he would be appointed a Federal Court Judge and an ex officio member of the Federal Court of Appeal a year after the Mégantic disaster.

So Burkhardt, while too penniless to repair his locomotives properly, had chosen to hire an expensive lobbyist. So far, our cynicism remains undiminished. What we want to believe is confirmed, though it brings us little comfort. And what came next was equally predictable: it seems certain that a few phone calls were made.

Yes, a few phone calls. Since 2003, Burkhardt had been wanting to introduce the single-person crew to Canada. Already, to his considerable irritation, he'd had to deal with rules and red tape. After he signed the contract with CP in 2012, Burkhardt was especially eager to glean some profits and reduce the company's costs. But he was receiving

letters from officials in the Québec regional services of Transport Canada (TC-Québec) insisting that he should observe the regulations. No penalties, just harassment. According to well-informed sources, Burkhardt was losing patience. He is then said to have enlisted the aid of the railway industry's chief lobbyist, Michael Bourque, CEO of the Railway Association of Canada, to lodge a complaint. The latter assured him that he would take care of the matter and immediately put in a phone call to the "highest level" of the ministry.

Several months later, officials of the Québec regional office would learn with astonishment (or, in some cases, resignation) that MMA was running its trains using a single-person crew. And, as Jacques Breton would discover, this had been authorized by the minister. Transport Canada had merely required MMA to install mirrors on one side of its locomotives.

But despite all this, the authorization of the single-person crew, as people finally understood to their consternation, was not the result of some skulduggery in the upper reaches of Transport Canada in return for some possible under-the-table reward. In fact, the minister – Denis Lebel, as it happened – never "directly" authorized the single-person crew, never signed anything to that effect.

No. That wasn't even necessary. This was because John Baird, a predecessor at the helm of the Transport Ministry, had handed the railway companies a most generous gift indeed. Completely disregarding numerous reports, including one from the Canada Safety Council [62] which expressed concern about a series of major derailments, Baird had allowed private companies complete control over the regulations governing railway safety in Canada, delegating to them the power to write their own safety rules and monitor themselves. As a bonus, Baird took care to make Transport Canada toothless.

As a result, according to our own laws and regulations, the single-person crew no longer needed anyone's authorization – not that of a minister or deputy minister, not of anyone. Burkhardt had been given a free hand. Government permission was no longer required. The big players in the industry, like Harrison and his associates, could pick and choose whatever regulation suited them. Would they comply with any? Only they can say.

Maybe one of those notorious "brown envelopes," the emblem

of corruption, would have been preferable. Then at least it might be possible to identify the rotten fruit, remove it, and feel safer. But in this case the rot was in the soil where the tree grew.

✖ ✖ ✖

Kathy and Lucie, my youngest daughter's two babysitters; Kevin, my cousin's son; Henriette, my uncle's lovely sister; Marie-Noëlle, the daughter of my great friend; Stéphane, my car salesman; Jean-Pierre, the contractor who was going to repair my roof; Sylvie, the president of the Scouts who I worked with for years; in all twenty-five people I knew very well and often met.

They all had lives. They were leading their lives. They were alive, living people. They were important. I lost them all. Gone in seconds. That's a lot of deaths. Too many. We're trying to find out why. We're digging, searching. Why did this happen? Who did it? Can it happen again?

—Robert Bellefleur

Our lives are full of peripheral figures – babysitters, garage mechanics, and grocery packers. We talk to them without giving them very much thought, we learn about them, we take an interest in them or are simply polite to them, we put labels on them: they're pleasant or grumpy, funny or shy. And they treat us in the same way, of course. They're just there, and we pay them a little offhanded attention.

But when many of these ephemeral figures vanish in a single moment, the hole that remains is bigger than the largest black hole in the universe. Normal life is diminished.

Proportionately, the forty-seven dead of Mégantic are the equivalent of sixteen thousand deaths in Montréal – as if all Westmount was wiped out.

TRANSPORT CANADA,
THE SUBSERVIENT ENABLER

I don't get it. You leave your keys in your car and they give you a ticket. But it's legal to abandon a train running at the top of a hill.

> —Isabelle Boulanger, mother of Frédéric Boutin, who was nineteen years old when he died on July 6, 2013

Just leave us alone ... and let us run our business.

> —Hunter Harrison, CEO of CP, addressing Canada's new Prime Minister Justin Trudeau in 2015[63]

Railway safety is a top priority.

> —Transport Ministers John Baird, Denis Lebel, Lisa Raitt, and Marc Garneau

ACCORDING TO TRANSPORT CANADA, THE FORTY-SEVEN FATAL-ities caused by the derailment of an oil convoy in Mégantic were due to an unusually unfortunate alignment of factors on a warm July evening in the Mégantic valley.

Railway Safety Down the Drain

On August 5, 2005, a CN train derailed about thirty kilometres north of Squamish, in British Columbia, spilling forty thousand litres of caustic soda (sodium hydroxide). Caustic soda, which is highly soluble in water, is used to unclog pipes. It is most familiar as one of the main ingredients in Drano. Needless to say, the environment paid the price, and the fish population of the Cheakamus River was

decimated. Between August and December 2005, four further major accidents would follow. Then, on June 29, 2006, a second derailment, near Lillooet, BC, caused two deaths, those of the train crew. "Several accidents during this period were spectacular," reported the Standing Committee on Transport, Infrastructure, and Communities. "Together they caused serious injuries and fatalities, resulted in serious environmental damage and a negative impact on the economy."[64] Between June 7, 2007, and March 5, 2008, a further fifteen major rail accidents would be reported in Canada. In response to public concern, Lawrence Cannon, minister of transport at the time, asked an advisory committee of the House of Commons to submit a report. The Canada Safety Council, a non-profit organization whose members are no more revolutionary than insurance companies, police services, or National Defence, made a presentation to this committee suggesting that "Canadians would be shocked to learn the degree to which the government had reneged on its responsibility for railway safety."[65]

In 2008, the final report of the advisory committee included more than fifty recommendations for the improvement of railway safety in Canada. It especially denounced the safety management system, the foundation of railway safety in Canada. The report would be carefully tabled without the media's knowledge. It was at this point, on October 10, 2008, that John Baird was appointed minister of transport.

✗ ✗ ✗

According to the Transport Canada website, the mission of the Department – and its minister – is to serve the public interest by promoting "safe, secure, efficient, and environmentally responsible transportation" within Canada.[66]

What tools are available to this federal agency and its decision makers to allow them to fulfill such a mission and avoid preventable fatalities such as those in Mégantic? They can use laws and regulations, including the Transportation of Dangerous Goods Act, the Railway Safety Act, and the Canadian Railway Operating Rules. But how can the Department and its minister ensure that companies respect the railway safety laws and regulations?

Do they do so by means of strict on-the-spot inspections, like the

police officers who mercilessly catch us out by setting up roadside checks in the holiday season? No, not really. Not where railways are concerned. In this domain the rule is, rather, "Inspections, but not really inspections." But why is this?

In March 2017, Robert Bellefleur asked Transport Canada a specific question about the number of inspectors in the field. He received the answer that the total number of supervisory personnel in the country, including researchers, engineers, and support staff, had been tripled in 2016. So far so good.

If we take a closer look, we find that three years after the Mégantic tragedy, it does, indeed, look as if 2016 was a good year for railway safety. From the forty-three previously existing inspection posts, the number had grown to 122 across Canada, meaning that approximately 250 individuals were responsible for ensuring transportation safety – for inspecting tracks, equipment, tank cars, level crossings, toxic or explosive materials, etc. – everything. Just 250 people responsible for fifty thousand kilometres of railway lines throughout the country.

However, according to Brian Stevens, former director of railway safety at Unifor, a union representing thousands of railway workers, Canada had once had as many as seven thousand inspectors.[67] Furthermore, by the time the reductions in personnel took place, between 2009 and 2013, there had been a 28,000 percent increase in the conveyance of petroleum on Canadian soil, and a 25 percent increase in the amount of hazardous material hauled by each train.[68]

Oddly, in Canada, the greater the danger on our railways, the fewer the personnel available to inspect and police the railway companies.

✕ ✕ ✕

In reality, this picture is not wholly accurate. Our railways are policed by numerous people, some of them very effective individuals. But there is a major problem: the police forces in question do not consider public safety their mission. The heads of CN and CP, long exasperated at having to rely entirely on security guards without much power to protect their property and land, called for the federal government to allow them to establish their own police. Authority to do so was established by section 158 of the Canada Transportation Act, amended

and applied in 2007 – incidentally, just when Hunter Harrison took the helm at CN. These completely private police forces are in the exclusive service of the railway companies to protect the property administered or owned by the companies. They have been accorded full legal powers, including the ability to make arrests, detain offenders, and impose fines. They carry arms. (In 2017, these private police would be granted additional powers by the government of Québec, including the ability to enforce the road safety code.) As was seen after an accident in Montréal in 2015 when a CN train unexpectedly burst into a house (!), they may even refuse access to an accident site, as they did on that occasion to officers of the Police Department of the City of Montréal.

Strange? No. Just rather feudal.

Here are a few illustrative anecdotes.

In 2014, a CN train derailed in the heart of Saint-Henri, one of Montréal's most populous neighbourhoods. On behalf of the Société pour vaincre la pollution (SVP), Daniel Green and I went to the spot to carry out a citizen's inspection, using a camera. It is the SVP's job to track pollution and polluters and, in this case, oil and diesel were spreading across a patch of land without CN making any effort to clean it up, though the land was used by pedestrians, dog walkers, and all the local residents, including children attending a primary school situated some two hundred metres from the railway track and the accident site. On his second visit to the scene, Green was intercepted by a private CN officer, who ticketed him for sampling and documenting the pollution. "Presence on private land without a lawful excuse," said the ticket. Worse, the police officer completely disregarded Green's request that he alert Urgence-Environnement* immediately. Not lacking in pugnacity, Green went on, in 2018, to personally challenge the fine in court, to the complete surprise of CN's well-paid lawyers, drawing public attention to this private pseudo-justice. However, CN enjoyed a clear advantage. It would cost Daniel Green over $3,000 to transcribe the proceedings of the trial, something the judge has now required – an exorbitant amount, of course, for a citizen lacking in

---

* The Québec contact of the National Environmental Emergencies Centre, the federal government's environmental emergency response program, which was created in 1973 following a major oil spill in Nova Scotia.

resources. Green v. CN, with its bottomless pockets. Still without a lawyer, Daniel Green managed to cover the cost … but lost anyway.

Concerned about the traffic of oil-carrying unit trains in her immediate neighbourhood, Nicole Jetté, a citizen of Saint-Hyacinthe as courageous as she is curious, wanted to ensure that the tracks passing close to her home were in good condition. This was after the Mégantic disaster, but also after two other major accidents had occurred in February and March 2015 in Gogama, Ontario, involving trains on their way to Saint-Hyacinthe and also hauling hazardous materials. In Gogama, thirty-eight DOT-111 tank cars derailed, setting off a spectacular fire. Nicole Jetté set out to review the rail infrastructure in Saint-Hyacinthe, including a tunnel. The photos and videos she published testified to the lamentable state of the equipment and infrastructure. Ms. Jetté asked CN to carry out urgent repairs to the tracks. The local municipal government supported her efforts, sending strong letters and passing resolutions, and also asked CN for assurances that its infrastructure was able to withstand the long, heavy trainloads of crude and other hazardous materials that were travelling through its jurisdiction. In a very extensive document she was preparing for the Court to obtain the results of the CN rail inspections that had not yet been made available to the public, Ms. Jetté explained:

> On March 11, 2016, following the reports and videos submitted, the CN police came to my home to "warn" and inform me that trespassing on CN's private property was illegal. I replied that for the sake of my conscience and the principle of necessity I considered it my right and duty to document the state of the rails and publicize conditions that might endanger public safety. The principle of protecting life and the common good should prevail over a private company's regulations.[69]

A TSB interim report on the two accidents in Gogama supported Nicole Jetté's reasoning, concluding that defective tracks very likely played a role in both accidents.[70] (A third derailment took place near Gogama in 2018 – the fourth derailment in northern Ontario that year.)[71]

Sometimes such cases are more subtle. In 2014, Robert Bellefleur decided to show the media photographs of the deteriorated track on which trainloads of explosive materials were travelling past his home in Mégantic. The response would be unusual, to say the least: it was left to the Québec Order of Engineers to intimidate Bellefleur. The Order accordingly dispatched an investigator bringing him a formal warning for "illegally practising the profession of engineer."

Okay. But then, if not inspectors or policemen, who is meant to look after our safety? How is it supposed to work?

"Without Us, There'd Be No Wealth"

Without the ability to transport freight, Canada – at least in the opinion of our politicians and financiers – would be nothing. Ours is a country of natural resources. Some of these resources had the foresight to reside close to port facilities, ready for export.

But, unfortunately for us, the country is so vast that many resources are landlocked far in the interior. Hence the all-powerful position held since Canada's creation by the transportation companies that haul our natural resources to ports and export markets. It is no coincidence that Canada has been built around its railways, the true backbone of the country.

Initially, the undertaking must have seemed exciting, even humanitarian, since it allowed prairie wheat to feed Canada and other parts of the globe. But soon wheat would be replaced by other mineral resources coming from central Canada – uranium, potash, iron, copper, lithium, nickel – which generated much larger profits. And then there was that fabled treasure trove of black gold in the ground beneath Alberta: the viscous tar sands bitumen, and the volatile, explosive shale oil, identical to what was being extracted from the Bakken formation in North Dakota.

So transportation is the very foundation of Canada's wealth. And as a result, rail transportation is at the heart of what is almost blackmail: Without us, there'd be no wealth, say the heads of the railway companies. And, in a way, they are correct.

Laws, rules, and regulations get in the way of profits. They mainly lead to expenditures, not revenues. "We tend to over-regulate a lot,"

Gérald Gauthier of the Railway Association of Canada recently repeated in a scandalized tone. Employing inspectors, maintenance workers, wasting time on environmental assessment, and what is worse, slowing "economic development" – such are the nightmares that haunt the sleep of some CEOs.

A great wave of deregulation, beginning in the early 1980s and lasting until the present, has sought to do away, little by little, with all such obstacles to "progress," for the benefit of industry. Reagan, Thatcher, Mulroney, and other proponents of neoconservatism or neoliberalism assailed the rules, regulations, and laws governing industrial activity, laid off thousands of inspectors, supervisors, and other employees of supervisory agencies, ultimately delegating to industry the power to police itself as it saw fit. This is still true today.

In the Canadian transportation sector, railway executives, skilled in the art of extortion, would undoubtedly be the big winners in terms of deregulation and the abolition of oversight.

Far from seeking to conceal the unique position of the railways, Transport Canada readily acknowledged this in the mission statement provided on its website at the time of the disaster: "TC promotes the safety and security of railway networks, air, rail, and road transport, and the safe transport of dangerous goods. To do this, TC develops regulations and safety standards ..." So far, there is nothing out of the ordinary, you say. The rest of the sentence was more embarrassing: "or, in the case of railways, facilitates the development of rules by the rail industry." It went on: "Transport Canada recognizes that the principal responsibility for safe operation lies with industry." It was all there, in black and white.[72]

✕ ✕ ✕

As the millennium began, the railways were well ahead of the game and masters of the transportation of Albertan oil. Over just five years, they would see an increase of around 28,000 percent in the amount of oil conveyed – an utterly spectacular expansion that had an equally dramatic impact on profits, shareholder returns, and, unfortunately, public safety.

For, more and more, this policy of deregulation was beginning to

encounter ever more snags, ever more inconveniences, in the form of accidents and derailments that were extremely visible to the public. It was becoming necessary to do something about safety concerns, for some people were becoming quite concerned about the issue, and the unions were getting media coverage. Railway safety was also a worry for a few conscientious legislators and public servants.

Yet the various ministers who succeeded one another at Transport Canada and could see what was happening felt that, as the ministry's website laid out quite clearly, "as traffic volumes increased, the total number of accidents would increase."[73]

Nevertheless, they did not adhere to "an exclusively prescriptive regulatory approach" (that is, laying down strict laws strengthened by inspections and sanctions). This was in large part because to do so "would have required a significant injection of resources for regulatory oversight, simply to maintain or further reduce the total number of accidents."

In other words, to avoid an increase in accidents, more inspectors on the ground would be required. But they had all, or almost all, been "let go." No: another solution had to be found.

✗ ✗ ✗

Over the course of twenty years, more than twenty reports appeared – accident reports, ministerial reports, House of Commons committee reports – almost all, describing concerns with railway safety in Canada and predicting that sooner or later a terrible accident was sure to occur. These reports were, of course, tabled.

But it was the 2008 advent of a new minister, John Baird, that really consolidated the railway industry's advances (and the profits these advances provided), plugging any leaks so that everything could continue to swim in oil. It can be said in Baird's defence that his predecessors had been equally servile in their dealings with the railway industry leaders. But in 2010, when Baird moved from the Ministry of Transport to the Ministry of the Environment, he famously said, in an interview with Radio-Canada, that it came as a considerable surprise to him to be told that human activity was the cause of global warming.[74] So it is easier to understand that he was able to relieve

completely the frustrations of CEOs and railway shareholders during his time at Transport Canada.

Baird was certainly the right man for the moment, always ready to fight against anything costly and unprofitable that did not contribute to economic growth. He had begun his career as Ontario's minister of community and social services in the Conservative government of Mike Harris with an aggressive crusade against welfare recipients – the embodiment of the "dead wood" of society. The ferocity of his hunt for welfare recipients gained him attention.

Baird had decided that it was necessary to reduce or even eliminate certain expenditures that were considered unproductive, such as social assistance and support for the disabled. At his first press conference as a new minister in 1999, he was already extolling the Harris government's record of reducing the number of welfare claimants, announcing that fifteen thousand people had exited the system since the initiation of the Ontario Works program. He naturally omitted to mention that 40 percent of the beneficiaries had been peremptorily removed from the list by his own department. Baird continued the hunt with the help of a confidential phone line which enabled people to report fraud by beneficiaries. If found guilty, the claimants would be excluded from the system for life and/or be sentenced to house arrest. This was a rather radical approach that, unfortunately for Baird, caused a tragic incident when, in the middle of a heat wave, a pregnant young woman who had been condemned to house arrest died in the apartment to which she was confined.[75] Baird naturally defended his position, but a report concluded that the heat in her apartment had contributed to her death. Another report also highlighted the necessity of providing food and medicine, as well as adequate housing, to those sentenced to house arrest. The same report recommended eliminating the lifetime ban.

Despite all this, Baird not only stubbornly defended his actions, but carried on in the same vein. He initiated a mandatory drug testing program for welfare claimants, threatening to ban them if they refused to submit. At one dramatic press conference, he threw a box of syringes on the floor, proclaiming that his ministry would prevent people from "shooting their welfare cheques up their arm"[76] and inject them instead with the secret of how to succeed in society. In 2000,

he expanded mandatory testing for alcohol and prescription drugs. He also tried to force claimants to undergo a literacy test before they could receive their cheques, probably to infuse his famous secret of success. This proposal eventually encountered resistance from various anti-poverty and human rights organizations active in Ontario, who publicly denounced Baird's offensive on the poor and disabled.

In May 2005, Baird joined Stephen Harper's Conservative federal government. He was appointed minister of transport in 2008. Once he took up his new post, railway safety seems to have been moved to the bottom of his agenda.

One of the first reports to be ignored was the official report of the Railway Safety Act Review Panel, an exercise launched in February 2007 by former minister Lawrence Cannon and intended to be repeated every five years. The report, issued in May 2008, had teeth. It also had indisputable credibility: its members, appointed to the committee by Cannon, had strong CVs. The authors pointed out that the Railway Safety Act, which had been passed in 1989 to protect the public and was ironically titled "Going Unimpeded," may have been a godsend for an industry hungry for deregulation, but in terms of safety, and given the frequency of accidents, it was time to do some "impeding."

Sixty recommendations were made in that report, and Cannon created a follow-up committee – which included representatives of the Department, industry, and the unions – to oversee their implementation. One suggestion was to tighten the rules. On becoming minister, Baird immediately dissolved this committee.

✕ ✕ ✕

Here, we look ahead to September 21, 2017, 9:30 a.m.

Scene: A dull conference room with a square table, in a Transport Canada building stuck at the back of the parking lot at Trudeau Airport (a.k.a. Dorval Airport). At one end sat the chairs of the Railway Safety Act Review Panel, in its second incarnation, 2017–2018. To head the review, Transport Minister Marc Garneau had appointed Richard Paton, former president of the Chemistry Industry Association of Canada, an association that claims to be "a global leader in

responsible care and deeply committed to all aspects of safety in its operations, including transportation." Sitting to his right as vice-chair was the respected Pauline Quinlan, the dignified former mayor of Bromont, Québec.

In theory, this was an important exercise. Its purpose was to suggest improvements to the Railway Safety Act while the ghosts of the forty-seven victims of the Mégantic disaster were still abroad. But improve it for whom? In some circles, disturbing rumours were rampant: the rail lobby would have the final say, the changes would all go the wrong way, and the "common good" would be flouted.

Seated at the table, on either side of the chair and vice-chair, were two clearly adversarial groups. On one side were those who must live with the consequences of goods trains travelling past their backyards: the mayor of Magog, where the track belonging to MMA's successor, CMQR, runs; representatives from the Pointe-Saint-Charles neighbourhood of Montréal, where everything from cereals to explosive materials travels through; Robert Bellefleur, from the Mégantic Citizens Committee; and Daniel Green, from the SVP.

On the other side sat two participants: Ryan Ratledge, the CEO of CMQR, who had flown in directly from Bangor, Maine; and Gérald Gauthier, of the Railway Association of Canada. That afternoon, but in the absence of those defending the interests of the general public, representatives of the two major players in the rail industry, CN and CP, were to attend.

The co-chairs were showered with suggestions from the citizens' representatives.

Make real-time information available on the transportation of hazardous goods in time to allow prompt reactions? Totally impractical, replied Gauthier. The risk of terrorism!

Install more level crossings because when people are cut off by a railway line they will cross wherever is convenient? Also impossible, retorted Gauthier. It is up to local authorities to discipline their citizens.

Slow down the trains? Perish the thought: it's not profitable; they need to go faster ...

And then, to crown it all, Green, in the presence of the horrified Gauthier, suggested renationalizing the railway tracks and subjecting

them to stricter oversight, similar to that provided by the CRTC for Canadian broadcasting and telecommunications. Ratledge, meanwhile, argued quietly that the fewer laws and regulations there were, the better for everyone.

The battle between the public and the railway industry and its lobby was completely one-sided in money, time, and resources. Would the chairpersons appointed by Garneau be able to restore some balance between the parties? Would the rumours be disproved?

It remained to be seen. That morning, Vice-Chair Quinlan had used several of the limited speaking minutes allotted her to praise and thank warmly – very warmly, indeed – the boss of CMQR, who had, with remarkable dedication, as she pointed out several times, flown in from Maine in order to reach Trudeau Airport by 9:30 a.m. – demonstrating, she said, the great willingness of the railway companies to collaborate. But she did not have a single word or glance for Robert Bellefleur, who had travelled at his own expense from Mégantic, a three-hour drive. (Perhaps Bellefleur would have done better to stay home that morning for, during his presentation on the still-undetermined causes of the disaster, Richard Paton nodded off.)

When the committee's report came out in 2018, its authors did mention Mégantic:

> Significant concerns were raised by participants ... on the need for more transparency ... to help reassure the public that the regulator is doing its job in enforcing compliance. As an example, it was noted that in Lac-Mégantic there was now a good level of collaboration between the railway company, the municipality, and Transport Canada, but the general town population is unaware of these good relations, or work being done to improve rail safety.

So, was this a public relations campaign conducted by Transport Canada to reassure the public? We can be quite sure that such an effort would have had no effect on a public that was now thoroughly disillusioned. This was because two minor derailments had occurred in Mégantic in 2019, including one that involved a train carrying

hazardous goods, even though just a few months earlier another Transport Canada report (not meant for public consumption but inadvertently publicized) had warned CMQR that it had more than 250 broken and dangerous rails on its line. However, Transport Canada was not requiring the company to carry out the necessary repairs – merely to keep it informed of its inspections.

As for the rail lobby, on May 27, 2019, it jubilantly thanked Transport Minister Marc Garneau for allowing it what it had been requesting for so long, namely video and audio recorders in the locomotives. To detect broken track and other defective equipment ... or to keep employees under observation?

✗ ✗ ✗

A turning point for the safety of Canadian railways came in 2008. All aspects of railway safety were on the table, awaiting review. These circumstances allowed John Baird to carve in stone the administrative procedures that made the Mégantic disaster possible.

Bruce Campbell, at the time the executive director of the Canadian Centre for Policy Alternatives, has studied the issue of railway regulation. He explains that in that year the Railway Association of Canada, the industry lobby, completed "a comprehensive redrafting of the entire Canadian Rail Operating Rules"[77] – which, as the TSB explains, are "the rules by which Canadian railways under federal jurisdiction operate."[78]

While this aligns with Transport Canada's policy of "facilitat[ing] the development of rules by the railway industry," the devil is in the details. The Canadian Rail Operating Rules frame the day-to-day working of railways, meaning that they have a direct impact on the cost of their operations. They determine essential factors, such as the number of brakes to be applied or the number of crew required. Corporate CEOs always take a critical view of these details, for the fewer the constraints put in writing, the greater the industry's freedom to reduce costs.

In 2008 Transport Canada reached a crossroads: it could choose to be strict, exercise greater control, and resume responsibility for railway safety – or not. The latter would be the case.

Of course, the Department did not abdicate its responsibilities overtly: "Transport Canada can order the development of a rule or the amendment of an existing rule." But then came the catch: "The RAC [Railway Association of Canada], in consultation with its member railways, would then draft the rule."[79] The TSB report on the Mégantic tragedy later highlighted this.

That report concluded that the "findings as to the causes and contributing factors" were that:

(1) MMA-002 [the train involved in the tragedy] was parked unattended on the main line, on a descending grade, with the securement of the train reliant on a locomotive that was not in proper operating condition;

(2) the seven handbrakes that were applied to secure the train were insufficient to hold the train without the additional braking force provided by the locomotive's independent brakes.[80]

Was this even legal? Yes, it had become perfectly legal since the revision of the Canadian Rail Operating Rules, "updated" by the industry, and finally adopted in December 2013.[81]

"There were no regulations," explained the TSB, "precluding trains, including those carrying DGs [dangerous goods], from being left unattended on a main track. When trains were secured at Nantes, they would be left on the main track with at least one locomotive running, the automatic brakes released, the independent brakes applied, and a number of handbrakes applied."[82]

A number? "At the time of the accident, Rule 112 (dealing with the immobilization of unattended trains, including the number and type of brakes that should be applied), merely stated that 'a sufficient number of handbrakes must be squeezed.'"[83]

A sufficient number? What *is* a "sufficient number"? Is that a precise safety rule, or simply empty words?

The meaning of words, however insignificant they may seem, can be very important. Take the case of words like "law," "regulation," "rule," "guideline," and "directive." For instance, railway companies operate according to "directives" where the number of brakes to be applied is concerned, but not "laws" or formal "regulations." The difference is considerable.

For instance, on March 4, 2012, a company called Les Atocas de l'Érable Inc. won a lawsuit against the Québec Ministry of the Environment after the ministry required the cranberry grower to provide compensation for the loss of some wetlands, following a ministerial directive in force since 2006.*

In his judgment, the Superior Court judge gave the ministry officials a stern lecture. The judge stressed that a directive or policy is not a law or regulation and therefore comes with no legal weight or measures to enforce compliance. The judge exhorted legislators to do their job by ensuring that a law or regulation was in place before trying to compel anyone to comply with a certain behaviour.

Laws and regulations are drafted with the input of impartial specialists and adopted by representatives duly elected by the public, responsible to the public, and acting in the sole interest of the public – at least in theory.

However, rules drafted by a company can change according to circumstances without any account being taken of facts or impartial findings that it considers irrelevant. Its authors are accountable only to the company, its managers ... and its shareholders.

✕ ✕ ✕

October 26, 2017.
Scene: Criminal trial of the three accused.
Michael Horan, one of those heading MMA in Québec, had been

---

* Since the name of the Environment Ministry has changed several times in the past few years, we will mostly use this generic name, but will also designate the ministry by its official name at the time, according to the circumstances.

testifying for several days, especially regarding the rules laid down in the MMA Operations Manual that dictate the best practices locomotive engineers are expected to follow in driving and securing trains.

On the morning of the twenty-sixth, the discussion, questioning, and technical cross-examination continue for at least an hour before a drowsy audience. Suddenly, the atmosphere becomes electric and the tone a little more heated. Horan is adamant that certain rules in the manual do not have to be observed by MMA locomotive engineers. And then an increasingly absurd exchange takes place, suddenly awakening the spectators: the lawyers are arguing a point.

"Look, Your Honour, it's in the manual."

"No, Your Honour, that doesn't apply to MMA."

"But it's written right here!"

"Yes, but it's not highlighted in grey ..."

"Highlighted in grey?"[84]

After much explanation, it emerges that the manual used by MMA locomotive engineers is the CP manual; the MMA authorities have used grey highlighting to distinguish the rules that are supposed to apply at MMA. In order to provide numerous photocopies for the defence counsel, jurors, and judge, the prosecution has used the original handbook seized from MMA by the police. But the photocopier failed to reproduce the grey highlighting – and the end result is that everyone in the courtroom has different versions of the rules that MMA locomotive engineers are or are not supposed to follow.

This is no trivial detail. Already, the fact that the rules were written by the companies and can differ from time to time was hardly conducive to the provision of clear, directive regulations. But this incident on October 26 shows how rules can be randomly applied, to the extent that even experienced lawyers and judges can be baffled and find it impossible to determine exactly which ones did or did not apply.

Just imagine a single locomotive engineer consulting a manual containing a few hundred primary and secondary rules ...

✖ ✖ ✖

Two days after the disaster, on July 8, 2013, officers from the Sûreté du Québec and Transport Canada finally "discovered" an MMA

train from the United States that had been forgotten at Vachon, high above Mégantic.

The locomotive's engine had been left running for three days, and only five handbrakes had been applied to keep the train's eighty-nine wagons and tank cars in place. Transport Canada Inspector Alain Richer, who was on site, requested five additional handbrakes, for safety's sake. Randy Stahl, an MMA manager in charge of locomotive maintenance, first carried out a handbrake effectiveness test by putting the train in forward gear. Nothing moved. The delighted Stahl turned to Richer and declared that the number of brakes was obviously adequate. However, MMA's official rule called instead for "10 percent of the cars, plus two" as the number of brakes to be applied – amounting in this case to ten brakes. Five additional brakes were therefore applied.

Michael Horan, who came on the scene a few hours later, decided to apply five more brakes, bringing the total number to fifteen. Stahl, who would testify at the trial in 2017, would say that he used a standard of 20 percent plus two and taught it at MMA. In that case, more than twenty handbrakes would have been required.

So what should it be: five, ten, fifteen, or twenty brakes? What level could be considered safe? A competent engineer, some impartial employee of Transport Canada, could have provided the correct answer. How many brakes are required to hold a convoy of 50, 100, or 125 wagons and tank cars? And on a steep gradient? For everyone's safety, would it not be possible to include the results of scientific studies on the physics of acceleration as applied to moving trains, accompanied by a clear, simple table and a binding regulation? A locomotive engineer, alone with their train, would probably prefer to rely on a scientific calculation (tonnage, gradient, etc.) instead of having to estimate randomly the "adequate number" of brakes required, guessing at somewhere between 10 or 20 percent.

For the sake of historical accuracy, the TSB did later – forty-seven fatalities later – conduct some tests, but only relating to the accident of train MMA-002. It concluded that between eighteen and twenty-six brakes would have been required. Richer, the inspector, confirmed in 2017 that he had never witnessed any such tests being carried out on trains of the current size and weight.

✗ ✗ ✗

In 2019, trains, even those carrying hazardous goods, could still be left on a main track with the engine running and without any mechanical means to stop them should they begin to roll. Worse, as is still the practice at Nantes, the triage operations, in which the wagons and tank cars are changed and moved around, are performed at the top of gradients. Why? Because the track is the property of the railway companies, so they can make whatever use of it they please. "This is private property and we are not entitled to interfere," Richer pointed out. Minister Garneau had himself confirmed this in the spring of 2017.

✗ ✗ ✗

> Regarding CMQR, we invite you to contact the railway officials to ask them how their practice in this matter complies with Rule 112.
>
> —Email reply from an official at Transport
> Canada to Mégantic resident Robert
> Bellefleur, February 28, 2017

The "matter" in question was the concern expressed by Robert Bellefleur, who in February 2017, four years after the tragedy, asked Transport Canada which new laws and/or regulations applied to the parking of trains hauling hazardous materials on the gradients on both sides of the little town where he lived.

Or, more simply, after so many reports, recommendations, ministerial visits, and reassuring statements, whether trains carrying hazardous goods parked at Nantes or Vachon were secured in a way that would prevent them from running unchecked downhill to Mégantic, as had occurred on July 6, 2013. Transport Canada's response speaks for itself: it suggested asking CMQR to explain how it observed Rule 112. Rule 112, dealing with the immobilization of unattended trains, had been drafted, like other rules, by the rail industry itself. It had been formulated to protect the interests of the railway companies.

But it was even worse than that, as Transport Canada's response shows. In addition to writing its own rules, the company also monitored itself, and did so according to a large volume it had written itself – a sort of in-house code of procedures called the "Safety Management System."

The reply provided by Transport Canada in 2017 thus reveals that nothing has changed since the Mégantic disaster. The safety of our railways, even after forty-seven fatalities, still rests on the same three pillars: the rules written by the industry itself, self-monitoring, and the above-mentioned Safety Management System. Even now, more than seven years after Mégantic, no one except the railway company knows whether its trains are adequately secured to prevent them from setting off uncontrolled toward populated areas.

On February 4, 2019, a train was parked at the top of a steep gradient in the mountains above Field, British Columbia, because one of its locomotives was malfunctioning. (Although the TSB report on the incident has not yet come out, it appears that this locomotive had been experiencing difficulties similar to those affecting the locomotive involved in the Mégantic disaster, namely engine hunting, when because the amperage was not constant the locomotive could not maintain a steady speed.) The three crew members attempted repairs. The emergency air brakes were applied, but the handbrakes were not, since no rule or regulation required the latter as an additional safety measure. The train began to move on its own, gathering speed as it raced toward the village of Field, at the bottom of the gradient. The last living action of the three crew members was to telephone advising that Field should be evacuated – especially since storage tanks of gasoline were located in the town. However, the train derailed before reaching Field. Result: three deaths, and two young children left fatherless.

The day after the accident, Minister Garneau discreetly issued a ministerial order requiring the application of handbrakes at the top of gradients – a precaution the people of Mégantic had been advocating for two years already. The next day, CN and CP appealed the Order. The matter is pending.

And Garneau's Order may be a moot point anyway. A close reading of the Order reveals that handbrakes are only to be applied on a slope of more than 1.8 percent. 1.8 percent? While the grade in the

Spiral tunnels, outside Field, comes in at 2.2 percent, the gradient at Mégantic, one of the steepest in an inhabited environment, only measured 1.2 percent. A cynic might almost wonder whether Minister Garneau and the senior bureaucrats of his ministry were not deliberately aiming for an almost non-existent degree of slope.

If the tragedies at Mégantic and Field were indeed disasters that could have been anticipated, the deaths that resulted from them were all the more odious. This is especially so of the three deaths at Field, since that accident occurred under the watch of a minister who was not only aware of the circumstances of the Mégantic disaster, but who, as an engineer and astronaut, must surely have been aware that the law of gravity and safe transportation are crucial factors in survival.

✗ ✗ ✗

Now let us return to John Baird, who, as transport minister in 2008 and the following years would face a major challenge: in the context of deregulation, budget cuts, and the increasing number of accidents, he had to provide the public with a plausible assurance to give the impression that even in the absence of inspectors and sanctions the government was taking steps to prevent disasters.

Transport Canada proposed Safety Management Systems (SMS) as a solution. SMS, written by the companies themselves, are a set of in-house guidelines that tell employees what to do, and when and how to do it, for trains to run safely.

And, to lend some measure of governmental legitimacy to these collections of theoretical rules, most of the few field inspectors remaining at the Ministry of Transport would be turned into SMS auditors – basically bureaucrats assigned to reading the thick volumes produced by the companies. This was now supposed to ensure that railway safety was "a Canadian priority."

The TSB's report on Mégantic – in addition to several other reports on the subject, including one by the Auditor General of Canada – would devote entire pages to the ineffectiveness of SMS.

> Many inspectors [from TC-Québec] felt that resources
> devoted to SMS audits were wasted; they believed that

there was little that could be done if an operator was not conforming to its SMS. This belief originated from TC's Railway SMS Regulations Enforcement Policy, which established that a railway company could be prosecuted for non-compliance with SMS Regulations, but not for deficiencies in the implementation of SMS ... [and because inspectors] were provided with few tools to require improvements if a company was unwilling or unable to effectively implement the processes required under the SMS Regulations.[85]

"I never looked at the MMA SMS, I never used it, it's just a sort of ideology," declared Alain Richer in 2017.

The authors of the TSB report were not deceived, saying that it had to be recognized that "administrative defences alone [were] not sufficient to maintain safe operations" and that "multiple layers of defence [were required] to reduce risks."[86] Clearly, this meant that an SMS was a paper tiger which, even if it was reviewed every five or seven years by a Transport Canada official, would never stop a train as efficiently as the application of twenty handbrakes or the addition of a derail device on the track. And that is something that the general public could easily understand – on condition it was made aware.

This was a problem for the ministry – and a disturbing sword of Damocles for the companies. For, despite the invention of SMS, the public was still not reassured, thanks to skyrocketing accident statistics. A convenient culprit was still needed. This was when, for once, Transport Canada turned to science.

The Swiss Cheese Model

In 1990, James Reason presented a now well-known model of accident causation (the Swiss Cheese model) that explained how human beings contribute to the breakdown of complex, interactive and well-guarded systems, such as rail transportation.

—Transport Canada website

It is well known that nature abhors a vacuum. In the absence of a credible explanation, without a clear culprit, the public might begin to ask inconvenient questions. For instance, should an accident occur, elected officials might be accused of negligence, or worse, the companies responsible might be sued. The very idea that citizens might be able to demonstrate in a court of law, whether criminal or civil, that a broken rail on a track belonging to CP or CN was the cause of an accident was highly disagreeable to railway CEOs. Companies wanted to maintain control of safety matters and write their own rules, yet not be held responsible for accidents, nor be obliged to pay compensation or damages.

James Reason, a researcher at the University of Manchester (and a darling of Transport Canada), would provide the answer to this delicate problem. Reason's research shows how "human beings ... contribute to the breakdown of complex, interactive and well-guarded systems, such as rail transportation."[87] His theory, called the "Swiss cheese model," is widely known; at the time of the Mégantic disaster and, until recently, was cited at length on the Transport Canada website.[88]

Reason argues, in brief, that although a system may function well, it can sometimes break down thanks to human behaviour, occasionally resulting in an accident. So how does that happen?

In Reason's Swiss cheese model, wrote Transport Canada, "defences against failure within an organization can be considered as a series of barriers, which are represented as slices of Swiss cheese. The holes in the cheese slices represent individual weaknesses or even breaches in individual parts of the system, which continually vary in size and position in any of the slices." When a hole in each slice happens to be aligned with a hole in each of the other slices, this allows risk to pass through, resulting, in Reason's words, in "a crash-friendly trajectory." "This model," wrote Transport Canada, "helps to understand how humans contribute to the breakdown of complex systems."

Here was the ideal solution, a simple but effective one. Who is to blame for accidents? Human beings. And not just anyone, especially not the person at the top. No, it is the very last in the series of holes in the package of Swiss cheese slices. In other words, the employee who fails to block the risk.

Hunter Harrison would confirm this: the accident in Mégantic was due to the negligence "of an individual who did not apply the brakes correctly." [89] "Regulation," he added, "cannot stop [such] behaviour." So the imposition of laws and regulations is a waste of time. "Let us run our business," he appealed to Prime Minister Trudeau in 2015.[90]

According to Transport Canada's theory, and in light of Hunter Harrison's comments, the deaths of forty-seven people were caused, on a warm July evening in the Mégantic valley, by an alignment no less improbable than that of all the holes in a package of Swiss cheese. This deadly event must therefore be the fault of a single person, the driver of the locomotive, the only one guilty of having threaded his way through the improbable alignment of holes: the broken-down locomotive, the unapplied and inadequate number of brakes, the gradient of the track, the unattended train, the too-fragile tanks, the lack of inspectors, etc.

Human error. Human failure.

ONE MAN ALONE

> The train engineer, Thomas Harding, was arrested and charged with criminal negligence causing the death of forty-seven people, having failed to apply a sufficient number of brakes.
>
> —*TVA Nouvelles*, May 12, 2014

WHY, ON SUCH A GRADIENT, WITH A LOAD OF THAT KIND, AND knowing he had a malfunctioning locomotive, would a normal human being not apply enough brakes? Pure folly? Negligence? Fatigue? And anyway, what *was* a "sufficient number of brakes"? Harding had applied seven, while the MMA rules called for nine and the TSB later estimated, after more comprehensive scientific testing, that between eighteen and twenty-six were required. "It's a good thing Harding has been charged. It'll teach the other engineers to be careful next time," said one highly respected and respectable individual, now retired, who spent his life on trains and furthermore has trained future drivers on safety.

"Would you, after thirty years as an engineer, leave an oil train on a slope with only seven handbrakes on?" I asked Fritz Edler, of Railroad Workers United in the United States, who came to the defence of the Mégantic accused. Edler had vehemently argued the importance of redesigning the famous rules that he saw as a menace to locomotive engineers and to the public. "You personally, Fritz, would you have ... just seven brakes?" Fritz, a huge man from Baltimore, stopped in his tracks. And finally he grimaced.

"I don't know. The guys always did that. Nothing had ever moved. And then there had been pay cuts, fatigue ... Anyway, there should have been a whole series of additional emergency brakes that should have been triggered."

"Okay, Fritz ... But only seven?"

Another grimace.

✗ ✗ ✗

It is midnight. Harding is on his own, soaked in oil, sick with worry. He is especially worried about the locomotive, which is spewing oil. But there is also something else. In 2008 he had received a letter from a man named John W. Schultz, who at the time was a vice-president of MMA in the U.S., about an apparently inadequately secured train. In order to avoid harming MMA's relationship with CN, MMA was asking Harding to quietly accept responsibility for an incident for which he was not to blame. Some actually say that he agreed to do so to spare a vulnerable CN employee.

Harding is viewed by his peers as a particularly careful, conscientious locomotive engineer, too cautious for his bosses' liking. It is said that when he drove passenger trains he would put a glass of water on his dashboard: "If the water's rippling too much, so is the passengers' wine," he said. But this admission of guilt in 2008 earned him a suspension.

And then, in addition, six months earlier, an email had come from Paul Budge, another high-up in MMA in the U.S., complaining to Jean Demaître, Harding's boss in Québec, that Harding was applying too many brakes at Nantes. "Yesterday I found the train with the automatic brakes applied. Talk to Harding," Budge had written.

In short, Harding, on his own up at Nantes that night, respected Rule 112, in part at least. He had carried out a handbrake effectiveness test on the train. It was conclusive: the train did not move. And why would it? He and his colleagues had always proceeded in pretty much the same way. Harding was forewarned: the company did not permit the application of a second system of brakes – the automatic brakes – because removing them cost time when setting off the next morning. Only the independent brakes on the locomotives were allowed by MMA.

What Harding did not know was that all the other supplementary brakes on his train, both the normal and the emergency brake systems, were either defective or had been rendered inoperative.

"Since there is no requirement for the RSC [Reset Safety Control] to initiate a penalty brake application in the event that the power to

the device is cut, there is no requirement for this function to be verified during shop inspections," as the TSB pointed out when explaining the failure of the functional emergency systems to respond during the disaster.[91] This brings us back to the same question: Why is a single individual, in sole charge of a heavy convoy of seventy-two cars, who has gone for seventeen hours without sleeping – twelve of them spent driving a malfunctioning locomotive across mountainous terrain – expected to decide how many handbrakes are "sufficient"? What does it mean to be "guilty"?

✗ ✗ ✗

It is April 2017, six months before the criminal trial begins. The courtroom is cold and soulless, as you would expect. Paradoxically, it is one of those rare places where, when people's souls are laid bare, they seem intensely present, naked, and vulnerable. Here, people's fates are decided. Thomas Harding and Richard Labrie, the MMA dispatcher who may have made a poor decision, listen to others debate their fate, four years after the disaster. Outside, a glacial rain is falling.

Of the thirty lined-up chairs, only four or five are occupied, one by the guard who applies the rules to the letter: no cellphones turned on, no legs stretched out. In a remote corner, Labrie, though a man of imposing build, nevertheless blends into this bleak decor. His features are drawn; the shadow of a mournful smile occasionally flits across his face when someone's eyes meet his, or when the exchanges between lawyers (including the one he finally found for himself after so many years) are especially incomprehensible. Yet, it is his life they are talking about.

If there is one person who seems to be suffering a fate too onerous to bear, it must be Labrie. His unkempt hair and worn clothes hint at a man cast adrift. "If God has sent me this trial, it's because I'm strong enough to get through it," he tells me one day when he is feeling less sad. He also gives me a newspaper article he takes from a large portfolio that he never allows out of his sight. It is an article about a renowned, much admired lawyer, Maître Bellemare, who has urged the Justice ministry to charge the three MMA employees as

soon as possible "so that justice may be done." I understand Labrie. He feels hunted.

Tom Harding is also in the courtroom, on the far side, sitting in the front row, not far from his excellent, effective lawyer. Harding is always accompanied by his brother, also a railwayman: the two are always well dressed, attentive, sitting erect. They, too, avoid conversations and curious onlookers, perhaps to avoid losing their self-control. "Justice must be done," Harding would say to me one day. "The case has to go on. I have to face up to things."

Harding would have preferred the trial to take place in Mégantic, in the presence of the victims' relatives and friends – not because he feels no shame, but because he wants to face them. He and Labrie have given up seeking the stay of proceedings to which they might have been entitled because of the "Jordan decision."* They want to go on trial.

Observing the six or seven lawyers (sometimes more) perform for the judge as if on stage, waiting patiently throughout the interminable procedural wrangling, listening to the lawyers for the prosecution and the learned responses from the defence, one has the impression that every legal authority in the country is hounding those two accused, that a sort of iron vice is closing on them, forcing them to defend themselves with tools they know nothing about and have no control over. Do they know that the O'Connor judgment allows lawyers to ...? That Baird and Lebel intervened to ...? That the evidence given by videoconference from the U.S. will have the effect of ...?

Labrie frowns, while Harding remains expressionless.

Harding stands accused of failing to apply enough braking power, and Labrie of failing to dispatch a qualified employee to the scene after the locomotive caught fire in Nantes.

By faithfully applying rules that had been laid down somewhere else, by conforming to the system that had merely afforded them a living, they had become trapped in a constantly narrowing channel

---

* In July 2016, the Supreme Court of Canada set aside the conviction of Richard Jordan, sentenced in 2008 for his part in a dial-a-dope operation. The Supreme Court determined that accused persons have the constitutional right to be tried in a reasonable time. The Jordan decision even led to the freeing of certain accused in murder cases whose trial was delayed beyond a reasonable time.

that had forced them toward the final move, toward the last decision leading to the victims' deaths. Did they have all the necessary data at their fingertips? Was it a crime to follow the rules blindly? We may think that sometimes it is. "I wouldn't have done things that way," we can tell ourselves. But hypothetical conclusions are easy to reach when one is snugly cocooned in safety.

✕ ✕ ✕

As the final hole in the package of cheese, there is just a single individual, all by himself: the solitary engineer.

This brings us back to John Baird, who had finally acquiesced to one of the most insistent demands the railway companies had been making for years: to be allowed to operate trains using only a single crew member without needing to obtain prior approval from the minister or the ministry. Baird went even further: he simultaneously abolished all the constraints and conditions previously in effect.

In 2008, the in-depth review by Transport Canada of the Canadian Rail Operating Rules led to the introduction of General Rule M, a loophole which, as the TSB wrote, "allowed railways to implement the single-person crew without any need to obtain Transport Canada exemptions from specific Rail Operating Rules, as was the case for Quebec North Shore and Labrador (QNS and L) in 1997."[92]

In 1997, QNS and L, which provides the rail link between Schefferville in northern Québec and Sept-Îles on the north shore of the Saint Lawrence, obtained the minister's permission to reduce the crew on its ore trains to a single locomotive engineer. On its second day, this mode of operation was responsible for an accident.

Transport Canada then asked the Railway Association of Canada to develop rules for single-person train operation. In 1998, the Railway Association commissioned an examination of the industry's wishes, and in 2000 it drafted guidelines for its member companies. However, these guidelines "were not approved [by Transport Canada], *nor were they required to be*"[93] (my emphasis).

Nevertheless, the report on the guidelines established sixty-nine preconditions to ensure the safety of trains operated by a single crew member. Among these were the completion of a pilot project to be

carried out on a safe section, closely following internal safety rules, the training of staff, and the addition of electronic detection equipment – conditions that were, in other words, quite complex and costly.

In developing the new Canadian Rail Operating Rules, written by the railway companies themselves, Minister Baird eliminated all those requirements. In doing so, he abolished any requirement to comply with the sixty-nine conditions, or to obtain approval. It was now enough simply to inform the minister and ministry that single-person train operation was being implemented. Period. That is how General Rule M was introduced. Raymond Robitaille, a retired manager for TC-Québec, told me that allowing companies carte blanche on single-person train operation in 2008 was the worst thing that could have happened.

✖ ✖ ✖

Ed Burkhardt, the CEO of MMA, who adopted single-person train operation in the United States in 1999, was among the first to welcome the advent of General Rule M. As early as April 2009, MMA informed Transport Canada of its intention to begin operating its trains with a single crew member. Three months later, the company submitted its risk assessment to Transport Canada, claiming that a crew member paid closer attention when working alone.[94] The Québec office of Transport Canada (TC-Québec) responded to Burkhardt a month later. It expressed a number of concerns, including, among other things, problems with equipment and with operations conducted by remote control.[95] The people at TC-Québec had not been taken in: it was one of them, Raymond Robitaille, who put a stop to single-person operation on QNS and L and began the process leading to the development of the sixty-nine preconditions. And TC-Québec had been keeping an eye on MMA for some time because of the lamentable state of its equipment.

Nevertheless, ten months later, in May 2010, MMA began to introduce single-person operation on a first section of track between the United States and Nantes, passing through Mégantic on the way. TC-Québec officials, as well as MMA employees, were uneasy about this. In December 2011, MMA informed Transport Canada that as of

January 9, 2012, it would extend the practice to Farnham, meaning that henceforth trains would complete their journey with only a single employee on board.

TC-Québec remained concerned. In February 2012, Transport Canada's Montréal office staff met with MMA and representatives from the Railway Association of Canada and informed them that Transport Canada did not approve of single-person operation. But MMA was adamant and persistent. In April 2012, the company renegotiated its collective agreement with its employees by forcing them to accept the principle of single-person operation, despite their reluctance. TC-Québec was powerless and was obliged to accept that MMA would proceed with single-person crews.[96]

In July 2012, MMA began to impose single-person operation between Mégantic and Farnham without changing anything else in its routine. The company offered its employees half an hour of training before they took their first train and gave them a belt pack, an automatic remote to control locomotives. Far from the sixty-nine preconditions, the only "ministerial" requirement would be the installation of a new mirror on the left-hand side of the locomotives. On August 29, 2012, TC-Québec learned that MMA had already begun to put single-person operation into practice all the way along its line.

In November 2012, MMA began hauling crude to Irving Oil in Saint John, using unit trains and passing through Mégantic. This was a major development: the new trains were much longer, heavier, and carried a more explosive type of crude. It would emerge later that they were excessively heavy, even according to the internal standards of MMA, especially considering the condition of the track. MMA did not bother to inform Transport Canada. (Theoretically, MMA no longer had to obtain ministerial authorization to implement single-person operation, but the company was still supposed to "inform" the ministry and the minister.)

At this juncture, did the officials at TC-Québec resist in any way? Did any worried mayors like Jacques Breton make phone calls to the ministry to complain about single-person crews? For now, it remains a mystery. It is known, however, that Burkhardt quietly made a phone call to Michael Bourque, the rail lobbyist, who in turn phoned "higher up." It is also known that during Transport Canada's discussions about

MMA's single-person crews, one of Transport Canada's representatives walked out, slamming the door as he went: "The dice are completely loaded," he complained, furious.

The dice were loaded?

What was the exact nature of MMA's request to the ministry? Who at Transport Canada intervened, and when? Who spoke to whom? More seriously, was Minister Lebel informed? Was he directly involved? If so, what part did he play? That, too, remains a mystery.

A mystery? Maybe not entirely, for Transport Canada's behaviour in the few hours and days following the tragedy, as well as Lebel's sudden fate, are troubling, to say the least.

✖ ✖ ✖

Alain Richer was a recent retiree after forty years of loyal service in the rail industry, including twenty-five at CN and fifteen as a rolling stock inspector in the wagon-and-tank-car section of TC-Québec. He knows his job. So he explained, haughtily, as he began testifying at the criminal trial of the three MMA employees. But his self-esteem would emerge severely battered from some vigorous cross-examination.

Richer was one of only three Transport Canada field inspectors working in Québec. A second inspector worked with him on wagons and tank cars. Alain Sauvé was the only inspector responsible for locomotives.

At noon on July 5 Richer performed the inspection of MMA train 002 in Farnham, twelve hours before the tragedy. In Mégantic on July 9, Lebel cited Richer's report when saying that, when inspected the day before, the notorious train was found to be in perfect condition.

It was a dishevelled Richer who learned, as he drank his morning coffee on the morning of July 6, that the train involved in the disaster was none other than the one he had inspected the previous day, and about which he had found almost no cause for complaint.

There was shock and stupor on the morning of July 6 in the offices of Transport Canada and at every level of the hierarchy. A frantic exchange of phone calls with the ministry ensued. After a few hours, Richer was asked by his superior to go to Mégantic in an official capacity and to keep the minister informed throughout the investigation

into the disaster. Richer explained that his assignment meant meeting with the TSB investigator, obtaining any new information, and immediately reporting back to the minister on the direction the investigation was taking.

How could this be possible? "There's an apparent conflict of interest here," TSB investigator Don Ross told Richer early on the morning of July 8. "You inspected the train, you're an important witness," he said. Being an important witness in an investigation is no trifling matter. And the possibility that a crime had been committed had been mentioned, for already on the morning of July 6, while the fire was still raging in Mégantic, the Sûreté du Québec was treating the disaster as a potentially criminal matter. This meant that criminal charges might well be laid. The fact that Richer had officially inspected the train twelve hours earlier was undoubtedly a significant fact in the eyes of the police.

Conflict of interest or not, starting on July 8, Richer accompanied various investigators from the Sûreté du Québec and the TSB at the disaster scene. This explains how, together, they would discover, and he would inspect, the train that had been abandoned at Vachon with its engine still running and held by a mere five handbrakes. Yet Richer did inform his superior, Luciano Martin, about chief investigator Don Ross's comment about a possible conflict of interest.

There followed a new round of telephone calls between Richer, Robitaille, and people in Ottawa at Transport Canada. As a result, Richer was removed as the minister's official representative, which was a more or less passive observational role, and reassigned as Transport Canada's official investigator into the Mégantic disaster!

To complete the picture, Transport Canada also appointed to its official inquiry team the inspector assigned to Québec locomotives and the hazardous materials inspector, also for Québec, together with their immediate bosses, Raymond Robitaille and Marc Grignon. These individuals were all directly involved in the disaster in their official capacities and were therefore important witnesses. They also had every interest in discovering whether any action of their own might be among the (criminal) causes of the disaster.

"You never felt at all that you had a conflict of interest in 2013?" Harding's defence lawyer, Maître Walsh, rapped out.

"It never occurred to me, never crossed our minds," Richer replied, very self-confidently. "Not even now."

Yet 2013 was a momentous year in Québec as far as conflicts of interest were concerned. Every day the media was revelling in the revelations of the Charbonneau Commission – never mind the arrests of Michael Applebaum, the interim mayor of Montréal, and Gilles Vaillancourt, the mayor of Laval. In short, in the summer of 2013, the term "conflict of interest" was on everybody's lips. And if there was one concept with which everyone was familiar, it was that of "independent investigator," referring to an investigation carried out by a police force well removed from the case in question.

Everyone, that is, except Transport Canada, apparently, which from the outset was kept informed on an hourly basis about everything that transpired in the course of the investigation. And which – why not? – decided to intervene directly.

One thing is certain: the Transport Canada investigators did not waste any time. On the morning of July 11, the Ministry's inspector responsible for hazardous materials supervised the sampling of oil in the still-undamaged cars – the same tainted oil that it was his job, as an inspector, to check for conformity. Sauvé, the inspector whose role it was to confirm that the locomotives – including those of MMA – were in perfect working order, assisted Steve Callaghan, the railway expert commissioned by the Sûreté du Québec, in his investigation. While Callaghan was at the controls inside the cabin, Sauvé and Richer, inspecting the lethal train from outside, transmitted to him the results of the tests carried out on the locomotives involved in the disaster.

Even worse, on the premises of Sûreté du Québec, Richer analyzed a large portion of the official statements that had been taken, even those of the locomotive engineers, including Harding and Labrie. Richer would also have access to the video recordings of the testimonies, as well as to many of the files and documents seized during the investigation. Everything. Was Richer's presence on the investigating team a godsend for Transport Canada officials? The word isn't strong enough.

And what did Richer report to the minister in the first days after the tragedy? It concerned single-person train operation. From the outset, Richer had viewed the single-person crew as the probable cause of the

tragedy, a view reflected in his official witness statement to the Sûreté du Québec. This was information that, in principle, would certainly be sent post-haste to the Transport Canada offices in Ottawa, to the very highest levels.

Let us return, then, to Minister Lebel who, just seven days after the tragedy, found it desirable to quietly relinquish his responsibility for the Department of Transport – while continuing with the other government departments in his charge. One consequence of this was that he would not be obliged to answer questions from parliamentarians and journalists. What questions was Lebel trying to avoid? Did they have anything to do with the phone calls made by Burkhardt and Bourque? Had an authorization come from high up in the ministry allowing MMA to introduce the single-person crew? Who had ordered that the protests by overly zealous public servants be silenced?

✕ ✕ ✕

"Mr. Robitaille, even today, you don't feel any conflict of interest when leading the investigation of the disaster, although you were one of the principal Directors with Transport Canada-Québec? Your subordinates were all directly involved ..."

"No, no conflict. There was no conflict."

"We find that very surprising ... We can't understand ..."

"We were carrying out a regional inquiry at Transport Canada–Québec ... So people from Québec were involved."

"Yes, but those were the very same employees who had to inspect the locomotives, brakes, etc."

"It was a regional inquiry into the breaches of laws and regulations. We didn't have to investigate the work of our employees."

"???"

"It was up to Transport Canada–Ottawa to launch an independent investigation into the causes of the disaster. And up to Ottawa to trigger an internal investigation into

the work of its employees. They didn't perform either of those two investigations."

Was this bureaucratic quibbling being used as an evasive strategy? No. Burkhardt had, indeed, made his phone calls to Ottawa – the place where decisions are made. And, instinctively, Raymond Robitaille, now retired, would highlight the problem: no investigation, neither internal nor administrative, was ever triggered at Transport Canada in Ottawa, absolutely none. Or if there was one, no one knows anything about it.

Nor was there any Royal Commission of Inquiry – any impartial body established, as outlined on the website of the Privy Council Office of Canada, to "fully and impartially investigate issues of national importance," and have "the power to subpoena witnesses, take evidence under oath and request documents."[97]

Yet in 2009 one such commission* did an excellent job when studying the decline of salmon in the Fraser River. After forty-seven fatalities and the destruction of a town by a railway disaster under federal jurisdiction, you might have thought ...

But so far each successive transport minister has stubbornly refused to hold such a commission. Worse, in 2019, when the Bloc Québécois MP Monique Pauzé offered Minister Garneau a copy of the original French edition of this book (*Mégantic: Une tragédie annoncée*, Écosociété, 2018), the minister replied in an irritated tone that it was all about "conspiracy theories." Clearly, there has been no desire on the part of the government to dig for answers.

✕ ✕ ✕

Answers – especially those concerning the single-person crew – are the Gordian knot that must be untied if we want to learn the truth about Mégantic and prevent a repetition of its story.

John Baird did the railway industry a huge favour when he changed the rules. Lebel thought it best to depart the scene and resigned as minister of transport. The adoption of single-person operation is an

---

* The Cohen Commission into the Decline of the Sockeye in the Fraser River, 2009–2010.

excellent example of how and by whom the rules that "protect" us here in Canada get written, and of the secrecy surrounding the pressures exerted by railway companies and their lobbyists. "If only you knew how all-powerful the rail lobby is," an anonymous Transport Canada official repeated ad nauseam.

Nevertheless, as early as July 23, just fifteen days after the tragedy, the first official action of the government, and the first emergency ministerial order issued by Lisa Raitt, the new minister, would ban single-person train operation. (This order, initially valid for six months, was renewed in 2014.)

However, the prohibition applied only to trains conveying hazardous materials. At the time of the disaster, the oil being hauled by train MMA-002 UN1267, which was mislabelled to indicate a low degree of flammability, may not even have been captured by the order.

Furthermore, the controversial practice of single-person train operation was not denounced outright by the TSB in its report on the Mégantic disaster. In that respect, the sequence of events is as troubling as Minister Lebel's departure. The authors of the official TSB report on the tragedy were also subjected to pressure about the single-operator system.

In January 2015, the Radio-Canada TV program *Enquête* and its reporter Sylvie Fournier obtained the briefing notes that had been brought to Lebel's attention in the wake of the tragedy. They stated expressly that allowing the MMA to operate trains with a single crew member "may have contributed to the accident and amplified the circumstances." Earlier versions of the TSB report also referred unambiguously to single-person train operation as a factor in the disaster. In the official report, these references were, however, buried among the "facts established regarding the risks and other established facts."

"Were you pressured to withdraw this [as a] cause?" Sylvie Fournier asked Kathy Fox, the newly appointed chair of the TSB. "No, not at all," she answered. "It wasn't conclusive enough" – but then she had the gall to add, without flinching, "But anyway, some people say that a single man on a train pays more attention."[98]

"*Some people say ...*"? Coming from one of Canada's top security officials, this was a peculiar observation. But she was right. There were

indeed some who said so – notably Edward Burkhardt, who had been repeating it over and over since the end of the 1990s. "A single man is less exposed to distractions," the CEO of MMA kept insisting in 2013, as he stood near the still-smoking ruins of Mégantic.

"Yes, there are studies that prove it," Kathy Fox added, unperturbed. For there are other studies, carried out in both Canada and the United States, including by the U.S. Federal Railroad Administration, which demonstrate the opposite. The list of accidents caused by this practice provides additional proof. They include one at Chatsworth, California, in 2008, that resulted in twenty-five fatalities. The cause of the accident? A momentary distraction of the single driver, who had no one with him to take over the controls.

So we may ask who was the mysterious person who gave the order to remove a direct reference to the practice of single-person operation as a possible factor from the most important report on the worst railway disaster in Canada? And who was it that struck from the TSB report the passage saying that the changes made to the rules in 2008 did not provide a level of safety equivalent to what existed previously?[99] Who was so powerful that TSB chair Kathy Fox, theoretically *the* upholder of transportation safety in Canada, could seem so complacent about the matter? Who was so powerful that the incoming Minister of Transport, Lisa Raitt, who took up her post seven days after the tragedy, declared loud and clear that "this tragedy occurred because the rules were simply not followed" – implying that they were not followed by some individual, a single person, a culpable employee, namely Tom Harding? If that was the case, why was Raitt in such a hurry, barely two weeks after taking up office, to ban single-person crews on trains carrying hazardous goods – the only major regulatory change introduced as a result of the tragedy? Who was this hidden actor powerful enough to threaten our safety?

✖ ✖ ✖

In 2014, another tragic accident occurred along the north shore of the Saint Lawrence. Alone at the controls of a 240-car ore train, Enrick Gagnon drowned in the Moisie River shortly after leaving Sept-Îles.

Gagnon, busy elsewhere on the locomotive, had failed to notice that a rockslide had destroyed a section of the track. His train plunged into the river.

In March 2017, during the renegotiation of its collective agreement with its employees, the mining company ArcelorMittal, of Port-Cartier, put on the bargaining table an initial draft plan to lay off half of its locomotive engineers in order to bring single-person train operation into effect on their ore trains. The mining company would later revive this proposal. In 2020, it is still permissible, without any special authorization and except when conveying goods labelled as hazardous, to run trains operated by a single crew member. This also applies to trains passing through Mégantic.

✖ ✖ ✖

On July 15, 2013, seven days after the Mégantic disaster, Minister Lebel was abruptly replaced by Lisa Raitt. Then, in the months following the derailment, many senior officials directly involved due to the positions they held also left the department, according to sources very close to Transport Canada. This allowed them to evade the questioning to which they should have been subjected about the parts they played and the links between the ministry and railway magnates. And that is aside from the fact that Transport Canada continues to reject out of hand all demands for an independent public commission of inquiry into the worst railway disaster in North American history.

As for Baird, in March 2015 he left politics for the private sector. Within two weeks of his departure, he had joined the boards of two major companies: Barrick Gold, the gold-mining company whose sinister reputation for disregarding life and human rights is unequalled on the international scene, and CP, where he would join Hunter Harrison and Bill Ackman. Neither CP nor the former minister disclosed how much he would earn as a board member.

FROM ONE TRAIN TO ANOTHER

JUNE 30 TO DECEMBER 12, 2013

JUNE 30, 2013

Just doin' my time ... If there's a light up ahead, well brother
I don't know

— Bruce Springsteen,
"Further On (Up the Road)"

"THE BADLANDS." THAT IS THE OFFICIAL NAME OF THE BAKKEN
region. Bare rock and earth as far as the eye can see. A naked landscape scoured for centuries by strong winds. A dead surface brought
alive by the mad scramble of tumbleweed – those rolls of desiccated,
friable vegetation often crushed under the wheels of tanker trucks.
There's nothing here, not even a tree: less than 1 percent of North
Dakota is wooded. Pale rocks – ochre, sometimes black – split by
crevices, sometimes bristle into amphitheatres ringed by bleached
promontories. Majestic landscapes, like Theodore Roosevelt National
Park, or distressing ones, redolent of loneliness and human devastation. A land with a scorched, lunar look, in the last hours of June 30,
2013, thanks to the thousands of flares burning above the production
platforms. A land at war with itself.

"Just doin' my time ..." Just doing their time, indeed. Springsteen
has captured the truckers' reality. Even before dawn on June 30, 2013,
254 drivers are already on the road in their DOT-407 tanker trucks.
Their destination that day, at the end of a ten-hour commute, is New
Town's transloading centre, where their cargo will be transferred to
a train bound for New Brunswick via Lac-Mégantic: train 606-282.

The truckers have slept in their vehicles or crowded into a seedy,
revolting motel at $700 a week, or maybe even in the open, at a gas
station or a McDonald's. "It's hell here," one of them will say in a video
posted on YouTube. The town's developers have driven the elderly
from their long-term care homes and poor families from their social
housing, preferring to rent the space to Bakken workers. Despite this,
it's difficult to find a bed in this part of the country. There aren't any

rooms or parking places available, or else it's too expensive. Wages had risen to almost $100,000 a year, but now they're beginning to drop, not only because of the decline in oil prices, but also because there is fierce competition between trucking companies. In June 2013, a few workers are starting to post videos on the internet. "Don't bother to come here," they warn. At McDonald's or Taco Bell, one of three or four fast food restaurants in the area, it can take over an hour to be served coffee and a doughnut.

The 254 trucks chartered for train 606-282 work for Prairie Field Services, which serves the eleven producers whose oil has been sold to World Fuel for shipping to its customer, Irving Oil. These producers are actually conglomerates with head offices in Delaware, Kansas, or Minnesota – a healthy distance from the inhospitable Bakken landscape. Marathon Oil, for instance, incorporated in Delaware for tax purposes but based in Houston, Texas, has $35 billion in assets, $15 billion in revenue and thousands of hectares of drilling in Dakota. The same goes for Arrow Midstream Holdings and Oasis Petroleum, two more of the eleven oil producers whose product will end up eight days hence at the bottom of the Chaudière River in Québec.

It's not raining today. This is a relief for the truckers, for mud is what they fear most. Reversing a tanker truck on a deserted road made slippery and furrowed by rain is a nightmare. The truckers know that their load will be extremely volatile oil, a potential bomb. An accident can be catastrophic. And accidents happen regularly on these appalling roads, caused by the mud, a sinkhole, or sometimes by a trucker falling asleep at the wheel. When they leave the main road, the trucks bounce for solitary hours along muddy, rocky roads, past the rigs that extend for miles around. Sometimes they encounter another truck transporting toxic water from storage tanks to the old abandoned wells where it will be re-injected into the ground, but that is all.

The Bakken region is dotted with oil rigs. There is nothing high-tech about them. The typical platform consists of an ordinary square of sand and clay, a few cisterns, and some pipes. Standing alone in the centre is the pumping unit, a metal structure that nods rhythmically the way we often see in movies. Next to it is a flare, furiously burning off the gases. That is all.

No one is to be seen anywhere around.

It takes fifteen minutes for the truckers to complete the transloading into the tanker trucks. The procedure looks odd, for this is a rudimentary industry: it uses just a branch pipe, often a measuring rod, some talcum powder, and a colouring liquid. There are few or no gas masks, even though, in the early days of fracking, poisoning was common due to hydrogen sulphide created by fermentation inside the holding tanks. Before the worker can start pumping, they plunge their measuring rod into the holding tank and pull it out again. The talcum powder and colouring liquid tell the worker the level of the heavier toxic water that sits at the bottom of the tank and from above which they must pump the oil.

Late in the afternoon, today like every other day, the 254 fully loaded trucks converge on the transloading centre, a few miles south of New Town. They drive through the northern tip of the Fort Berthold Reservation, past the Four Bears Casino, where too many of the truckers go astray, shedding their boredom and their earnings. They cross the Four Bears Bridge, decorated with Native American spiritual symbols – a meagre tribute to the greatness of the Three Affiliated Tribes – and drive by big Lake Sakakawea, which is not a natural lake but the third-largest artificial reservoir in the United States. (Before the territory of the Three Affiliated Tribes became a checkerboard of drilling, their land was flooded by a dam across the great, legendary Missouri River in 1956.)

When the trucks reach the transloading centre belonging to Dakota Petroleum Transport Solutions (affiliated with World Fuel and CP), train 606-282 is already assembled and waiting on the track. It consists of seventy-eight DOT-111 tank cars, leased to six different suppliers, and two locomotives.

The trucks empty their cargo directly into the DOT-111 cars, each of which can hold three truckloads. As World Fuel will later tell TSB investigator Don Ross, the oil from different wells is mixed, which makes it very difficult to accurately identify the product's properties, including its liability to catch fire or explode.

All this oil has been purchased by World Fuel (or, more specifically, by World Petroleum, one of its many subsidiaries) and resold to Irving. Like all the players in Mégantic's tragedy, World Fuel is a huge company and counts its assets in billions: billions of gallons, billions

of profits. A Fortune 100 company with eight thousand service points worldwide, in 2016 the company reported $27 billion in revenue from the sale of twenty-one billion gallons of oil. It is World Petroleum that has leased the dangerously vulnerable DOT-111 cars of train 606-282.

On June 30, 2013, it is also to a World Fuel / World Petroleum employee named Eli Jasso that the truckers hand in their Safety Data Sheets, the SDSs, with details of the oil they are carrying. These sheets, which are mandatory, show that the product delivered is Class 3 Petroleum Crude Oil (UN1267) – in other words a flammable substance.

The data sheets also provide other crucial information for first responders in the event of an accident: this oil, as shown on most of the sheets, is classified as PG I, the most dangerous category. Just two sheets out of ten show PG II, which is still very dangerous.

A few hours later, as the train moves off, the level of risk presented by the oil has been changed – falsified – to PG III.

✕ ✕ ✕

Train 606-282
Class: 3
Packing group: PG III
Hazmat STCC: 4910165
...

I, Eli Jasso, acting for Western Petroleum CO, hereby declare that the contents of this consignment are fully and accurately described by proper shipping name(s) and are classified, packaged, marked and labelled/ placarded, and are in all respects in proper condition for transport according to applicable international and national government regulations.[100]

In June 2013, Eli Jasso was the new manager of Strobel Starostka Construction, the transloading centre of World Fuel, in exclusive partnership with CP. Jasso is a pleasant man, a hunting and fishing enthusiast, proud of his work and his family, according to his

Facebook page. He is just a normal employee, an ordinary guy, far from the oil tycoons and their tax havens.

Yet, acting on behalf of World Petroleum, his employer, Jasso appears to have changed the product identifier on the data sheets for train 606-282 to indicate that the cargo was crude petroleum belonging to the much less hazardous category PG III. We can see that this is an obvious falsehood, considering that we know that the documents that the truckers handed over identified the oil as PG I, meaning that it was extremely explosive and flammable, or PG II, meaning that it was very dangerous.

Was Jasso's name used without his knowledge? Was he following his employer's instructions? Or, on the contrary, was he acting on his own initiative? Did he understand the terrible consequences that this falsehood might have on the lives of people who, eight days later, would experience a living hell?

✗ ✗ ✗

They told us that this oil was like molasses. That you could throw a match in it, and even then it wouldn't catch fire.

—François Daigle, locomotive engineer
with MMA

We knew right away that this oil didn't burn like the others, not like the oil whose number was shown on the placards on the tank cars. It wasn't ordinary oil; it didn't burn that way! We should have evacuated much more widely. The firefighters were very close to the blaze. Mr. Lafontaine was right there with his machinery ... We were a hair's breadth from having a hecatomb of victims. When the terrible explosions happened at 1:30 a.m. and 4 a.m., the mushrooms of flames rose one thousand feet in the air. We could have lost a lot more people.[101]

—Jacques Breton, mayor of Nantes and the
person responsible for public safety

BLEVE stands for "Boiling Liquid Expanding Vapour Explosion," an explosion caused by the rupturing of a container containing a liquid at a temperature well above its boiling point.[102] BLEVEs are common in accidents involving Bakken crude. At Mégantic, according to the TSB, there would not have been a BLEVE properly speaking, but a variant caused by droplets of gas catching fire. It was like a pressure cooker exploding – but a pressure cooker the size of an entire train.

The risk that Bakken crude might explode had been known, recognized, and documented since 2011. The rapid increase of oil production in the Bakken formation and the corresponding increase in trains passing through communities led the Federal Railroad Administration to send its inspectors to North Dakota to investigate the carriage and explosion risks of Bakken crude. Their report, entitled "North Dakota: The Next Hazardous Materials Frontier," was published in 2011 and broadened in 2012. It was alarming. In it, the inspectors confirmed that the oil pumped in this sector carried a high level of risk. They also highlighted the rudimentary nature of the transloading centres (the fact that the hoses did not even fit the openings properly, for instance), and pointed out that the tank cars were overloaded with liquid, thus increasing the internal gas pressure. Finally, they stressed that the DOT-111 tank cars being used had several major deficiencies (including walls that were too frail) and recommended that they be taken off the rails.

In addition, the Federal Railroad Administration inspectors found that the oil companies were falsifying the danger rating. But why would they do that? The explanation resides partly with the term "PG." PG stands for "Packaging Group," a term that specifies the appropriate type of container for the substance concerned. The more dangerous a product, the more imperative it is that it be "packaged" in a sturdy container capable of resisting the particular risk involved. But the companies were not consistently adhering to these standards.

Following an investigation into a fatal accident at Cherry Valley, Illinois, in 2009, the National Transportation Safety Board recommended in 2012 that authorities require companies to use more robust

tank cars for the conveyance of hazardous goods rated PG I and PG II, such as Bakken crude. Similarly, the Board asked companies to reinforce the tank cars already in use. Experts unanimously agreed that it was necessary to reinforce the walls – which were liable to rupture on the slightest impact – and to modify the ineffective escape valves for explosive gases, as well as securing and fortifying the attachment of the cisterns to their metal cradles. So the government gave companies a choice. They could either upgrade their DOT-111 cars or replace them.

The companies procrastinated, playing for time. The Association of American Railways (AAR), the U.S. railway lobby, argued initially that it was impossible to repair the existing DOT-111 cars. And, after all, they objected, the derailments of previous years had cost the industry only $64 million, while bringing the DOT-111 cars up to standard would cost $1 billion[103] – making it too costly.

Yet the AAR was not unaware of the risks of using DOT-111 cars to haul PG I and PG II rated hazardous materials. As accidents and explosions made headlines, public pressure intensified. The oil and railway companies therefore decided to compromise: for the more dangerous crude oil graded PG I and PG II, and on a strictly voluntary basis, they would, whenever possible, use upgraded DOT-111 cars which, after 2012, would be called "standard" tank cars. In addition, the companies agreed to replace by attrition the old DOT-111 cars with the improved version – in other words, when the old cars reached the end of their lives, they would be replaced with cars designed to carry PG I and PG II rated hazardous goods. (One slight hitch: the lifespan of DOT-111 cars could be up to forty years.)

So, starting in 2012, the companies were theoretically supposed to prefer the use of upgraded DOT-111 cars to ship Bakken oil. But the higher rental cost was a problem. In 2014, after the Mégantic disaster, CP applied a $300 surcharge when the use of newer cars became more common. But in 2013 there was still no surcharge, and, to remain competitive, companies needed to keep the cost of hauling crude oil by train to a minimum. The rail industry had to find a solution.

× × ×

There is only one way to discover how dangerous a petroleum product is: laboratory analysis. In 2013, some Bakken oil producers did have such analyses performed. The U.S. government authorized the use, in some cases, of generic Safety Data Sheets, since the Bakken crude was already recognized as being, at best, highly dangerous. Anyway, whether they were generic or specific to a given shipment, the SDSs should naturally be truthful. All the records prepared by the eleven oil producers and submitted during the transloading of oil for train 606-282 had been accurate. They had classified the oil correctly as PG I or PG II, the most dangerous categories. But a few hours later ...

Eli Jasso, whose name would appear in documents filed in a Québec court, had done what his employer World Fuel asked him to do – what the employer's partner, CP, had called for, and what most carriers, including CP, had begun to do: Jasso fraudulently changed the oil risk category from "very dangerous" to "normal." On the safety sheets of train 606-282, he put a PG III rating, the least dangerous or, in other words, the least explosive or flammable.

Of course, there are regulations in Canada (and the United States), the Transportation of Dangerous Goods regulations, that require carriers to properly classify the properties of the product they are transporting. Mislabelling a product is illegal. So oil and rail companies like World Fuel, Irving Oil, and CP were taking a risk by falsifying the oil classification. The authorities understood that the tendency to falsify the classification was becoming more widespread on the railways. In March 2013 the U.S. government began preparations to launch "Operation Bakken Blitz"; it was initiated in August, when surprise samplings of tank cars began in order to monitor compliance.

But World Fuel, CP, and Irving seem to have considered the risk of being caught to be minor compared to the benefits, including the ability to transport this dangerous oil in the aging, inexpensive, and widely available DOT-111 cars – especially since in June 2013 "Operation Bakken Blitz" had not yet been launched. If the falsification was to be unmasked, it first had to be noticed. But the risk of an inspection in the United States was very slim, and on the Canadian

side, train 606-282 was safe. Canadian inspectors, equipped with the Transportation of Dangerous Goods Regulations, concentrated their starved resources on transloading centres, and therefore at Irving Oil.

Except that it was not until October 2017 that Irving, in an unconvincing act of contrition, agreed to pay a $400,320 fine after facing thirty-four charges of failing to classify Bakken crude as hazardous goods ever since delivery of it to its refinery began in November 2012. Irving, the owner of the crude that passed through Mégantic, had utterly falsified the classification, and not a single Transport Canada employee had noticed, at least officially, prior to the tragedy on July 6, 2013. This speaks volumes about the effectiveness of the Canadian inspection system. It is true that Irving Oil, in addition to paying a small fine, was required to contribute $3.5 million toward research programs on federal safety standards and regulations under the Transportation of Dangerous Goods Act. But that was all rather vague. It is not known precisely what was meant, where this famous – or nebulous – research program is located, who directs it, what it does, etc. But according to Marc Garneau, the minister of transport, these millions provided an assurance that "the sort of tragedy that happened in Lac-Mégantic would not reoccur."

Be that as it may, considerable mystery still surrounds the false classification of the oil being transported by train 606-282. For instance, in 2013, railway companies were not legally required to use the new upgraded tank wagons (as is still the case today). There was therefore nothing illegal about train 606-282 with its aged DOT-111 cars. So why were the documents falsified? Was there another reason to want to mislead about the danger?

In relation to this mystery, the TSB would formulate one of the most convoluted, confusing sentences in its report: "While proper classification of the petroleum crude oil would have allowed the railways to identify the true hazards of the product they were transporting, it is not known what effects (if any) this identification may have had on MMA's operating plans."[104]

Did MMA have the appropriate insurance or permits to run trains hauling cargoes labelled PG I or PG II on rails in poor condition? Could Transport Canada employees have found a way to prevent MMA, with its very poor safety record, from transporting

this explosive material? Impossible to know, said the TSB – a rather hasty conclusion.

Another issue was – perhaps – the somewhat nebulous question of "excepted tracks," that is, railway lines in such poor condition that, according to the regulations governing railway safety, it is forbidden to use them to transport dangerous goods. Some of MMA's tracks were indisputably in a disastrous condition, and this was common knowledge. Could the company have been banned from transporting Bakken oil on them if it had been correctly classified as PG I, thus depriving CP, World Fuel, and Irving of their most direct and cheapest route? In theory it could, according to the regulations. But in practice? In practice, it is left to the company itself to decide whether its tracks are "excepted" or not, and to designate them as such – the fox in charge of the henhouse! Obviously, MMA had no interest in enforcing any regulation that would have dried up its major source of income.

So why did World Fuel, Irving, and CP falsify those safety sheets in June 2013? The only explanation that has emerged so far is distressingly banal and petty: it was to save money. The companies – the customers and the haulers, etc. – were economizing on the type of container cars and saving a surcharge payable because of the hazardous nature of the goods conveyed. Were there any other reasons? And what about today? Do Safety Data Sheets still get falsified?

✕ ✕ ✕

The safety of individuals ... depends in large part on an accurate description of the product being transported.
—TSB report

"Mr. Breton," I asked, "as a mayor and the person responsible for emergency measures in the region, do you know exactly what hazardous products pass through your town right now? Canada's Minister of Transport Marc Garneau has publicly stated that yes, he has changed the rules."

To which Jacques Breton answered: "No. Zilch, absolutely nothing. We don't know anything. We have to take pictures of the trains to find out what is going through. And then that doesn't let us see the safety

sheets. Only the family the products belong to. It's as dangerous as ever for my firefighters when they arrive on the scene of an accident." He hesitates. "In fact, yes. You can find out. If I asked, I could find out what passed through here last year!"

✕ ✕ ✕

On the evening of June 30, 2013, train 606-282 and its oil- and gas-filled tank cars left the windswept Badlands to start their long journey across the greener plains of the American prairies before crossing the Canadian border. Its first destination was Minneapolis, Minnesota.

Just before midnight, train 606-282 stopped in the CP yard at Harvey, North Dakota, just over 160 kilometres east of New Town, where it underwent its first inspection by CP technicians. A first defective DOT-111 tank car was taken from the train, and a brake test was carried out on the cars. That was about 3,500 kilometres before disaster struck in Mégantic.

JULY 1, 2013

CANADA WAS CELEBRATING ITS 146TH BIRTHDAY AS THE column of black tank cars made its way across the plains of Minnesota and Wisconsin before heading for Milwaukee. Denis Lebel, the federal minister of transport, was celebrating in his Québec riding of Roberval–Lac-Saint-Jean, where he would remain until four days after the disaster. "Television reaches Lac-Saint-Jean perfectly well," he would explain to justify his failure to visit the scene of the disaster.

While most Québécois feel rather lukewarm about Canada Day celebrations, they never fail to take advantage of the long weekend. Québec government ministers, including Yves-François Blanchet, minister of the environment, and Premier Pauline Marois, weren't attending any political events, but they did show up at popular celebrations. After all, it was quite possible that the minority Parti Québécois government might have to face an election within a few months.

In Mégantic, some activities were scheduled to take place on the shores of the big lake. But above all, just as it was all over Québec, July 1 was moving day, the day when, each year, Québécois play musical chairs with their places of residence. It was a red-letter day for young Kathy Clusiault, who had just moved into her first apartment, directly facing the Musi-Café. Thomas Harding, a hundred miles away, was enjoying his day off. In CP's accounting department, the routine was uninterrupted; the invoice for train 606-282 bill was issued – a two-page document that included the numbering of each tank car. "Loaded to full visible capacity," it said – in other words, full to the brim.

✖ ✖ ✖

CANADIAN PACIFIC

Freight Invoice

CPR Invoice Number	Invoice Date
610016405	2013/07/01
Account Number	Total Payable
52019412	496,527.64 USD
Customer Reference	Due Date
NS	2013/07/16

Bill To

WORLD FUEL SERVICES INC
NO PAPER ACCOUNT- EMAIL
ATTENTION: LAND CRUDE BILLING
DORAL FL 33178
USA

Remit to:
Canadian Pacific Railway Company
DEPT. 77299
P.O. BOX 77000
DETROIT MI 48277-0299

Inquiries to:
Margaret Bahen
Tel: (514) 395-8235
Fax: 1 877 395 7413

Please remit payment to Canadian Pacific Railway. Payment must be received in our office by the due date. If exception is taken to the charges, please remit according to your records to maintain payment terms. Indicate the reason for the adjustment through MyAccount or contact as listed above referencing the CPR Invoice Number. Payment terms and interest charges on late payments are in accordance with applicable CP rules, Tariffs, and may be amended from time to time at the sole discretion of the carrier.

Waybill Number
243537
Waybill Date
2013/06/29

Shipper
WESTERN PETROLEUM CO
9531 W 78TH ST STE 102
EDEN PRAIRIE   MN 55344

Consignee
IRVING OIL LTD
10 SYDNEY ST
SAINT JOHN   NB E2L4K1

Route
CPRS STJNS MMA

Shipper's Routing

Contract Numbers

Tariff Reference
CPRS 2248 100.000
FSC 1

Origin
917 NEW TOWN   ND

Destination
1200 SAINT JOHN   NB

Commodity Code
4910165 PETRO OIL CRUDE

Weight Agreement
TAW

Remarks
TO BE PREPAID

Charge Description	Quantity	Weight	Rate	Rate Type	Curr.	Charge	Exch. Rate	Total
Commodity: 4910165								
Detail(1) 1 TANK CAR PETROLEUM CRUDE OIL CLASS 3//UN1267//PG III PETROLEUM CRUDE OIL COUNTRY OF ORIGIN US COUNTRY OF DESTINATION CA TRN ID 606-282 FUEL SURCHARGE 2267.1 MILES	79	14,852,000 LBS	5,435.0000 Per Car 0.3750 Per Mile Total Charges	USD USD	429,365.00 67,162.64		429,365.00 USD 67,162.64 USD 496,527.64 USD
				Total Payable				496,527.64 USD

No Tax Applied

References
Bill of Lading No.:   NS

Instructions
LOADED FULL VISIBLE CAPACITY
DANGEROUS
BROKER LIVINGSTON CUSTOMS BROKERAGE
REVENUE PROFILE 6681

Unit	Unit Type	Rated Weight	Shipment Weight	Unit	Unit Type	Rated Weight	Shipment Weight
Rated Unit Details							
Detail(1)							
CTCX 735572 L	T	188,000 LBS	188,000 LBS	NATX 310471	T	188,000 LBS	188,000 LBS
WFIX 130616	T	188,000 LBS	188,000 LBS	WFIX 130664	T	188,000 LBS	188,000 LBS
WFIX 130630	T	188,000 LBS	188,000 LBS	TILX 316523	T	188,000 LBS	188,000 LBS
TILX 316639	T	188,000 LBS	188,000 LBS	TILX 316613	T	188,000 LBS	188,000 LBS
PROX 44224	T	188,000 LBS	188,000 LBS	TILX 316616	T	188,000 LBS	188,000 LBS

BDADMIN   Copy   Page 1/2

JULY 2, 2013

AT 12:30 P.M. ON TUESDAY, JULY 2, THOMAS HARDING BEGAN his shift. He took the controls of MMA train 002 departing from Farnham and travelling to Mégantic along the very route that would be so fateful on July 5. This time, however, he was not alone, but accompanied by a conductor. At 12:30 a.m. he left the train parked unattended on the same spot, at the top of the gradient, with its engine running, just as he would late on the night of July 5.

Harding was no greenhorn. He had joined CP in January 1980 and been a qualified locomotive engineer since 1986. He had remained faithful to the same routes throughout his career, moving to Quebec Southern Railway (QSR) when that company purchased the CP line in 1996, and then to MMA after Rail World, Burkhardt's parent company, acquired Quebec Southern in 2003.

Harding had undergone training with CP, Quebec Southern, and, over a ten-year period, with MMA – though the TSB would later conclude that MMA's training was utterly useless. For instance, said the TSB, MMA provided almost no training in single-person operation: merely thirty minutes before the locomotive engineer took the controls for the first time, as has been noted previously. Nor did MMA – like Transport Canada – concern itself with the nature of the terrain, even when it presented a high risk, like at the top of the steep gradient leading down to Mégantic.

Harding was thoroughly acquainted with the terrain. He had made hundreds of trips between Farnham and Mégantic during his career. During the previous twelve months alone he had travelled that stretch more than sixty times, including at least twenty as the sole operator. He repeated the same procedures each time. And each time his train did not move.

FROM ONE TRAIN TO ANOTHER

JULY 3, 2013

THE DIE WAS CAST. IT WAS ALREADY TOO LATE FOR THE CAN-adian government authorities responsible for our safety to prevent the tragedy, too late for them to deploy the tools, measures, or inspectors who might have defused the time bomb heading toward Mégantic. The leading actors in MMA's tragedy, in Bangor, Maine, now had complete control. All the decisions were in their hands.

First, the owner of MMA, Edward Burkhardt. At his side was his right-hand woman, Lynn Labonté, general manager of transportation, who ran the company. She controlled all the budgets – for track maintenance, equipment, and training – and did so with a tight fist. She also gave the final orders. Then there was her assistant, Kenneth Strout, director of operating practices, who was responsible for MMA's rules and regulations (including the immobilization rules that Harding was supposed to follow), as well as for the (virtually non-existent) training program. And, finally, Robert Grindrod, CEO and president of MMA, at the apex of the decision-making pyramid.

Then we come to Paul Budge, Jean Demaître's superintendent and Québec boss. It was Budge who would tell the police that the whole disaster was the fault of the employees, whom he described as lazy. He was also the individual who had had Harding reprimanded for applying too many brakes to oil-carrying trains at Nantes.

Lastly, on the mechanical side were Randy Stahl and James Harton, in Derby, Maine, responsible for inspecting and repairing the locomotives, including 5017. It was Stahl who would make a few terse statements about Harding during the trial, and who oversaw the workshop in which locomotive 5017 was repaired with polymer. Judge Gaétan Dumas would denounce Stahl at the trial of the three accused in the fall of 2017, exclaiming ironically, that if Stahl "had been as careful about repairing his locomotives as he is said to be about applying brakes, we'd be driving in a Cadillac and nobody would be in the courtroom today!"

Labonté, Grindrod, Strout, Budge: it was they who decided to leave locomotive 5017 as the lead locomotive. It was also they who allowed oil trains too heavy for the tracks to travel on the MMA network. These protagonists are all U.S. citizens, comfortably ensconced on the other side of the border, who would never be held responsible for criminal negligence or assigned any real responsibility for the disaster. Burkhardt was another, like MMA-USA, Rail World, World Fuel, CP, and other companies of the same stripe. The bosses of MMA-USA would refuse to testify at the criminal trial of their three Québec employees. They would even refuse to meet with the Sûreté du Québec investigators. Grindrod, Labonté, and Strout would each be fined $50,000 in 2018, *in absentia*, for regulation breaches of the Railway Safety Act. That was all. And their fines were paid in full by the company's insurance.

On the Canadian side, a few days ahead of the tragedy, the actors in the drama were Jean Demaître, the Québec director of MMA, and Richard Labrie, a qualified locomotive engineer, who acted as dispatcher at the Farnham Control Centre, and who would be on duty the night of the tragedy. And, of course, Tom Harding who, on July 3, took charge at Vachon of the empty train MMA-001 coming back from Saint John to Farnham, via Maine.

As for train 606-282, it was entering Canada via Windsor and Sarnia on its way to Toronto.

JULY 4, 2013

The [Crown's] case will be restricted to the events that occurred between July 4 and July 6, 2013.

—Crown Prosecutor at the trial of Harding, Labrie, and Demaître, charged with forty-seven counts of criminal negligence causing death

THE PREVIOUS DAY, FRANÇOIS DAIGLE, A LOCOMOTIVE ENGIN-eer with MMA, was the locomotive engineer on the train of eighty-one tank cars heading for Maine, which he parked at Nantes. He applied twelve handbrakes to the train. On the morning of July 4, at Vachon, he took charge, as sole operator, of the empty tank cars of the previous train, MMA-001, on its way to Farnham.

Locomotive 5017 was the train's lead locomotive. Daigle first drove the train from beyond Mégantic to Nantes, where he had to "pick up" some wagons, that is, take some cars waiting on the secondary track and attach them to his train on the main track. According to Daigle, that would be the first occasion when he was required to use a belt pack without assistance.

Years later, Daigle would have to question himself: was that day really the first time he used a belt pack? But never mind. The belt pack is a gadget much beloved by railway companies and which they use to justify, among other things, single-person train operation. It is used everywhere, more and more. What is it exactly? A remote-control device carried on the belt, it can be used to operate a train: to stop it, start it off again, and slow it down, all without direct human intervention – a kind of video-game controller without any game.

This was the only tool available to Daigle in carrying out his shunting operation at Nantes. This was an impressive operation, taking place over more than a kilometre, on a gradient. Imagine a train of almost a hundred tank cars or wagons and a single engine driver. Leaving the train on the main track, the driver disconnects

a locomotive and moves it downhill, stopping halfway down. The locomotive engineer then returns on foot to change the switch, which is located at the top, several hundred metres away. Returning to the locomotive, they then reverse onto the secondary track where the new wagons are parked. They attach the wagons to the locomotive. This new train then moves downhill and stops, again on the gradient. The engineer goes to return the switch to its original setting. The new train reverses and is attached to the column of cars on the main track. These two snakes moving back and forth on the gradient measure over a kilometre in length. The driver is completely alone.

In February 2014, a CN train controlled by a belt pack collided with another train in the densely populated Montréal neighbourhood of Saint-Henri. The TSB, which attributed the accident to the use of a belt pack, recommended – with the support of many American studies – to never use the device except within enclosed marshalling yards. More than a dozen trains hauling oil and other hazardous products pass through Saint-Henri daily, but that day, fortunately, the train was only carrying grain.

Today the rail industry is still intensively lobbying Transport Canada to promote the increased use of this gadget and the automation of operations.

× × ×

From Nantes to Farnham the train descends the slopes of the Appalachian foothills. All along the route, on July 4, 2013, locomotive 5017 experienced mechanical difficulties. "The amperage isn't holding," reported François Daigle at the controls. This phenomenon, in which the speed is not constant, is called "engine hunting":

> With the 5017, you were losing too much amperage, and therefore speed. You had to let off the brakes; we used what we call "cycle braking." Except you can't do that all the way down, because at some point you have no air left in the brakes, so you could stop. That was the problem with the 5017. At one point, on July 4, I had no air left in the brakes, so I had to use something else.[106]

Daigle arrived at Farnham at 9:45. He filled out form 5001, which each locomotive engineer must submit at the end of a trip. He provided a clear explanation of the problem with locomotive 5017. Although it was contrary to the directions he was given, he faxed the report to the MMA repair shop in Derby, Maine, for which Randy Stahl was responsible. "I faxed it because if I had handed it over here, to Demaître, nothing would ever have been done. I tried to have something done. Here, nothing ever gets done."

In Maine, Harton would not pay any attention to this fax until July 8, two days after the tragedy. Why? Because that was where the sequence of "everything that can go wrong" began. Daigle faxed his report on July 4, Independence Day in the U.S. The workshop in Derby was closed for the holiday. But why didn't someone see the fax on Friday, July 5? Pure incompetence, too few mechanics, an inadequate budget ...

Locomotive 5017 should have been scrapped long before, and it should certainly never have been used as the lead locomotive of a train. The problems with it were known and recognized by the engineering management: the locomotive's useful life was done. On October 7, 2012, again on March 15, 2013, and in the week before the tragedy, locomotive 5017 was in the MMA workshop in Derby, where several components were repaired, including the engine block. Oil leaks were "caulked," and bolts were tightened. In its autopsy of the locomotive, the TSB determined that "the cam bearing had fractured when the mounting bolt was over-tightened after the cam bearing had been installed as part of a non-standard repair to the engine block," and that "this *temporary repair* had been performed using a polymeric material, which *did not have the strength and durability required for this use*"[107] (italics added for emphasis).

The engine of a locomotive assigned to haul about a hundred tank cars containing dangerous goods had been given a temporary repair – using a sort of glue. Ironically, two weeks earlier, in June, an inspection by Transport Canada found that "the employees performing the safety inspections were not qualified as certified locomotive inspectors."[108] So? So nothing. To the knowledge of one locomotive engineer, no one checked the locomotives in Montréal. "The cars, the brakes, yes, not

the locomotives." Not MMA. Not CP. So where was Transport Canada in all this?

In answer to a question he posed about Transport Canada's locomotive inspections in 2017, Robert Bellefleur would be told that "it is very difficult to inspect locomotives, equipment that travels all the time across Canada and the United States."[109] And after all, in Québec, there is only one inspector.

✕ ✕ ✕

On the evening of July 4, train 606-282 arrived in Toronto, at the CP workshops where the cars' air brakes were inspected by a qualified inspector. The train left Toronto on its way to CP's Côte-Saint-Luc triage yard in Montréal, via Kingston and Côteau-du-Lac. At this point the train consisted of two locomotives and 120 wagons, including seventy-seven tank cars of Bakken crude.

Train 606-282 reached Côte-Saint-Luc while the populous neighbourhood was still sleeping soundly. MMA took over the train for the last leg of the journey to Saint John. It then underwent a "regular safety and mechanical inspection." This was the third inspection carried out by CP inspectors on train 606-282, following one by Harvey in North Dakota and one in Toronto, both of which were of the brakes. After the inspection in the Côte-Saint-Luc yard, five tank cars were removed due to mechanical problems. Now there remained only the seventy-two cars that would explode in Mégantic.

✕ ✕ ✕

In less than twenty-four hours, train 606-282 would reach the gradient that descends to Mégantic. By then, it will have undergone four inspections in all including one by Transport Canada, in Farnham. In almost all cases, the focus will have been on the brakes. Yet the brakes failed.

In theory, the brakes function according to a well-designed mechanism which, despite its apparent complexity, is actually made up of a number of simple components, supplemented by a complete backup system in case one of the systems should fail. But in practice … take

a toy train. Set the wagons to one side and the locomotives to the other. There are two components: the locomotives and the wagons. Each component has two brake systems, making four different braking systems on a single train. You can choose to apply one, or two, or all, or none, on the wagons and on the locomotives. They can also be inspected independently, or not inspected at all, or one may be inspected but not others.

On each of the two components, the wagons and the locomotives, there are two types of braking system: manual brakes and air brakes. The manual brakes are found on both the locomotives and the wagons. They are simple: everyone has seen them in the movies: those big wheels that the engineers turns by hand. They must keep turning until the wheel is tight – like the handbrake of a car when you pull the lever.

The second system – that of the air brakes – is found on both the locomotives and wagons. In simple terms, they operated by decreasing or increasing the air pressure in the brake line. There are two types of air brake. The first, called the "automatic brakes," can be applied on the wagons and the locomotives, or on the wagons alone. The creation of a vacuum in the brake line stops the train, which explains why they can hold for a long time. The other air brake system, called the "independent brakes," are also applied by the creation of a vacuum. They block only the locomotive wheels.

All these braking systems, manual or air-operated, work independently of one another. Again, the air brakes can be applied on the locomotive alone and not on the wagons, or on the entire train. The same is true of the manual brakes. (The independent brakes are only on the locomotives.) In addition to these four systems, there are redundant or emergency braking systems, also known as "penalty brakes." For example, the mechanism that representatives of MMA had mentioned to Jacques Breton: if a train starts moving by itself, and no human intervention is available to reapply the brakes, the train stops quite soon of its own accord. This is called the "dead-man switch." If the independent brakes, which hold only the locomotives, are not reset after a while, the emergency brakes come on and stop the train. If the electrical system shuts off, the emergency brakes also come on immediately.

Finally, in addition to the braking systems that are part of the train

itself, other physical defences may be available. The first and most important is a siding. If a train left standing begins to roll, the siding and its derail, if so equipped, which plays a crucial role in safety, automatically send it off the track.

Finally, there is a panoply of other physical defences, including different kinds of holding devices and derails attached to wheels or trains. "Simple and available in all Canadian Tire railway stores!" says Thomas Harding's lawyer, Thomas Walsh. So a train has several independent systems to slow it down or stop it, whether intentionally or in an emergency.

JULY 5, 2013

AT 5:30 A.M., THE SUN RISES OVER DOWNTOWN MÉGANTIC FOR the last time before the disaster. At the same moment, locomotive engineer Thomas Harding is getting out of bed. Seven hours later he will be at the controls of freight train MMA-002, which has just left Montréal's Côte-Saint-Luc yard for Farnham, in Montérégie.

× × ×

On Tuesday, October 24, 2017, a man is going through hell in the witness box at the trial of the three accused, Labrie, Harding, and Demaître. For more than ten hours, Demaître's lawyer, Maître Bourassa, has been pounding François Daigle, hammering him, harassing him. With each new question, the witness slumps a little more.

From the back, as seen from the room, Daigle's pink shirt is creased from the tension of his muscles and from the pressure of his hunched-up back. His big, strong hands won't keep still. Head bowed, he seems to await the next question like a coup de grâce. The man everyone in the courtroom is looking at has never recovered from the disaster and is reliving the nightmare. It will be no surprised to learn that he did not sleep a wink all night.

François Daigle's big mistake – "Your Honour, the only thing I know how to do is drive trains!" he pleaded – was to have confronted his boss, Jean Demaître, on the morning of July 5, 2013, in the MMA office. Daigle had advised Demaître to take locomotive 5017, which was in a very dangerous condition, out of service and not allow Harding to set off with an oil train drawn by it. Demaître's lawyer has a clear objective: to discredit this witness in the jury's eyes. Using a lot of trick questions, Bourassa sets about undermining the witness until he becomes confused:

"Does the MMA office measure one thousand square feet?"

"I really don't know ..."

"One thousand, two thousand, five hundred square feet?"

"I don't know, I'm not good at that ..."

"Aha!"

Daigle is on the hot seat like this for ten hours. He is a beaten man. Bourassa has won. He has managed to demonstrate, four years after the fact, that the witness contradicts himself, doesn't remember whether he arrived at the MMA office at eight o'clock ... or maybe at nine, on the morning of July 5. But why is that so important?

Bourassa is trying to get the jurors to forget about Daigle's attempts to improve safety at MMA. He wants us to forget that Daigle urged Demaître to have all the locomotives repaired – all of them, because they were all dangerous. Bourassa is trying to erase from history the argument between an honest man and his boss fifteen hours before the disaster about taking locomotive 5017 out of service.

Above all, what Bourassa – a very humane individual, but a lawyer devoted to his client – wants us to forget is the answer the man received from Demaître: "Griping again? Well, put up with it, it's all you're getting!"

Demaître left a worn-out engine as the lead locomotive of an oil train. It can be said in his defence that it was his bosses in Maine who made the decisions and that he had no choice but to go along. That was probably so. It will also emerge that his superiors often scoffed at Daigle, as they did at other cautious locomotive engineers. But the fact remains that Daigle had tried ...

"Your Honour, when I saw the pictures, the dead, your Honour ..." François Daigle is in a state in the witness box, his large, trembling hands groping for some support. "I couldn't sleep anymore ... I should have done more ... should have done something so that that locomotive wouldn't be used ... I should have warned Tom [Harding] ... Your Honour, I didn't do enough to prevent all those deaths, and that's kept me awake at night ... I didn't do enough ..." Yet, to the annoyance of his bosses, he had even given a verbal warning to some Transport Canada inspectors. "I wasn't satisfied with their answers."

During all his years at MMA, Daigle felt responsible for his colleagues' health and safety, fighting for them to have a first-aid kit in

the locomotive cabins – railway workers often suffer cuts and bruises. At MMA, he never got anywhere.

In October 2017, François Daigle was still working fifty to sixty hours a week for CMQR, MMA's successor company. He was still fighting for the first-aid kit. But he found a solution: he bought some Ziploc bags, which he filled and taped to the cabin for his buddies. A truly fine human being.

✕ ✕ ✕

As was later stated by Steve Callaghan, an alumnus of the TSB and a Sûreté du Québec–mandated expert for the technical autopsy, "If any one of the other four engines had been the lead locomotive that night, there would have been no tragedy. They all had braking systems and functioning penalty brakes. Only locomotive 5017, given a Mickey Mouse repair by MMA, lacked an emergency braking system." Daigle was quite right.

Locomotive 5017 was left as lead locomotive by the MMA bosses because it had apparently been modified to accommodate a single-person crew. But, above all, according to a witness, they wanted to have their logo on the locomotive at the front of the train: the other locomotives had been leased and bore no logo. It was just a matter of branding.

✕ ✕ ✕

On the morning of July 5, train MMA-002 is being assembled in Farn-ham in preparation for its journey through Maine and on to Saint John, its destination. It is hauled by five locomotives: locomotive MMA-5017, in lead position, followed by a special-purpose caboose (VN car), locomotives MMA-5026, CITX-3053, MMA-5023, and CEFX-3166, then a buffer car and seventy-two tank cars whose labels show that they contain UN 1267 crude oil, class 3, PG III. The train measures one and a half kilometres and weighs 10,290 tons.

This morning, in Mégantic, an MMA track maintenance employee inspects the rails, especially at Mile 0.0. This point is located in down-town Mégantic, at the start of a very sharp four-degree curve that

wraps around the downtown area a few metres from the Musi-Café – "When it hit that fucking curve it must have derailed," Labrie will say later.

Since 2009, due to the risks associated with poor track condition, the risk represented by this "slope and curve" section of MMA track had been classified by Transport Canada as the thirteenth highest out of fifty-five, and the permissible speed, normally between sixty-five and forty kilometres per hour, had accordingly been reduced to between forty and fifteen kilometres per hour. In October 2012 Transport Canada had even sent a letter to MMA noting "urgent track geometry defects, rail corrugation, gauge corner shelling and rail surface collapse, excessive rail end batter with marginal track surface profiles, and excessive vegetation."[110] The track was in lamentable condition.

The TSB will later say that the rails at Mile 0.0 were defective, that only temporary and "non-standard" repairs had been carried out without the use of any machinery. "Non-standard" would also be the euphemistic term used by the TSB to describe the engine's polymer repair. On the morning of July 5, the MMA employee who carries out a visual inspection at Mile 0.0 has not detected anything abnormal – but that does not matter, because in any case the company would not provide the means to correct the problem.

● 11:00 A.M.

At MMA in Farnham, Alain Richer, the Transport Canada inspector, performed a mechanical inspection of train MMA-002 as it prepared to depart. "Minor defects were noted on 2 cars, and these were corrected," says the TSB report on the accident.[111]

Five days later, federal Transport Minister Denis Lebel would state that a Transport Canada inspector had reviewed the locomotives on July 5 and found nothing of concern. That was true. However, the inspector had never actually looked at the locomotives, nor had he examined or tested all the braking systems, including the invaluable automatic brakes – which was impossible anyway, since apparently the locomotives had not yet been hooked up to the cars. Yet Farnham is actually a designated location for brake inspections.

FROM ONE TRAIN TO ANOTHER

● 12:00 P.M.

The weather forecast confirms that it will be a lovely, warm day in Mégantic. At the Musi-Café, after serving lunch on the terrace, they start preparing for a busy evening: several birthday parties are scheduled, in addition to the regular customers and the tourists who are beginning to arrive for the first day of the summer vacation. Dr. Gérard Chaput, from the Granit Hospital Centre in Mégantic, is on call at home. At the Lac-Mégantic Marina, under the leisurely gaze of the people sipping their drinks on the terrace of the Citron Vert, boaters are hoisting sails and swabbing down the decks. The early-morning fishers have come in, and the evening ones will go out around 5 p.m. The catch has been good: lake, speckled, and rainbow trout, and the celebrated yellow perch.

● 1:00 P.M.

Following the mechanical inspection, Richer carries out a "brake continuity test" to ensure that the brake pipe pressure was properly released or created simultaneously in all the brake pipes throughout the length of the train, but finds nothing to report. The train is considered perfectly safe and fit to leave.

● 1:30 P.M.

In Farnham, Harding begins his shift, which he has delayed by an hour. He will take the controls of MMA-002.

● 1:40 P.M.

The train starts off. Harding has a relatively difficult journey ahead of him, taking him through several urban areas, including Sherbrooke, so that he will encounter a lot of level crossings. The route is also very hilly, passing through the foothills of the Appalachians, which in this region include some of the highest summits in Québec.

● 1:57 P.M.

Harding has barely taken the controls when he initiates a series of phone conversations with the control centre in Farnham. The lead locomotive is unable to reach full power, he says, and is struggling to keep going. He asks if anyone has ever reported the same problem

with this locomotive. He is afraid it will not be able to cope with the climb. He is instructed to lower the speed to spare the locomotive. Harding will have four telephone conversations on this subject over the next few hours.

● 3:00 P.M.
Harding again informs the control centre in Farnham that locomotive 5017 is losing power, affecting all the locomotives behind.

● 6:00 P.M.
Richard Labrie, familiarly called RJ (for Richard Joseph), a qualified locomotive engineer, starts his shift as a controller in Farnham. Harding will be talking to him over the next few hours.

● 8:00 P.M.
Harding, becoming increasingly anxious, informs the U.S. Bangor control centre directly of the locomotive's difficulties.

● 10:49 P.M.
Harding has reached Nantes and is beginning to secure his train for the night. His actions over the next fifteen minutes will be the final triggers of the tragedy.

✕ ✕ ✕

"You really feel alone out there in the middle of the night," says Randy Stahl, thus making a partial admission that for the solitary crew member the stop at Nantes was no cakewalk.

Harding has reached the top of the steep gradient at Nantes, despite the smoke being spat out by locomotive 5017. He traverses the village and, given the length of the train, advances it to the far end instead of leaving it on more level ground. This puts the train at the start of the steep gradient that descends to Mégantic, but he has no choice. The obligation to leave level crossings unobstructed during the night is a concern for MMA: in August 2012, the company had received a non-compliance letter from Transport Canada about parking trains on level crossings. The train must leave the level crossings in Nantes

clear, but Harding cannot "split the crossing," for that would require uncoupling the wagons, and two people are required for such a task. And MMA did not want to attract the ministry's attention, as the locomotive engineers, always liable to sanctions from their bosses, were perfectly aware.[112]

Harding parks the train on the main track, which has no derail device, alongside the siding which, as usual, is completely blocked by wagons belonging to a local company, awaiting triage. He first stabilizes his train using the automatic air brakes, which are activated along the entire train. Then he applies the second, pneumatic system, which hold only the locomotives (the "independent brakes").

This is where the plot thickens. To park a long, heavy train, nothing beats having two people, the locomotive engineer and a conductor, for the manoeuvre is carried out *simultaneously* from inside and outside the cockpit. The locomotive engineer, at the controls, first performs a manoeuvre called "pull-push to crunch the cars," in other words stretching and relaxing the couplings between all the cars. Outside, the conductor watches to make sure that the couplings have responded as they should, then goes along the train applying the handbrakes on the wagons and locomotives one by one. After a certain number of brakes have been applied (it is up to the conductor to decide how many), the conductor radios to the locomotive engineer to perform the handbrake effectiveness test. The driver, still at the controls, releases all the air brakes, puts the locomotive into forward gear, and attempts to move. From outside, the conductor observes first-hand if the train has shifted, even by a millimetre. The necessary adjustment is then made so that nothing can move on its own.

That night, though, Harding is alone.

There will be no visual confirmation of cars "crunching" or of the train moving. Harding therefore applies the independent and automatic air brakes on the entire train. Then he goes outside and starts to apply the manual brakes on the five locomotives, the buffer car, and the VB car. What Harding does not know is that the manual brakes on the second locomotive are defective and only work if a certain procedure is followed – but MMA has not informed him of this. The manual brakes of the second locomotive will not work properly. In addition, the brakes on the other locomotives are worn.

Harding applies seven handbrakes in all. Why only seven? This question will haunt him for the rest of his life. Why not nine, as the company requires? "Because the manual called for 10 percent of the brakes," Harding would later explain. "Seventy-two cars, seven brakes ... And then I had the independent brakes on ..."

Except that nine brakes wouldn't have changed a thing. As we have seen, an expert named Callaghan would confirm that at least fourteen brakes were needed; the TSB would conclude after testing that between eighteen and twenty-six would have been required.

The criminal negligence charges facing Harding would include a failure to apply enough brakes (two more than he did apply). But doing so would not have made any difference either, because during his review of the brakes Harding turns off the engine of the four locomotives behind locomotive 5017. In doing so he is following the instructions contained in paragraph L of MMA's Rules of Operations Manual, intended to save fuel. By shutting down the engines, Harding deactivates the locomotive's emergency system. Of the emergency braking systems on MMA-002, only that of number 5017 are left on. But Harding can't know that number 5017's emergency brake will not work because it has been connected improperly. As a result, no system to stop the train in an emergency will be functional when it begins its deadly run.

Now Harding has finished applying his manual brakes. Covered in oil, he returns to the lead locomotive, which is emitting thick smoke. He is about to carry out the brake effectiveness test. He disengages the air brakes on the entire train – the automatic brakes. At the time of the test, only two braking systems remain operative on the entire train: seven manual brakes and five independent brakes on the locomotive.

Harding will also be accused of leaving the locomotives' air brakes on while performing his test, something forbidden by Rule 112, which is concerned with the immobilization of unattended trains. Those air brakes are unreliable; they can leak off without notice (something that will indeed happen that night), making the test invalid. So why does Harding, a man described by his peers as so cautious and professional, not comply with this basic rule? Why does he leave the air brakes on when performing his test?

Once again, perhaps it was because he has no choice, according

to sources familiar with the parking of trains at Nantes. If Harding pushed the engine to the limit in carrying out his test and the train moved forward, it would have blocked the next crossing. This crossing, at a roundabout, is where four important roads intersect. If he blocks it, he will be unable to reverse the long train without assistance: such a manoeuvre is absolutely forbidden, and in any case no locomotive engineer worthy of the name would reverse a train of that sort without someone at the rear to check.

But that is not all. It will emerge during the trial that no locomotive engineer, when parking a train at Nantes, ever used the eighteen to twenty-six brakes that are said to be necessary to keep the train in place. They point out that they would apply barely ten or twelve, and, apparently, never used the independent brakes, contrary to what Harding did that night. Yet the trains never rolled.

How could that be possible? What if it was the engineers' custom to contravene the rule and always activate the independent brakes? Perhaps, in the trial, they all tinkered a little with the truth? Nevertheless, that night Harding would leave his train with a braking power two and a half times what was needed to keep his train from moving. When he later said that his train was "safe," he was correct.

So we come back to the man who was all alone one night at Nantes – to a man who needed to be both outside and inside his train to check the couplings and brakes. A man who was not allowed to apply extra brakes but was also not allowed to back up his train if it moved. A man on the horns of a dilemma, caught between contradictory regulations.

We return to the man who must at the same time shut down a locomotive and leave it running – for MMA officially required its locomotive engineers to shut down the locomotive engine to save fuel, yet unofficially required them to leave one of the engines running for the sake of the Americans who would take over the trains the next day, as U.S. regulations stipulate that a brake test is mandatory if the air brakes are disengaged for more than four hours without a locomotive running – and that costs time.

So Harding carries out his handbrake effectiveness test with the independent brakes applied. Nothing moves. The well-established procedure certainly worked. Harding, a cautious man, has done this

dozens of times, and no train has ever rolled. Certainly, in the past, he used to take greater care; in fact, he once used to observe the North American industry standard for trains parked unattended. He had applied the air brakes, the automatic brakes, on the entire train. As an additional precaution.

"Application of the automatic brakes ... likely would have kept the train secured, even after the eventual release of the independent brakes," wrote the TSB in a sentence buried on page 105 of its report. If Harding had pushed a certain lever from left to right in his cabin – a procedure that required only ten seconds – the air brakes would have been applied to the entire train, including the seventy-two tank cars. For more than a century that has been one of the safest backup systems for securing a train.

It seems completely logical to follow this procedure, especially in the case of a train as heavy and flammable as MMA-002, which was, moreover, parked on a gradient. But that night Harding did not apply those brakes. On the contrary, he deactivated them as soon as he stopped his train. Why? Simply because MMA formally forbids its locomotive engineers to use this braking system to immobilize a train. Paul Budge, Harding's superior in the United States, had even had Harding lectured by his superior in Farnham. Budge had written in an email six months earlier that when he came to the train at Nantes one Saturday morning he had found it with the automatic brakes enabled, and that Tom Harding should be spoken to about it. And Harding had been spoken to. Use of the automatic brakes was forbidden at MMA, as the controller Steve Jacques, an MMA employee, would later confirm; profitability had to prevail, trains had to travel, and do so without wasting any time. Both applying and releasing the air brakes can be time-consuming.

Yet those brakes would have held MMA-002 at the top of the gradient for several hours, until the driver began his shift the following morning. This was especially so since the longer the train, the longer it takes for air brakes to disengage. MMA-002 had seventy-two cars. Some experienced locomotive engineers confirm that those brakes can hold a long train in place for almost a week.

How could MMA have banned such an essential measure, the use of the most effective backup safety system for immobilizing a train?

Who gave them the right to do so? How can it be that no law or regulation has been introduced to countermand this prohibition? This question remains unanswered, and the TSB has buried this sensitive subject on page 105 of its report, where it has survived only in an unobtrusive paragraph which admits that those ten seconds could have saved forty-seven lives.

It would not be until 2016, three years after the Mégantic disaster, that an anonymous and highly praiseworthy source drew the attention of the *Globe and Mail* to this crucial little paragraph.[113] The industry responded resoundingly to this article about the "ten seconds" with a reaction of fury, total fury. Michael Bourque, the chief lobbyist working for the Railway Association of Canada, responded immediately in an open letter to the daily newspaper affirming that the application of the automatic air brakes would have changed nothing and that, roughly speaking, those brakes were useless. A few days later, the *Globe and Mail* reported that a considerable number of railway employees had responded indignantly to Bourque's letter. He decided to withdraw it, while continuing to protest strongly.[114]

The TSB's lack of frankness and Bourque's reaction speak for themselves. Even today the industry maintains its vehement opposition to any law or regulation requiring the application of that braking system to all parked trains. Nevertheless, those ten seconds would most likely have saved forty-seven lives, as the TSB would admit.

✕ ✕ ✕

Transport Canada's reply to the *Globe and Mail* article would be sadly predictable. The spokesman for the ministry would simply answer that their role was merely to "monitor" the observance of the rail industry's rules by means of audits and safety inspections. And anyway, the spokesperson would add, Transport Canada was not required to approve or enforce instructions formulated by the companies.

How can our laws and regulations allow such unsafe behaviour? Only Ministers Baird and Lebel, or officials from Transport Canada, can answer that question. But they have all remained silent, or departed the stage. Even today, the application (or non-application)

of this tried and true braking system is the result of a decision left entirely to the railway industry itself.

✕ ✕ ✕

Now let us return to July 5, at 10:55 p.m.

Harding, alone with his train, disengages the automatic brakes, following the instructions he has been given.

At this moment, a few hours before the tragedy, train 606-282, renamed MMA-002 when MMA took it over from CP, has accumulated the following failures and potential dangers since its journey began on June 30:

- falsified Safety Data Sheets that vastly underestimate its cargo's flammability and risk of explosion

- failure to carry out surprise inspections by the authorities to verify the SDSs

- transportation of extremely dangerous goods that should not have been allowed on MMA's tracks because of their poor condition, if only the company had been willing to recognize its own "exempted sections"

- use of tank cars too fragile to meet the "pre-2012 standard" (six tank cars with mechanical problems were removed during the journey)

- use of a single-person crew

- failure to adequately inform the locomotive engineer about technical defects

- failure by both MMA and Transport Canada to recognize the high-risk factor associated with the gradient

- use of a defective locomotive, reported as such, upon which "non-standard" repairs had been carried out

- use by MMA of uncertified mechanical inspectors, a problem previously recognized by Transport Canada

- parking the train on a main line, on a gradient, with no emergency derail device

- inadequate and defective brakes

- non-functional emergency braking system

- poorly executed handbrake-effectiveness test

- prohibition of the use of automatic brakes

- failure to repair a track in poor condition and recognized as such

- threatening to sanction employees for failure to apply the company's orders

The responsibility for all these risk factors, without exception, is borne by Transport Canada (and its U.S. counterpart), World Fuel, and the railway companies CP and MMA; to a lesser extent, three factors also involved the three MMA employees who would be charged with criminal offences.

THE NIGHT OF JULY 5–6, 2013: THE FINAL COUNTDOWN

OVER THE COMING HOURS AND MINUTES, RICHARD LABRIE, alone at the Farnham control centre, will be bombarded with phone calls. All of these are recorded, making it possible to follow what occurred during the final minutes before the disaster, as well as its consequences, in all their horror.[115]

● JULY 5, 11:04 P.M.

Harding to Labrie: "5017 W-E-S-T siding switch, Nantes right now."*

Locomotive 5017 is parked for the night. Harding leaves the cabin and carries out his tour of the brakes.

● 11:15 P.M.

Harding to Dave Wiley, rail-traffic controller at U.S. Rail Traffic Control in Bangor, Maine: "Tom here. I'm up here at Nantes. Shut down four of the five units, got the handbrakes applied. Do you have any questions for me?"

"No, no," replies Dave.

"The 5017," Harding continues, "I worked pretty damn hard coming up here ... I know it's going to settle down once she cools and stuff like that. I don't know how good it's going to be on the eastbound. When I left Farnham, I had engine hunting on it ... this last little pull here from the bottom of the hill at 26, down at Scotstown, all the way up, to here, she worked pretty damn hard. Once I got stopped here, I noticed ... she was smoking excessively, both black for a minute or so, and then she would go white for a little bit, and then go back to black again."

---

* The conversations cited have been abridged. They were sometimes in English, sometimes in French. In the latter case, they have been freely translated.

"Well you probably cleaned her out, Tom."

"Okay, yes. I cleaned her out. ... Maybe if she sits here for another hour or so, she'll cool right down."

"Well that's all we can do, Tom. We'll check it in the morning and see what she says and see what she comes up with. Diagnose her then, I guess."

Harding goes over to André Turcotte's taxi, which is waiting for him. Locomotive 5017 is running, the cabin door is unlocked, with the train starter key in plain sight on the front seat. The taxi starts off at 11:39. Harding calls Labrie: "RJ, me here. ... I'm off the clock at 45."

André Turcotte, the taxi driver, asks a few questions. His windshield is smeared with oil, as is Harding. Turcotte is even afraid that all that oil will make the road dangerously slippery.

Barely a minute later, at 11:40, a 911 call comes in, reporting a fire on a locomotive at Nantes. The call is transferred to the Nantes Fire Service. Flames were rising between two and three metres into the air, the caller said.

Harding, in the taxi, does not look back and does not notice the glow in the sky. If only he had turned around, made a simple movement of the head, he would have seen, returned to his train, and the disaster could have been avoided.

● **11:50 P.M.**

Eleven minutes after Harding leaves with Turcotte, Gilles Bertrand, a Sûreté du Québec dispatcher, informs Labrie of the fire. The firefighters are on their way, he says.

Labrie is concerned: "Where's the fire? In the wagons? The locomotives? Because there's oil there ... seventy-two wagons of crude ... "

"I don't know, I know nothing," Bertrand replies.

Labrie calls his boss, Demaître.

"There's a fire at Nantes, but that's all I know."

"Have you someone from the railway who can be there?" asks Demaître. "Lafleur?"

Labrie calls once, twice. Dédé Lafleur lives in Marston, less than ten kilometres from the burning train. A railwayman and a qualified locomotive engineer, Dédé knows all about trains. But he is on leave, and his phone is turned off. It is 11:53 p.m.

In Nantes, the firefighters David Grégoire and Martin Dumont are already on the scene. They aren't in uniform – they just happened to be passing. A few minutes later, the Sûreté du Québec and a fire engine pull up on Route 161. The firefighters turn their hose on the burning locomotive. But water on oil is a bad idea, so they spray a special foam. Unfortunately, it fails to extinguish the fire, because the fire is inside the exhaust. Sébastien Pépin happens by; he tells the firefighters how to find the cut-off switch to turn off the locomotive. The locomotive engine stops, halting the flow of oil to the exhaust. The fire is soon out. Firefighters also turn off the circuit breakers on locomotive 5017.

The firefighters try to reach someone from MMA. Dumont, who has the phone number of Daniel Aubé, MMA's track maintenance manager, calls him. It is 11:58. Aubé gets in touch with Labrie who, in Farnham, is still trying to reach Dédé Lafleur: "Lafleur's on leave, but the fire's under control. 5017's engine was cut, the locomotive's dead."

Aubé also informs Labrie that the Sûreté du Québec is requesting the presence of some responsible person from MMA on site. Firefighters, once the fire is under control, are not permitted to leave the train without handing over the responsibility to a qualified representative of the company. "Call Jean-Noël Busque," Aubé asks Labrie.

Busque lives in Mégantic, ten minutes away. The track maintenance supervisor for the sector, he has a forty-year career in railways behind him. He is a specialist on railway tracks, but he is not a mechanic. Labrie calls Busque, who will go to Nantes. Everything is under control.

● JULY 6, 2013 – MIDNIGHT

The locomotive fire has been put out and an MMA employee has been dispatched to the scene, so Labrie calls Harding at his hotel. The reception hasn't seen him arrive. Labrie tries to call him in Room 5.

"Sorry to bother you. Hey, uh, did you kill the units before leaving?" asks Labrie.

"Yes, four of them," replies Harding.

"Which one did you keep running?"

"5017."

"The leader?" continues Labrie. "Okay, apparently it's – it caught fire."

"It caught fire?" Harding replies, surprised.

"Yeah ..."

"I had problems with that. I reported it to Dave. Have you talked to Dave?"

"No," answers Labrie.

"Okay. I told Dave that I worked it hard coming up there and she was smoking pretty good when I left her ... Now you're telling me she caught on fire? ... Okay, somebody up there to take care of it or ...?"

"Yeah, well, the firemen were there," says Labrie. "And the fire is, is all gone ... and that's all I know about it."

The second part of the conversation will haunt Harding and Labrie at the trial and for the rest of their lives.

"Do I have to go back up, start ...?" Harding asks.

"No, no, no, no," answers Labrie. "Jean-Noël Busque is. He went there to check if there's any damage and he's going to call me back. Go to bed."

"Okay, call me back, RJ." says Harding. A brief silence, then Harding, at a loss, continues: "There's nothing to do, hey?"

"There's nothing to do," confirms Labrie, "We won't start up an engine now. Tomorrow morning. He's going to start them up, the American will start them up."

"Okay," says Harding. But both are worried, and don't hang up.

"So she caught on fire then ..." repeats Harding.

"It might be a minor fire, mind you," the controller replies.

"Yeah, yeah."

"But you killed the four units, you kept only 5017 running?" Labrie is still uneasy.

"That was the only one that was running, 5017," Harding confirms again.

"Yeah, and it caught on fire," says Labrie.

"And she caught on fire ..." ends Harding.

Neither man is aware at that moment that Daigle had done all he could to have the dangerous locomotive removed, without success. Labrie informs Bangor about the fire and that locomotive 5017 has been shut down.

Labrie advises Harding not to return to the train: "No, go to bed." Labrie is concerned that Harding have his regulatory hours of rest. Those words will be held against Labrie at the trial, and he will also be blamed for not asking Harding how many brakes he had applied.

At Nantes, Busque is looking over the locomotive. The fire is now out. But one thing worries him: all the locomotives are shut down. He calls Labrie and, repeating word by word what he is told by the firefighter Grégoire, who is standing beside him and who tells him about the actions that have been taken, that the locomotive fire has been put out, and that the circuit breakers of locomotive 5017 have been turned off. Labrie confirms that everything is fine: "That's exactly what's supposed to be done, according to the protocol."

"My instinct told me there's always a locomotive kept running." Busque would say later. "I thought it strange that they were all shut down."

Labrie repeats Busque's words to Demaître who, unlike Busque, is surprised to learn that Harding had left the 5017 running. "To avoid having to do a test on the air brakes before starting off, like the Americans require," explains Labrie. "But we'll see tomorrow," had said Dave, in Bangor.

"There'd have been no stars in Mégantic anymore," says a relieved Labrie to Gilles Bertrand of the Sûreté du Québec, who confirms to him officially that the fire has been put out and the locomotive shut down.

"Fortunately ... With eighty tank cars of crude, there'd have been an apocalypse in Mégantic, if that train had rolled down," Labrie explains to Gilles, "the whole thing would have blown up. You've no idea ..."

Labrie gives a little relieved laugh and hangs up.

✖ ✖ ✖

The firefighters shut down the engine of locomotive 5017. In doing so, they shut off the air to the locomotive's air brake, which went slack. After that, the seven manual brakes applied by Harding were no longer enough to hold a train weighing over ten thousand tons.

What is beyond doubt is that, with the closing of the circuit breakers on locomotive 5017, the train was left entirely without emergency

FROM ONE TRAIN TO ANOTHER

brakes. Shutting down the circuit breakers on any of the other four locomotives attached to this train would have triggered the train's emergency brakes immediately – but not on locomotive 5017, which had been tampered with by the MMA mechanics in Maine. And 5017 was the lead locomotive; the others were out of the picture, having been shut down by Harding, following orders.

✕ ✕ ✕

● 12:43 A.M.
The firefighters, the Sûreté du Québec, and Busque leave Nantes. The air pressure in the brakes is falling.

● 12:58 A.M.
Train MMA-002 starts its run downhill. "There'd have been no more stars in Mégantic ..."

● 1:07 A.M. – FORTY KILOMETRES PER HOUR
At a level crossing, firefighter Jean-Luc Montminy, on his way home from dousing the flames on 5017, is very nearly hit by a dark train that vanishes into the night. Distraught, he returns to the fire station in Nantes.

● 1:10 A.M. – EIGHTY KILOMETRES PER HOUR
André Turcotte, the taxi driver cruising along Mégantic's main street, sees the runaway train heading for the town centre.

● 1:13 A.M. – ONE HUNDRED KILOMETRES PER HOUR
The train reaches Mile 0.0, in the heart of the downtown Mégantic. Impact.

Forty-seven fatalities.

There will be no details. We fall silent.

Let us simply honour the victims' memory.

Let us remember the survivors' tragic nights.

And remember, too, the agony of those who, with bodies intact but souls seared, will also not survive: the suicides.

× × ×

Respect and peace.

And our apologies, too, for failing to notice anything, foresee anything, prevent anything.

MILE 0.0

AN EARTHQUAKE, THEN A SECOND. THE TANK CARS DERAIL,
pile into one another, are disembowelled, and emit their toxic gases.
Streams of liquid oil and tiny droplets envelop the town centre in a
fiery haze. A transformer is mowed down, the electricity fails; it's total
darkness. At the Musi-Café, in the dark apartments, an intense orange
glow suddenly lights up the melting walls. The town centre flares up,
explodes. A multi-storied wall of fire consisting of liquid oil and gases
escaping from the gutted tank cars heads toward the lake at four kilometres an hour, mowing down everything in its path. The surface of
the lake is on fire. Barely a few seconds remain to survive, to escape
the deadly, asphyxiating gases, the explosions, and the wall of fire,
which reaches a nearly inconceivable three thousand degrees Celsius.

● **1:17 A.M.**
Several 911 calls come in about a fire on rue Cartier in Mégantic.
The calls are transferred to the Mégantic Fire Department. The town
centre is in flames.

✕ ✕ ✕

Mégantic, which sits on a valley bottom, overlooks a lake, the source
of the Chaudière River, which cuts the little town in two with its tur-
bulent, ten-metre width. A dam and a single bridge connect the two
banks. On the western bank, on the Nantes side, are the town centre,
the shops, and the Musi-Café, overlooked by the imposing Sainte-
Agnès Church. The railway makes a tight four-degree curve around
the main street at Mile 0.0, circling the downtown core. Higher up,
toward Nantes, on a plateau a kilometre away, are the hospital and
the police station.

On the eastern bank of the river, toward Vachon and the state of
Maine, stands the rest of the little town: the parish of Fatima, modest

houses, little shops. About a kilometre, the length of the downtown, separates Fatima from Sainte-Agnès Church on the far side.

The derailment takes place on the western (Nantes) side, just below Sainte-Agnès Church. The only other bridge connecting the two parts of the town is near the industrial park, a ten-kilometre detour into the countryside. The emergency services and the inhabitants are cut off, each on their own riverbank, by a sea of fire, left without any way to cross from one point to another in the town, without making that detour.

✕ ✕ ✕

● 1:20 A.M.

Dr. Gérard Chaput has been asleep for some time in his house by the lake, a few kilometres from the town. He is on call tonight, for the hospital. A medical practitioner with thirty-eight years of experience, Chaput is head of the department of medicine. As if in a scene from a B movie, he is awakened in the night by the strident ringing of his phone.

"The town's on fire, the town's on fire ... Save yourself!" his son is shouting at the other end, while on his second line the stunned Chaput hears the order: "Code Orange, Code Orange at the hospital."

"Code Orange" means that a major disaster has occurred. Chaput, who can see nothing from his home, has not yet taken in the full measure of the drama. But he knows he will have to initiate emergency procedures when he arrives at the hospital.

On the western side, Denis Lauzon, Mégantic's fire chief, rushes to the fire and immediately grasps what has happened: "It's the cocktail train, it's the cocktail train ..." he shouts over the radio to the first responders. The worst scenario, the worst nightmare, one that has been feared for a long time, a train carrying hazardous materials derailing in the town centre.

But what kind of materials? There is no way to find out.

Everywhere, before the advancing inferno, survivors are fleeing the heat and flames, helping their relatives and neighbours to escape. Gilles Fluet, almost brushed by the train as he was leaving the Musi-Café, is knocking on doors, waking people, yelling to them to run. At L'Eau Berge, the sleeping guests are evacuated by the Sûreté du

Québec. "Come out now, NOW": they have only seconds to cross the river and find safety in Fatima.

"Send someone, it just exploded, everything's burning in Mégantic," shouts a Sûreté du Québec officer on the phone to the aghast Labrie in Farnham. "It exploded, what do you mean?" he responds. "Is it us? My train is at Nantes!"

"Call in the Fire Departments from ..." Fire Chief Lauzon, whose quick thinking will later come in for praise, calls on the emergency service to send every fire department within a radius of over a hundred kilometres. More than a hundred fire departments will respond. Lauzon has grasped the magnitude of the urgency, the scale of the catastrophe. But he could never have guessed what would happen fifteen minutes later, and again at around 4:30 a.m.

The downtown area is melting. Fire and toxic gases are spreading through the town, under and above it (the gases will rise a kilometre into the air, as would be learned later). A half-dressed crowd, including old people and children, goes barefoot to the farthest points from the inferno; panicking people search for one another everywhere.

Dr. Chaput is speeding; to reach the hospital he will have to make that ten-kilometre detour and cross by the other bridge. When he reaches the far side, he can finally see. A wild-eyed crowd is gazing at a sea of fire. "Sodom and Gomorrah and Hiroshima in one," says Chaput. He understands the magnitude of what will surely await him at the hospital.

● 1:25 A.M.

"Hey, RJ. Tom here. Listen, emergency. The town of Mégantic is on fire ..." screams Harding to Labrie on a borrowed phone.

Harding, on the Fatima side, can't see where the fire began. "Do we have tankers in the yard anywhere? ... Tankers, any kind of tankers, of any kind?"

"No," answers Labrie, who can be heard rummaging through his papers. "What's the problem? Is it with us?"

"Everything is on fire, from the church all the way down to the Metro,[*] from the river all the way to the railway tracks ... The yard is

---

[*] Metro is a supermarket chain based in Québec.

gone. Flames, RJ, flames are two hundred feet high ... It's incredible, terrible, RJ ..."

"Is, is, is it the train that run, run down?" Labrie asks.

"No, I had all the police here around me because they know I work for the railway. We got [my] loaded train up at Nantes, it's okay ..."

Labrie stammers: "Tom, there's only the, the, the oil, the tank there for the, for the machinery, so the ..."

"Okay, that means it's got to be the natural-gas pipeline that's been ..." Harding breathes a sigh of relief.

Labrie wakes his boss, Demaître:

"It's not us ... but Mégantic's on fire ... It's an apocalypse ... it's an apocalypse."

Alone in his little glass cubbyhole in Farnham, Labrie instinctively understands that the situation is critical. He wakes Aubé, who rushes to Mégantic.

It is impossible to get close to the inferno. The heat is unbearable. There are explosions everywhere. The firefighters cannot get close. They try to evacuate the nearest residents to remove them from the fire zone and turn their hoses on homes and buildings further up that are being attacked by the flames shooting up everywhere. The police close off every access point, every way through. Everyone is confined to his or her own area, not knowing, not seeing, prevented from moving about.

At the hospital, the power goes off and the generators kick in. Chaput and everyone else who has responded to the Code Orange have been able to prepare things in twenty minutes. Eight teams, each with numbered stretchers, a doctor, a nurse, an attendant, and a helper. Among them are four respiratory therapists, a surgeon, and very soon a radiologist summoned urgently to Mégantic from Sherbrooke. Only a few cellphones are working. Nothing is visible from the hospital, which stands high on a plateau a kilometre away from the fire, except from the upper floors where Father Steve Lemay, the parish priest, himself an evacuee, is trying to calm the distraught patients. In the emergency department, they're waiting, in the dark. But a few personal cellphones belonging to members of the medical team are beginning to ring.

Suddenly, there is an earth-shaking blast, with the force of a small nuclear explosion. A fiery mushroom cloud rises into the air to one thousand, two thousand, or even five thousand feet, according to the petrified onlookers. Lauzon and Breton, responsible for Nantes firefighters, are appalled: their men, their firefighters, are close to the explosion: the security perimeter isn't wide enough. "That oil doesn't burn, doesn't explode like others," Breton would say later. But both men understand what is happening. Under the effect of intense heat, the tank cars full of gases are exploding instead of pouring out their oil in sheets of fire. The escaping gases are igniting and exploding. And despite the blaze, they can make out dozens and dozens of tank cars. The same, agonizing question reoccurs: What can be in those tanks? "UN crude oil 1267," is what Labrie repeated to them, for he can only confirm what is written on his "consists," the documents that identify the contents of the tank cars.

In Farnham, on the recordings made that night, the overwhelmed Labrie's wheezing breath is audible. He calls Busque, who is in Mégantic, and Aubé, whom he can't reach. Labrie is terrified, he wants information. He tells everyone: "I'm stressed shitless ... I've got to find out if our train's still at Nantes ..."

The Sûreté du Québec calls again: "Are you sure your train is still at Nantes?"

Then, a sudden downpour. Rain is falling furiously on the distraught survivors, on the inferno. Harding is on the bridge, seeing "sheer hell" around him, as he describes it later. He is trying to understand what is fuelling the fire, and finally realizes that it is coming from the west, from what he thinks must be the MMA yard. Had some tank cars been forgotten there?

Busque is fleeing the downpour in his MMA truck. A man in rain gear knocks on his window: "It's your train ... I saw it go past in the dark at a hundred miles an hour," says the man, before disappearing into the rain.

Busque calls Labrie: "It's our goddam train ... Someone saw it going past ..."

"I don't get it," Labrie answers. "The police said it was at Nantes."

Busque calls back a few minutes later: "It's our train, Richard, I'm

sure ... the guy must have forgotten to apply the brakes ... It's our train that derailed ..."

"I don't get it," repeats Labrie, though he's beginning to understand.

"There'll be deaths, Richard, a whole lot of deaths ..."

"Can you go to Nantes to check if the train's still there? Can you go?" gasps Labrie.

"I'll try, but I can't budge from here, we're stuck everywhere ... I'll try to get to Nantes ..."

Sheets of burning oil are rushing through all the underground pipes, water pipes, sewer pipes, melting plastic pipes and spreading everywhere beneath the town. In Fatima, the burning oil, which crossed under the river through conduits, is shooting manholes fifty metres into the air on jets of flame.

Fire Chief Lauzon, his world gradually organizing into sub-teams with the help of the Sherbrooke fire chief, is trying to obtain the phenomenal amount of foam they need to put out this sea of fire. The foam, which comes from the Valero refinery, in a suburb of Québec City, will not arrive until around 9 p.m. on Sunday, forty-five hours after the derailment. Breton, meanwhile, is struggling to set up a functional telecommunications centre. The news is getting out, to the media, to the Transportation Safety Board, to Urgence-Environnement.

Eighty kilometres to the west, in the quiet village of Cookshire-Eaton, Jean Clusiault is sleeping like a log. He can't hear his phone, which continues to ring in the back of his apartment.

As required, the Mégantic town councillors and municipal employees have an emergency plan – except that the binder, containing the phone numbers, is kept in the town hall ... in the middle of the firestorm, inaccessible. The Hydro-Québec facility is also in the heart of the fire; its fibres and wires have melted.

In the hospital, the team is working blind, with no radio, no TV, unable to know what is occurring a kilometre away, in the town below. But the personal cellphones of the team members never stop ringing:

"Dad, have you heard from ...? He was at the Musi tonight with ..."

"Mom, did he call you ... I can't get him ... His phone just keeps on ringing ..."

A son, a sister, a husband ... Despite the anguish and the dark,

the medical team remains stoic. But it is 2:20 a.m., and no casualties have reached them yet.

On boulevard des Vétérans, construction contractor Raymond Lafontaine, his son Christian, and his employees are demolishing still-erect houses and buildings to create a firebreak. "Where there's fire, you stop, where there's smoke, you get on with the demolition," said one of the employees. Lafontaine is directing his men. He is only too aware that he had sons, in-laws, and employees at the Musi-Café that evening.

The water treatment plant, a few kilometres distant, becomes a landmine, invaded by gas and tongues of fire driven along the sewer system. The operator reacts to save it by opening the valves, sending everything directly into the river.

● 2:30 A.M.

A first ambulance arrives at the hospital. A body. Dr. Chaput, who knows everyone, offers to identify it and notify the family. He is not allowed to approach and is told that only the official forensic team will look after such matters later. This would be the first sidelining of the Mégantic medical staff, whose offers of assistance during the disaster will be rejected, "even if it's only to carry stretchers, to help out a bit," the distraught Chaput would argue later. "After all, we have the expertise," he adds, sadly.

In Cookshire-Eaton, Jean Clusiault finally gets out of bed and answers his phone. It is one of his two daughters calling: "Dad ... There's no answer from her cell ..." He turns on the radio, hears the description given by a horrified reporter. He understands. He knows that his other daughter lives right there, in the very heart of the conflagration.

At the MMA Control Centre in Farnham, Labrie receives a flurry of phone calls. Aubé, Demaître, and Bangor want information. "But we're so far away," Labrie will say to his opposite number in Bangor. They are all wondering the same thing: "Is it the train from Nantes?"

Then comes a different call: a strangely calm voice, the voice of Clément, the proprietor of the taxi stand in Mégantic:

"Richard, Mégantic is on fire, and it's your train ..."

"No ... no," Labrie answers, stunned.

"It's your train, my driver saw it going past ... Don't call me any-more, I've no taxi stand left, everything's burning ... Richard ... there'll be dozens and dozens of deaths ..."

Another call comes from Busque who has managed to reach Nantes: "Richard? The train's not at Nantes anymore ... it's your train that's burning ..."

"The Nantes train isn't at Nantes anymore ..."

● 2:45 A.M.

"We're in deep shit," repeats Demaître, whom Labrie has just informed. Demaître dashes to Mégantic from Marieville. He'll take Michael Horan, his deputy, who is camping on Lake Champlain, along with him. Everyone at MMA in Québec, as in Maine, is wondering how many handbrakes were applied by Harding – Harding, who is on the bridge in Mégantic, in the rain, with no phone.

The five locomotives, including locomotive 5017, did not derail. Travelling at one hundred kilometres per hour, they ran across and up the slope on the other side. Abandoned to their fate, they descended into the night without anyone knowing and, fortunately, came to a stop a short distance before the bridge.

● 3:29 A.M.

"RJ, it's Tom ..." Back at the Esso station's phone booth, Harding asks Labrie for information.

Labrie cuts him off: "My friend ... It's your train that rolled down."

"NO, NO, RJ! Holy fuck!"

"Yes, sir. That's what I got, it was confirmed at 2:30," says Labrie.

"The fuel train rolled down here? ... Ah, *tabarnak de tabarnak*! And it was secure, RJ, when I left! ... She was fucking secure," Harding protests.

"That's what, that's what I got as news," replies Labrie.

"... Oh, Jesus Christ ... Oh, fuck. So that means ... holy fuck."

A moment of silence from Harding, and then: "How the fuck did that thing start to roll down, RJ?"

"I don't know. How many brakes did you put on?" asks Labrie.

"The units, the V.B., and the first car, seven brakes."

"... Were there any railway people that went up there to put the fire out?"

"Jean-Noël Busque."

"And everything was secure when he was there? Everything was fine? Everything was ..."

"Everything was fine, yeah," Labrie confirms.

"And then it rolled, what, two hours later? Three hours later? The police," pleaded Harding, "they confirmed to me, RJ, when I talked to you at the very beginning – they confirmed that the train was up there, that it ... I don't understand, RJ, if it rolled down."

"Apparently it rolled down."

"... Where did it stop?"

"At the curve, at the crossing there?" said Labrie. "That's what I think, but it would be the only thing that would ... When it hit that fucking curve there, it must have derailed."

Harding falls silent, then says: "Call me ... call me, I'm here, next to the phone ... I'm in the rain and the cold ... Don't leave me alone in the cold ..."

⬤ 3:30 A.M.

Jean Clusiault rushes to Mégantic with his brother, who came to pick him up. His mind is entirely focused on a single image: that of his daughter, his surviving daughter.

Labrie, in his glass cubbyhole, can hardly breathe. He's on the phone to Busque again; he asks: "Why did no emergency braking kick in?"

On the emergency line, Chief Lauzon is asking Labrie to find ways to move the tank cars that haven't yet exploded away from the fire. But the MMA guys in Mégantic are all cut off from each other, unable to move about, and Labrie is having difficulty contacting them. And the MMA locomotives are in Montréal. There is just one in Sherbrooke, a good way off. Labrie has it brought all the same.

"Tom, where are you?" asks Labrie.

"Taken refuge in the convenience." This time, Harding's voice is flat.

"Alone?" worries Labrie.

"Yes. I don't feel too good," says Harding.

"I don't feel too good either," says Labrie, sounding equally distraught.

"I can't even imagine ... I don't even want to imagine the hell I've caused," Harding murmurs.

"Because it's hell, Tom?"

"Yes, RJ, it's hell ..."

Everywhere in the little town people are looking for their loved ones, begging for news, asking around if they have been seen. Many begin to walk up the hill toward the Sûreté du Québec parking lot, eager to find answers and contact their family.

At the hospital, it's waiting and anguish in the dark corridors. No casualties, no more bodies have arrived, nor has any news ... not about the fire, nor about the family members from whom people are hoping for a call. The team goes out into the parking lot to breathe. All they can see is the intense orange glow of the fire.

● 4:30 A.M.

Another brutal explosion, almost like a nuclear bomb ... another gigantic, fiery mushroom cloud that again rises several hundred metres into the sky, spreading its flames and toxic cloud across the whole region. "A din like the end of the world," Father Lemay will recall, "but inside me I've a silence that still chills my blood ..."

Harding, who has been picked up from the far side of town, is brought close to the scene of the derailment. He dons bunker gear, the firefighters' protective clothing. With the help of one of the Lafontaine boys, he sets about hauling back to Nantes the unexploded tank cars that are still close to the fire, three at a time, using a pull-car belonging to the Tafisa company and a payloader belonging to Lafontaine. He'll make three trips. The firefighters stop Harding at the fourth trip, which would have been fatal.

● 6 A.M.

Jean Clusiault arrives in Mégantic, looking for his daughter, for his daughters. He finally finds the surviving one: a miracle. In the light of dawn and the fire, before the still-raging conflagration, a dazed crowd remains standing. At last, everyone can see the extent of the

FROM ONE TRAIN TO ANOTHER

loss that has been inflicted on them. There is nothing but pain in the police station parking lot.

Dr. Chaput decides to go home. In the devastated town he can hear the hiss of the unexploded tank cars' safety valves. Then the remaining tank cars, swollen with toxic gases, reach breaking point.

"When we saw that, at 4:30, that explosion ... when we saw it from the hospital parking lot," Chaput would say later, "we all looked at one other ... we cried a little ... we understood that no one would ever come ... ever. We knew we wouldn't have anyone to care for ..."

THE TRAIN RETURNS

I've got six orphans, my grandchildren. Four members of my family were suddenly gone, my son, my daughter-in-law, my secretary. And you, sir, do you have children? If you've got children, you can understand how it hurts like hell ...

There was no reason to allow an atomic bomb from the west to travel through us. In 2013, we should be able to feel safe in Québec. In 2013, a train that starts off by itself and crashes into a town at a hundred kilometres an hour, if that's normal, what's the use of carrying on?

We knew. They were hauling oil through at faster and faster speeds, too fast for those rails to bear ... Those tracks weren't in a fit condition, it's 150 years since those rails were laid, and the sleepers are all rotten. I know that, I work on it. Last week, we went to an accident, a locomotive that broke down as it was leaving town. Two weeks ago, we went to lay two feet of missing track at Scotstown. The train had only just gone by. Is that normal? Our governments are just working to gag us and to let these companies operate with no public safety ... no safety ... There must surely be somewhere else these bombs could travel where there's no population, for God's sake ...

I'm not angry ... I just feel defeated by events that could have been avoided ... avoided. Politicians are supposed to protect us. They don't protect us, because everyone's chasing after money.

Today, it's my boy, my in-laws, that are gone, it's our life that's been cut short halfway, and we're supposed to carry on, to overlook that? If the people of Québec stand up, it'll have to stop, so it will, leaders will have

to listen, make different decisions ... We can't go back, but we must put a stop to this ...

We've no choice but to go on living, if we stop eating, we'll die too ... But it's got to change ... We've got to get rid of the danger ... We've got to stop those bombs ... stop those bombs and get on with our lives ... Our kids have to rebuild their lives ...

We must put a stop to those bombs; our leaders have to get their act together ... People have always told me, "Don't talk about it, leave it to the politicians ..." Now my grandsons have no mother, no father ... and we're supposed to go on living, just cross it all out and move on? No way! Can you tell me you're going to make them change this? This oil mustn't pass through towns anymore, I swear, it's a bomb ... Let me tell you something ... one thing ... Where they were, they were sixteen feet from the track, where the tank cars piled up ... They had no chance of surviving. If they'd had a chance to say, "We have three minutes to get out" ... then you could choose to live or not ... but in there, they had no choice ... it's like when you shoot a deer, it looks at you with a smile and when you shoot it, it dies on the spot ... But what grieves me is how long was it hell in there before they were gone?

—Raymond Lafontaine, general contractor
in Mégantic, interviewed on Radio-
Canada thirty hours after the impact

✕ ✕ ✕

IN THE DEVASTATED TOWN CENTRE, THE FIRST THING TO BE rebuilt was the railway track. And 132 days after the tragedy, on December 20, 2013, trains began travelling through downtown Mégantic again. On February 12, fifty-two days after that, trains hauling hazardous materials were back. In 2020, their sirens are still heard in the night as they haul their tank cars filled with propane and other gas and petroleum products.

THE SECOND
DEVASTATION

Fire-charred tanker cars in the wreckage of downtown
Lac-Mégantic, July 7, 2013
Photos: Transportation Safety Board of Canada

FROM POLLUTION TO "RECONSTRUCTION"

THE RUINS CONTINUED TO BURN, SMOKING, EXUDING A STENCH – surely imaginary – of charred flesh. A short while before, near the edge of the destruction, one mother continued to wait for her daughter to return from her evening at the Musi-Café.

We all parked – how could we resist? – on the high ground in front of Sainte-Agnès Church, which afforded a perfect view of the disaster – as if, sardonically, the fire wanted to ensure that no detail would remain unnoticed. The fire had also spared the statue of Christ that stood with hands outstretched toward the crater in which forty-seven human beings had been incinerated. Was Christ offering comfort or pain? I don't know. In any case, it provided a picture the media found irresistible.

Journalists from all over the world crammed into a large marquee. The mayor was trying to get her press briefing into shape; government ministers, on vacation, had not yet visited. I have always had a suspicious nature, always feared that public health and environmental authorities were inclined to conceal facts from the public. And unfortunately, my suspicions have too often proved to be correct. Things have indeed been hidden deliberately. But this time, I told myself, the tragedy was so overwhelming that surely everyone would unite in the effort to recover from such a loss and to rebuild what had been destroyed. The presence of Colette Roy-Laroche, the mayor of Mégantic, and of Pauline Marois, the premier of Québec, was reassuring.

However, from the very outset there was a discrepancy between the official information and what was revealed by a simple web search. Daniel Green (my toxicologist colleague from the SVP) and I set about the task of providing reliable, independent data to those affected by the pollution, and of explaining what had happened to

them. We had the necessary receptacles and sampling equipment ready to use.

But there was a problem: we couldn't take any samples from the site of the destruction. We couldn't dig up the soil or scrape up a single fragment of ash, for we felt that this would mean disturbing the flesh of the dead, profaning their graves. Shaken, we resorted to the river, from which, sometimes by the bucketful, we took the crude oil that was beginning to sink to the bottom.

The way that Mégantic's tragedies (in the plural) developed subsequently conformed to the same pattern as the great tragedies of history. There were heroes. But there were falsehoods too, smokescreens, misplaced blame, blindness, and incompetence. And predators. A lot of predators.

MACHINATIONS

IN THE EARLY HOURS OF JULY 6, THE EMERGENCY RESPONSE
teams representing the various governmental authorities and other
actors involved in the disaster rushed to the scene. Then began a
sequence of intense machinations in every quarter affected by
the tragedy.

First, of course, MMA, CP, Irving, and all the companies with an
interest in the railway industry sent representatives. The saga of the
various investigations began at the same time, mostly carried out by
the Transportation Safety Board (TSB) and the Sûreté du Québec – the
latter operating from the outset on the assumption that some criminal
negligence had occurred.

Specialists from the Public Health Agency for the Québec region,
whose new director, Dr. Mélissa Généreux, had recently assumed office,
took complete control of all the operations and decisions related to
the residents' physical and psychological health, rejecting outright any
collaboration with Mégantic's own medical officials. The coroner's office
also moved in. The team dispatched by Réjean Hébert, the Québec
Minister of Health and Social Services, was already at work by dawn on
July 6. Mégantic resident Robert Bellefleur, who was also attached to the
Ministry of Health, moved into the hospital with an interdepartmental
coordination team especially concerned with keeping local firefighters
and first responders away from the disaster scene – a sensible precaution, but one that did not prevent the suicide of a young firefighter
the following November: like several others he had come upon the
remains of someone close to him.

The Québec Ministry of the Environment, which had been the first
to announce the spill, was an early presence at the scene of what would
turn out to be an unprecedented environmental disaster. Others also
rushed to the scene for various reasons: to document, to help, to offer
a variety of specialized skills. But also as predators. Among the latter
was a whole range of more or less nefarious individuals, including the

famous Texan "ambulance chasers," hoping to loot the victims' compensation.[116] Starting from the first days, the little town of Mégantic was so crowded that it was impossible to find accommodation within a radius of thirty kilometres.

A close examination of the events that occurred behind the scenes in various government departments in the aftermath of the tragedy is essential. This is because the case of Mégantic raises two fundamental questions, seemingly distinct, but which will turn out to be related.

First, what was the response of the various governments, and how are they likely to respond in the future to human and environmental disasters of this sort?

And second, a vital question for the people of the town: How did that initial shock lead, in under two years, to the obliteration of their town and their history? How could their town be annihilated without their knowledge?

"Decontamination was used as a weapon of mass destruction in Mégantic," comments Daniel Green of the SVP.

× × ×

Here, Let Us Pay Tribute

Among those present on the scene of the tragedy from the earliest days were the forensic investigators working to identify the victims' remains. They would spend three weeks searching through the rubble with infinite patience and concern, in the most horrible conditions – benzene vapour, extreme heat, and pouring rain – for any trace of those who had perished. The local people were full of praise for their efforts and their compassion.

They included a small handful of Mégantic young people who assisted the forensic identification specialists officially, providing their knowledge of places and people to prevent absolutely anyone from being forgotten. Those young people were literally looking for their friends. Medals, honours, and other forms of recognition would be awarded to some in the years following the disaster, but I am not aware of any recognition for these young people. We honour them here. Surely they would also have deserved more concern for their

subsequent well-being – at the very least a brief visit from the post-traumatic stress specialists of the Public Health Agency.

× × ×

On that July 6 morning, the people of Mégantic had their lives shattered, splintered into a thousand concurrent tragedies. No one yet suspected that years later those tragedies would still be playing out.

There were a thousand traumas requiring a thousand responses, a thousand fragments of lives and souls to be healed. But, first and foremost, the site had to be cleared and the environmental disaster cleaned up. Of the eight million litres of oil being transported by the train, six million litres had been dumped on Mégantic, soaking the soil and the underground infrastructure and finally flowing into Lake Mégantic and the Chaudière River – six million litres of oil, laden with carcinogens, that would mingle with the toxic substances already present in the downtown, which had once been an industrial triage zone developed over decades by building up the flood plain alongside the Chaudière River. In addition to all those contaminants would be added the enormous amount of foam, diluted by water and rain, required to extinguish the blaze.

At any given moment, more than forty companies were working on the environmental cleanup of the town and the Chaudière River, which would suffer "permanent consequences," according to Yves-François Blanchet, the environment minister, who was officially responsible for cleaning up the environmental damage.[117] But was he really responsible?

Who Is in Charge?

> We were walking in the red zone and it stuck to our feet,
> it was like mud, and gooey.
>
> —A witness from Mégantic[118]

As soon as the fire subsided, there began a race against the clock to confine as much as possible of the spilled oil and the polluted water before they spread through the rock fill and underground pipes and

reached the lake and the river. It was mostly workers from Mégantic itself who made the initial efforts, using their mechanical equipment. These men were familiar with the town and its buried infrastructure, and they knew what needed to be done first: digging catchment and diversion trenches, plugging pipes, and creating holding ponds. Ultimately, there would be nearly 350 trenches, 116 boreholes, 1,250 soil and water analyses, and 84 observation wells.

> On the morning of July 7, we rushed with our excavators to the riverbank. We tried to dig trenches to redirect the water to lower ground instead of flowing into the river. A channel was inadvertently open, and everything was emptying into the river right away. The river literally caught fire. It was scary. We used our diggers to stop the fire. Then up came a little guy with shiny shoes and a new white helmet telling us to stop, saying we weren't allowed to fell trees thirty feet from the river. I was mad. I'd been dealing with the fire for twenty-two hours. We lost an hour because of him. That's how the environmental people suddenly appeared, with all their programs.

So explained one worker, who remains, five years later, a disillusioned resident of Mégantic. Clearly the initial contact between those on the spot, those in charge, and the specialists, was botched.

For, unfortunately, this was not just one sad, isolated anecdote. It was the first indication of a failure of confidence and credibility that would arise from the outset between, on the one hand, the various authorities (provincial and soon municipal) and, on the other hand, the victims – a crisis fed by the gigantic rumour mill that goes into action during any crisis. Conspiracy theories were running rampant in Mégantic, centred on a lack of transparency on the part of the authorities.

Yet Yves-François Blanchet, the minister of the environment, and his team had been almost the first to arrive on the scene, preceded only by Réjean Hébert, the minister of health. At noon on July 6, Blanchet was asking his senior officials the right questions, requesting, for instance, a definition of the highly toxic PAHs (polycyclic aromatic

THE SECOND DEVASTATION

hydrocarbons), high concentrations of which were present in the air. He expressed concern about the wind direction and the presence of other dangerous materials in the tank cars. He also focused on one priority: following the oil slick down the Chaudière River as it threatened the drinking water supply of all the towns and villages for more than 185 kilometres downstream, including Québec City. On July 9 he took a helicopter flight over the river, confirming on Twitter the "low risk of impact." But this was already far too reassuring. And the few more alarming tweets he sent went unnoticed.

From early on, rampant distrust – easy enough to sense on the spot – began to grow among the citizens. This was, firstly, because of the broader context. The Mégantic disaster fell like a malevolent thunderbolt of fate into an already unhealthy, sensitive atmosphere. At the time, Québec was in turmoil, up in arms against the crude petroleum that had been inflicted on it for months. In the poisoned atmosphere of the impending elections, villages united and held demonstrations, brandishing placards saying "*Coule pas chez nous*" (No oil spills here) and "*Non aux hydrocarbures*" (No to hydrocarbons). The Marois government had put oil at the centre of its electoral program, as was indeed the case for the other major parties.

In the months prior to the derailment, the pace of events picked up. In July 2012, the National Energy Board had approved reversing the direction of Enbridge pipeline 9B, and in November of that year plans were put forward for a pipeline leading to Montréal. There was opposition: while the government favoured the pipeline, the population was against it.

At the same time, there were heated public exchanges about oil exploration in Gaspésie and on Anticosti Island, which also involved shale oil. The announcement of the sale of allegedly petroleum-rich Anticosti to the Petrolia company for a paltry sum came just a few weeks after the Mégantic disaster. A few months later, heaping insult upon injury, Marois announced an investment of $115 million of public funds in private oil consortiums of doubtful viability.

In short, both the victims and the ordinary townspeople immediately suspected that the authorities, whose favourable view of oil was common knowledge, were downplaying the reality and consequences of the disaster. Worse, people felt they were being completely misled.

Public distrust became even deeper when, on September 1, 2013, another oil spill choked the very fragile Bay of Sept-Îles with heavy crude. The official figures on the quantity of oil spilled posted by the Ministry of the Environment – barely five thousand litres were supposed to have reached the bay – were easily debunked by a visual inspection of the scene.

Another bone of contention was the credibility of the authorities' spokespersons. From the outset, everyone sensed the heavy hand of the premier's office in the public statements about the tragedy – Marois was clearly very pro-oil and already in difficulty with the electorate. An email confirmed this suspicion: at 10:56 on the morning of July 6, when a message instructed the Ministry of the Environment's director of communications that "Madame Marois, who has taken the case under her direction, together with the office of Stéphane Bergeron [the minister of public security], *asks that no one comment on these events*" (their emphasis). The civilian population and the victims suspected that information about the tragedy put out by the authorities was tainted by electoral concerns.

On reflection, it is only fair to recognize that, given the incredible scale of the disaster, it might have seemed logical for the premier and her minister of public safety to assume control of the crisis and of the public statements about it. But in those early days, in those first weeks, no one was in a frame of mind to give it any thought.

Furthermore, a gulf opened up very quickly between the reality as it was seen and experienced on the spot on the one hand, and on the other hand the way that the authorities, including the Ministry of the Environment and Minister Blanchet, its official spokesperson, depicted it. Perhaps it was not always a gulf, but at times it became an abyss, and for very obvious reasons. Initially there was the claim that only 100,000 litres of oil had been spilled, when anyone could clearly see that each of the disembowelled tank cars contained about 100,000 litres. And a good forty such tank cars were visible on the initial photographs. The math was obviously erroneous.

Above all, there was the official obstinacy, lasting more than a week, in denying that the oil in question was Bakken crude – the very kind of shale oil that there was such a desire to develop in Québec. Yet, there again, and from the very outset, given the clues of the two

terrible BLEVE-type explosions that occurred that night, one only needed to trace the route of the railway network on a map to determine with total certainty – exactly as Daniel Green of the SVP would do – that the oil in question had originated in North Dakota and was therefore the highly volatile, explosive product of fracking. Moreover, the paperwork related to the train, which was seized from MMA on July 6, indicated clearly that the oil had originated in New Town, North Dakota. Yet Blanchet continued to deny these facts.

So a lack of trust soon developed. But what would prove even more devastating for the credibility of the Environment Ministry, the minister himself, and the government apparatus in general, especially in the eyes of suffering individuals, was the so-called incident of July 11 and its aftermath.

✕ ✕ ✕

Starting from the initial hours of the tragedy, the devastated little town was rife with rumours. Many people muttered, for instance, that the whole thing was a huge conspiracy by the oil companies to make the case for a pipeline. People were said to have been seen sneaking off the locomotive after dark – which could well have been true – or strange taxis seen driving along the dark streets. As the rumours became inflated, death and assassination threats were made "because I know too much," and "letters left to third parties, just in case ..." circulated clandestinely. Later still, muted complaints about the disrespectful disposal of victims' remains – rumours that still subsist, even today, as soon as some incident casts too harsh a light on the drama. It was "the understandable irrationality of distress," as Yves-François Blanchet justly put it.

All these rumours, which merely added to the anguished atmosphere, were inevitable symptoms of a severely traumatized community. From the outset, greater consideration should have been exercised. The townspeople were not crazy; they were upset.

Instinctively – perhaps because the loss was too acute – the explanation that not enough brakes had been applied seemed too banal, and because no true culprit has ever been punished, many people, seeking to endow their loss with a broader significance, still fall back

on those rumours of a socio-industrial conspiracy. And they are not mistaken, for underlying their tragedy is the universal story of greed and indifference to the suffering of others.

Except that, for the authorities who are required to issue directives, including in the field of public health, a loss of credibility, even in the eyes of those who reject rumours, is a major handicap when a crisis has to be managed, or when one is speaking as an expert. For instance, advising people that they do not need to boil their water can convey exactly the contrary message, that is, that the drinking water is *not* safe – but that nobody had thought of this earlier.

The credibility of a spokesperson, of an organization, is fragile. Without a match between perceived reality and official reality a spokesperson's words come across as mere fiction, a story that we sense is false, a part learned by rote and regurgitated to deceive us.

The Big Cleanup: the Chaudière River

There is almost no remaining trace of hydrocarbons in the river.

—Email from the Ministry of the Environment[119]

In the early days of the tragedy, having been shut out of the town centre already partitioned off by tall fences draped in black plastic, the traumatized townspeople began wandering from the west to the east of town, from the square in front of Sainte-Agnès Church to Fatima, taking the bypass bridge five kilometres downstream. Many lingered on the bridge to contemplate the state of the river. The Chaudière, the only disaster-stricken area that remained truly accessible, had become the symbol and symptom of what was being done, clandestinely, to their town.

The afternoon of July 11 was no exception. The bridge was crowded with townspeople, aghast to see the film of oil covering the river and carried along by the fast current. "Here," someone told Daniel Green and myself, "here and a little lower down, there are trout, beautiful trout! Ah, Monsieur, if you only knew!" And they ended by asking, heartbrokenly, "What's going to happen? What's going to become of

us?" We know that humans sometimes go to pieces, as if rendered defenceless, when confronted by some sight less appalling than the actual appalling reality. Under the bridge, the sorbent booms deployed by ECRC, those familiar yellow "sausages," which were already turning black, were powerless to contain the oil against the strong current, which allowed it to flow beneath them. A series of green booms placed by another company, Opflex Solutions, was also attempting, unsuccessfully, to contain the oil.

For anyone looking down from the bridge, there could be no doubt that the river was polluted and that oil was still flowing from Mégantic at a high rate – which was only to be expected, after all, considering the dozens of gutted tank cars lying a little higher up.

As has been documented from too many such incidents around the world, light crude spilled into water normally behaves in approximately the same way. In short, when the oil is stirred up – oxygenated – by the current, and once its volatile components have evaporated, it settles, first on the banks and then on the bottom of the body of water, in the form of what is called "chocolate mousse" – in scientific terms, an emulsion. In rivers, this "chocolate mousse" settles where the current is slower, in inlets and at bends.

Was that so in this case? We needed to check. Of course, we first had to accept that we were, indeed, dealing with light crude, with shale oil. Unlike the ministry, the SVP was keeping this hypothesis in mind. So it was that, led by townspeople of Mégantic looking for one such quiet bay, and on a beautiful hot summer afternoon, Daniel Green and I would end up at Monsieur R.'s.

A fine, stalwart gentleman with a big heart, Monsieur R. is the owner of a precious gem, a beautiful little paradise that he has laid out and cultivated on his riverbank. Sheltered from the tumult of life is a tiny house surrounded by trees, more like a cottage, with a wood-burning stove, a table with a red-check tablecloth, and a rocking chair, where he has come to find happiness with Madame R. Through an attractive grove of young pine trees – a decade-old family project ("They're fairly tall now," says Madame R., "I could use one as a Christmas tree") – a trail leads to a riverbank shaded by healthy, dense foliage. Monsieur R. has placed a few benches, a few tree trunks, to allow this beauty to be admired in silence. "In the middle of the

river, there's a beautiful trout pit. I'm no fisherman, but I let some friends come, and I watch them," he says, wearing the inscrutable mask of a vulnerable man, with the hint of a smile in his eyes.

That day, Monsieur R. was in mourning. His young niece was in the Musi-Café on the night of the disaster. To add to his loss, on this superb but ominous July 11, under a large pine tree whose needles limply caress the oil on the water's surface, he looks on as we try to remove bucketfuls of the thick, clinging, smelly chocolate mousse that is fouling his riverbank, his paradise.[120] According to the samples taken on July 11 by the SVP, the hydrocarbon level at Monsieur R.'s was thirty-four times higher than the acceptable standard set by Environnement Québec.[121]

That same day, Opflex Solutions, the company that deployed its green sorbent booms under the bridge, would detect the presence, in large quantities, of thirty carcinogenic and non-carcinogenic poly-cyclic aromatic hydrocarbons (PAHs). And yet that same day, July 11, the environment ministry's website would state that, just two and a half kilometres from the spill site – closer, even, than Monsieur R.'s riverbank, there was no trace of oil in the river: "NQD" (non-quantifiable data) – in other words, too insignificant an amount to be measured.

Yet in plain sight of all those gathered on the bridge, three kilo-metres farther down, the oil was visibly still flowing. That was an indisputable fact, one that totally contradicted the official statements.

✕ ✕ ✕

Over the following days and weeks, the ministry continued to insist that the river's condition was improving steadily. There was still some oil, of course, but the public announcements gave the impression that it was dispersing rapidly.

While the red zone in the town centre was being rapidly enveloped in a deafening and extremely unwholesome official silence, the river had suddenly provoked a battle of transparency and credibility. On the one hand, the SVP (which would later be joined by Greenpeace), supported by some residents, was denouncing the official statements about the cleanness of the river. On the other hand, the Ministry of

THE SECOND DEVASTATION

the Environment and its minister, Yves-François Blanchet, tried to be reassuring. For many people there could be no remaining doubt that a cover-up was taking place.

What was at stake was far from trivial: polluted drinking water, petroleum fumes, and contaminated soil. The residents of Mégantic were fearful. Hurrying to the scene on August 6, 2013, Blanchet was asked several probing questions. Not only were the townspeople afraid, they simply wanted to *know*, to be informed about what was going on, about what the future held, and what options there were. They wanted to be provided with some straightforward, documented, verifiable facts – just a little transparency. "I was asking myself, 'Am I getting information because it's real, or are they just saying things to reassure me?'" commented one resident. "I don't need reassurance in life, I'll always find a way. I just need to know."

Here, a parenthesis. Following the media event on July 11, the SVP's phone hardly stopped ringing. Some of the questions people were asking had to do with the atmosphere surrounding the houses and the air inside them. "It smells of oil indoors, they're telling us that if it smells inside we should open the windows and if it smells outside we should close the windows, but it smells both inside and out. What are we supposed to do?" asked one resident – a pertinent question, if ever there was one! Whatever the authorities' response, trust had obviously shifted away from the official authorities and toward organizations belonging to civil society. "Participants in the INSPQ[122] study of the tragedy say that they no longer have confidence in some government authorities." In November 2013, at the request of some townspeople who were planning to raise funds to help with SVP members' living expenses, the SVP held a public information session about the pollution, speaking plainly to an almost full auditorium. The first citizen's committee was created that evening.

By July 12, 2013, the media war between the SVP and the minister about the condition of the river had become embittered – even more so when the SVP discovered that, apart from some samples collected two kilometres from the downtown area, the only other data published by the ministry came from eighty kilometres downstream. No data taken from between those two sampling points was provided – none,

for example, from close to Monsieur R.'s, where the battle against the "chocolate mousse" was still being fought.

Even worse, as Daniel Green and I argued, the oil, which by this time had been relieved of its volatile components, had sunk to the river bottom, requiring that urgent action be taken. The ministry and the minister denied this. On July 24, 2013, in a press release reinforced by a media diatribe by Blanchet, the ministry stated bluntly that there was "very little oil remaining in the river."[123]

But facts are stubborn. The issue was finally settled by a riverside résident named Yves Laflamme who, at SVP's request, checked the river bottom on July 24. He was accompanied by his daughter, planning to make a video recording. At one point he accidentally fell into the water. An eloquent aquatic reaction followed. His fall dislodged the oil lurking on the river bottom, making it suddenly spread on the surface and create a beautiful rainbow that was perfectly visible in the widely viewed video. On it he can be heard exclaiming: "People say that there's no oil any more ... well no, there *is* oil, it's all on the bottom!"[124]

Those images did not lie. They contradicted the ministry and the minister. Worse, said many, the minister had known all along – he *must* have known. ECRC, the company whose staff was working on the river and had also stirred up the oil, must have informed him and his officials of the situation.

This provided the people of Mégantic with the proof they had been waiting for: it was clear that the minister and the authorities (in the broad sense of "those who govern us") were responding to political, not environmental, imperatives. In this case, especially on the eve of a provincial election and in a Québec that seemed about to venture into oil, drilling, and pipelines, they considered it essential to minimize awareness of the damage done by oil in Mégantic. It appeared that every available soldier, including Blanchet, had been enlisted for this fight.

✕ ✕ ✕

If ECRC knows, the ministry knows.
Are they withholding information?
Are they protecting themselves?

THE SECOND DEVASTATION

What interests are at stake?
We need an action plan in order to intervene immediately
on this serious, politically toxic issue.

—Email from Yves-François Blanchet to
Éric Cardinal, his director of
communication, July 30, 2013

Except that the minister didn't know. The minister responsible for the largest cleanup site in Québec history had been kept in the dark. Despite all the officials on the ground, he had not been told things that Monsieur Laflamme, Monsieur R., and all the others could see with their own eyes.

Even worse, he would be obliged to resort to indirect means to become informed, for that email dated July 30 was the last in an exchange of messages that allow us to track his attempts, as he turned to resources outside his ministry to verify the possibility that the SVP was correct and that the oil had indeed sunk to the river bottom. This was confirmed by an email from which he learned this "most disturbing fact." The minister was rightly asking himself who *did* know: ECRC did, naturally. But what about his own officials?

"If ECRC knows, the ministry knows. Are they withholding the information?"

Curiously, we would later learn from another email that by July 10 an environmental emergency officer named Joëlle Généreux-Godbout, who was unhappy with the booms' failure to contain the oil, had mentioned the emulsion problem – the notorious "chocolate mousse" whose presence she suspected – to representatives of ECRC, as well as in her report. But apparently this information was never passed up the chain.

Other information was, however, passed upward, serving, in theory, as a basis for ministerial decisions and statements. These briefings, to use the military term, traced the evolution of the environmental situation. They were updated continually and based largely on the findings of private companies working on site. A few years later, reading these briefings gives the impression that they were vaguely reassuring – too reassuring – without being clear about what evidence they were based on.

Indeed, a few falsehoods did gradually creep into them. Thus, one dated July 9 noted that "the banks on the Frontenac side show no evidence of pollution" – information that probably originated with ECRC – even though I personally had filmed orange filaments and efflorescences of petroleum in places where the water was still.

The minister's email and the efforts he had to make outside his ministry to discover the truth are troubling, but the questions they raise are even more disturbing: Who *did* know? Who was *really* directing events in Mégantic? Who was overseeing the disaster response and the cleanup sites? And what was happening in the red zone, which had soaked up even more oil than the river but from which no information was allowed to filter out?

✕ ✕ ✕

"Mr. Blanchet, as minister at the time, why couldn't you admit from the outset that it was shale oil?" I asked in April 2018.

"I only found that out later, and indirectly," he answered in an interview with me. "Someone from one of the companies came to see us in a restaurant in Mégantic and hinted at something about the documents that accompanied the tank cars, and that set us thinking – about that, and about CP. We tried to find out independently ... And yes, it's possible that in the apparatus of government, there were people at a much higher level than me who didn't want the word 'shale' to be used right away. Or that I be informed right away. With hindsight, that's possible. It's possible that when it became political, it was on a different level than us."

✕ ✕ ✕

An innocuous anecdote amid the utter tragedy is nevertheless revealing. How much oil was there in the Chaudière River? It was crucial for the decision-makers to be fully informed as they raced against time to save the source of drinking water of towns and villages extending all the way to Québec City.

From the outset, Blanchet sought information about the quantity of oil that had spilled into the river, noting Environment Canada's

questioning of the figures provided by ECRC. "ECRC's method, which consists of flying over the river by plane, gives very inconsistent results," explained one of Environment Canada's Québec officials. "The estimates range from fifty thousand to two hundred thousand litres ... It makes you think that the plane maybe didn't notice the accumulation of material at the edge of the bank." Never mind that the plane also failed to see the material that had already sunk to the bottom.

Where the Chaudière River was concerned, the difference would be split, with the figure of one hundred thousand litres becoming official – though this figure was contradicted by workers on the ground, speaking anonymously: "A hundred thousand litres? Give me a break! No way! And the river fills up every night when they open the gates of the dam above, in Mégantic."

As for Environment Canada, it would use another model, from a software program that simulates data. Apparently, it arrived at the magical figure of 509 litres emptied into the river. 509 litres!

× × ×

On July 11, 2014, the Québec Ministry of the Environment, under the new Liberal Premier Philippe Couillard, announced that it was updating the profile of sedimentary contamination using a broad characterization – in other words, by sampling and analysis. In accordance with the principle of "polluter pays," World Fuel would be responsible for this characterization – World Fuel, the owner of the lethal oil, World Fuel, which lacked any independence or credibility in this field – except when it was looking after its own interests.

× × ×

Following an epic battle with the authorities, Monsieur R. finally managed to attract the Ministry of the Environment's attention to his polluted riverbanks. After a public call for tenders was cancelled at the last moment, the ministry gave the mandate to clean up his riverbank to none other than World Fuel, which is, of course, entirely devoid of expertise in cleaning up oil spills in rivers.

The cleanup operations cost approximately $800,000 – a huge sum for cleaning up a mere three hundred metres of river, which gives an idea of the true costs of the damage to Mégantic. But it was a pittance for World Fuel, which enjoyed revenues of $33.7 billion in 2017, and which could – or should – have borne, at least in part, the overall cost of the pollution.

In October 2014, the major cleanup operation began at Monsieur R.'s, when two American contractors with no expertise in dealing with oil or decontamination descended on his polluted paradise. With trailers, pumps, and heavy equipment, a fence and a padlocked entrance gate, and dozens of men mobilized, the cleanup was about to start. A bulldozer would carve out an access to the river from the formerly bucolic riverbanks, and, in an operation requiring a significant amount of patience, the river bottom would literally be scooped up, almost pebble by pebble, and all of it carried to higher ground to be washed.

The washing would take place in huge basins excavated on the very spot where the plantation of young pine trees had stood, now cut down and pulped. Today, Monsieur R. no longer sets foot in his ruined paradise. He says he can't bear to look at it. Like too many other citizens of Mégantic, he is torn between staying on and selling up to move elsewhere.

The Big Cleanup: the Cesspit, the Red Zone, and the Town Centre

The red zone was over a square kilometre of mud, sticky and black ... about forty tank cars, piled up, disembowelled ... benzene vapours hanging in the air, hastily dug trenches ... buried pipes, like so many unexploded bombs ... a broad corridor cleared level ... a ground zero extending downward to the lake that would be nicknamed the "coulée de la mort" – the "ditch of death."

Half the downtown area was left standing after the disaster: its shops, its modest homes, the Knights of Columbus hall, the recently renovated L'Eau Berge, all amazed to find that they still existed ... together with a carbonized debris that had to be tamped down with shovels, but gently, since Forensic Identification was skimming off the

THE SECOND DEVASTATION

soil so that no victim would remain unidentified. It was a cesspool that would gradually be enveloped in secrecy, modestly concealed behind large sheets of black plastic that flap in the wind.

✕ ✕ ✕

Who was officially in control of the two cleanup sites, the red zone and the river?

MMA. Yes, that MMA – the same fox but a different henhouse. This was a perverse consequence of the "polluter pays principle," according to which, if you make a mess, it is your responsibility to clean it up. And on the river it was MMA's subcontractor, ECRC, a "private management company, owned by several of the major Canadian oil companies" according to its website.[125]

A few hours after the derailment, MMA contacted its insurance company, which required it to hire an obscure management company from South Carolina called MEREDITH Group. ("There was this company trying to tell us what to do but we paid no attention," a worker in the red zone would comment later.)

MEREDITH hired subcontractors, dozens of companies, some of them required by Environnement Québec. A real web of private companies would be woven around Mégantic. It was their workers on the ground, their operation. Some would be very competent, others less so, but all were under the thumb of MMA, through MEREDITH, which controlled the site and the information.

✕ ✕ ✕

From the outset, the red zone was a hive of activity. Companies pumped and dug trenches under the official direction of MMA. "Information [about the contamination of the water treatment plant] is being sent to MMA to explore other options [for decontamination]," wrote Assistant Deputy Minister for the Environment Michel Rousseau on July 9, displaying extraordinary confidence in such a polluter. So it was up to MMA (and its subcontractors) to choose between various ways to clean up the pollution.

A routine became established. Every morning, the field teams

started work. At 11 a.m. there was a conference call between the ministerial coordinator Michel Rousseau and "the executives concerned," most of them representing private companies, followed at noon by a conference with the Québec Ministry of Public Safety. In the early afternoon, information was collated for the briefings that were routinely sent to Blanchet.

Blanchet, for his part, reported on the situation to the office of Premier Marois in two phone conferences each day, with other key ministers concerned participating, including Stéphane Bergeron of public safety, and Réjean Hébert of health. "To ensure that environmental issues remained within the purview of the environment ministry when other ministers began meddling on the site for entirely legitimate reasons, but ... it bothered me a bit," Blanchet would say five years later in an interview. "People who offered their expertise, claiming to be knowledgeable, saying this was how it was going to be done, and you'd say okay, but there were other issues ... Things were becoming more political; at one point it became difficult; structural hypertrophy played a part; the governmental and political apparatus would gradually take over. No real centre of authority had been established on site, with the necessary ramifications; we weren't all on the same page at the same time. Things weren't becoming any more coherent."

In short, in the struggle between human nature and power, government control was gradually being eroded. This created a vacuum, which would be filled, to their great delight, by actors and decision-makers who had objectives other than the public good.

On the scene of the disaster, on July 12, while holding and diversion trenches were being dug, the situation was still dangerous, for the sewers were sometimes almost 100 percent explosive. Nevertheless, if the oil was to be contained, the pipes had to be closed off. That day, twelve police officers suffered benzene poisoning. "Our firefighters were working there and suddenly, quickly, quickly, we were told to get everyone out," explained Jacques Breton, the mayor of Nantes, who was responsible for civil security. "We were working without

masks and no one warned us about the risk," a worker confirmed. The CNESST* would intervene.

Also on July 12, MMA submitted "an action plan for the work required in the red zone." The ministry was to evaluate the plan with the partners, said the briefing. The magnitude of the task was starting to become clear: "By 1 p.m. approximately four million litres of oily water were recovered (7 percent of this was oil, meaning that approximately 280,000 litres of hydrocarbons were recovered)." This was nowhere close to the approximately six million litres of oil that had been spilled. Unfortunately, the next day, July 13, this 7 percent was lowered to just 5 percent, amounting to "about 150,000 litres of oil" supposedly removed from the site. These figures may also be inaccurate, since it was widely rumoured (though without independent confirmation) that to speed things up certain subcontractors, once they had pumped a little oily water, would finish off with clear water before going to have their truck weighed for the invoice.

Be that as it may, still on July 12, in response to a question from the minister requesting information about the situation and about the available options to deal with the contaminated soil, Deputy Minister Michel Rousseau candidly confessed: "We are developing scenarios for the soil, but we have almost no information ... We can't enter the red zone yet." Yet, of course, MMA, MEREDITH, and their consultants had unrestricted access. No wonder that less than three minutes later the minister, visibly unhappy, suggested to his deputy: "Can we imagine getting authorization for you, a specialist, and myself to enter the red zone for a short time on Tuesday in order to make an initial visual survey allowing us to form some notion of the magnitude of the challenge?"

The choice of words was judicious: the magnitude of the challenge was indeed enormous. On the previous day, July 11, confronted with that magnitude, a state of emergency had been declared by the town council of Lac-Mégantic. This made it possible to ignore several regulations. The first to take advantage of this were the principal companies located in the industrial park (including the important

---

* The Commission des normes, de l'équité, de la santé et de la sécurité du travail, an official Québec agency responsible for the health and safety of workers and the laws protecting them.

Tafisa), which were allowed to resume operations and discharge their wastewater directly into the river – a necessary measure which allowed workers to be rehired until the water treatment plant was back in action. The state of emergency also allowed the granting of untendered contracts, which would prove quite rewarding for some.

So the pumping and digging continued, following guidelines supplied by ... whom? By Golder, an MMA subcontractor? By Lafontaine, a local company familiar with the underground infrastructure? By ministry officials? Or by the municipality? There is no clear answer.

But then on July 17, a dramatic intervention took place: the entire site, both on the river and in the red zone, was shut down.

✕ ✕ ✕

Right now, the major challenge is to maintain the recovery teams, the consultants, and ECRC, all hired by MMA. Work has stopped in Mégantic, ECRC is talking about stopping work on the Chaudière for today ... All the contractors are looking to MMA to discover if they will be paid.

—Briefing 36, July 17, 2 p.m.

At 3 p.m. that day, the Railway Committee, an ad hoc committee of various participants, held an urgent meeting. The situation on the ground was deteriorating; violent thunderstorms were forecast, and water mixed with oil was everyone's nightmare, for it flowed in enormous quantities, infiltrating everywhere and escaping toward the river. There was one obvious imperative for the environment: "We must keep pumping twenty-four hours a day."

But now companies were refusing to continue their work. They went even further. At the meeting they wanted to know who controlled the site, whether those delegated by MMA were still responsible. They were concerned. These were relevant questions that MMA's representative, MEREDITH, was unable to answer. Faced with a deadlock, Denis Lauzon, Mégantic's fire chief, asked the MMA representative to remain on site, "even if the situation is difficult to take." He flatly refused to "continue working on the site under such conditions."

THE SECOND DEVASTATION

On July 18, things were still at a standstill. MEREDITH was ordering all the contractors not to resume work. "We are having a minor disagreement with our insurer, but we are hoping for a quick resolution," wrote MMA's lawyers to the Ministry of the Environment. The ministry would discover that, in fact, MMA had insurance coverage amounting to only $25 million, which was totally insufficient to cover the consequences of the disaster.

At 3 p.m. on July 19, another meeting was held to coordinate operations between the partners, the consultants, and the municipal government. "The last meetings were very uncomfortable," as the minutes record with somewhat ironic discretion. The consultants wanted to know who was going to pay them.

The impasse continued. Since no work was being done, the situation on the ground was deteriorating even further. But relations were also worsening between the so-called partners. This was because, despite the chaos, MMA had never lost sight of its own interests. One of its unspoken priorities was to recover the intact oil from the unexploded tank cars. It was reported on July 17 that MMA had mentioned that it reached car 19 in checking the contents. An Environnement Québec official was concerned about oil being spilled during the transfer to tanker trucks, and asked MMA to notify him when the tank cars were being dealt with.

Nobody had yet guessed MMA's intentions with respect to the tank cars – nobody, that is, except World Fuel, which apparently shared MMA's cupidity. In fact, MMA was reported to have emptied thirty-six of the tank cars.

On the afternoon of July 19, silence reigned in the red zone, where work was at a standstill. In this strangely sombre atmosphere, young B. from Mégantic, along with his colleagues, continued clearing away the debris from one of the blue zones, where the search for victims' remains was continuing. For their part, the small merchants who had been displaced were looking for somewhere they could return to earning their livelihoods. In the secondary school and in Sainte-Agnès Church, the bereaved families, especially the twenty-seven children orphaned by the disaster, were still numb with grief. Father Steve Lemay was preparing for the heartbreaking series of funerals.

At the same time, in an office at the sports complex a few hundred

metres away, a ridiculous dispute was taking place during a meeting called to discuss pressing decisions that needed to be taken concerning the very survival of Mégantic. The representatives of World Fuel, in a virulent confrontation with MMA, were claiming that the oil in the tank cars belonged to them – but not the contaminated oil, so that MMA alone should be held responsible for the latter.

In short, they were asserting their claim to the remaining clean oil, while at the same time disowning any responsibility for the environmental damage. Was this really such an urgent a matter, in the very heart of a disaster scene and when all activity has come to a standstill? Apparently so.

Three days earlier, Thomas Tancula, a former representative of MMA, had called Neil Plug, a vice-president at World Fuel, informing him that MMA intended to take possession of the intact oil recovered from the damaged tank cars and sell it at $0.05 U.S. per litre. World Fuel had objected strenuously. How, wondered World Fuel, could it prevent this and recover its property? World Fuel's representatives, from a firm called ENVIRON, had no access to the site, which was still under MMA's strict control, as ENVIRON's executives would complain to the Ministry of the Environment.

Nevertheless, ENVIRON's representatives had turned up to speak on behalf of World Fuel at the coordination meeting of July 19 and, against all odds, was allowed to attend. They raised the subject of the salvageable oil, but MMA refused to discuss the tank cars. The oil was to be *theirs*. The dispute became venomous, and finally, before the dumbfounded onlookers, the MMA representative, beside himself, shouted at the ENVIRON representatives to "get the fuck out of the trailer." At another meeting on July 22, World Fuel renewed its offensive. Again, its representatives were expelled, this time by the police, at MMA's request.

The intact tank cars that were salvageable would remain parked on rue Frontenac until July 31, when they set off, in most cases, for Nova Scotia. World Fuel, frustrated at the theft of its oil, complained to the ministry that forty thousand litres of crude petroleum had been recovered and handled entirely by MMA, with the obvious complicity of the Ministry of the Environment. MMA made a profit of almost $370,000 thanks to this operation. No amount of

profit is too insignificant, apparently. It seems laughable. But it was no laughing matter.

This July 19 incident was the first official indication that the priorities determining the decisions and the operations were not of a purely environmental nature, but were dictated by other, possibly private, interests. The situation would not improve – a further indication that in the aftermath of this major disaster the power to make decisions was very likely in the wrong hands – the hands of people with little concern for the public good.

✕ ✕ ✕

July 21 came and went without work having resumed. In a confidential memo, a public servant warned the deputy minister of the environment that "the government [would] have to cover a good portion of the costs [of the disaster]," and that "MMA [would] likely seek protection under the Companies' Creditors Arrangement Act."[126] In other words, it would declare technical bankruptcy. Indeed, how could anyone have doubted, from the very outset, that this would be so?

The contractors had not been paid since July 13. On July 23, the Town of Lac-Mégantic, which had already paid out $7,796,948 to various businesses, sent a formal demand for reimbursement to MMA – a vain gesture, as was correctly anticipated. According to the town's lawyer, who would later plead before the Tribunal administratif du Québec (TAQ), the bill was growing by a million dollars per day, an amount the town was blindly paying to MEREDITH without even being able to examine the invoices. Without the assistance of the government of Québec to pick up the bill, the town would inevitably be bankrupted.

On July 13, however, the Ministry of the Environment had come up with an initial plan: "The Civil Protection Act permits the Town of Lac-Mégantic, which has declared a state of emergency, to award contracts directly to the companies on site to continue the work." These costs would subsequently be reimbursed by the government of Québec, and ultimately by the federal government.[127]

So the ultimate regulatory responsibility for the tragedy would

be borne by the federal government. Did it ever actually reimburse Québec? And by how much? This remains unclear to this day.

The Québec public servant's briefing note went on: "However, this solution has the principal disadvantage that the costs of the spill are borne by the public rather than by the companies responsible or the owners of the contaminants." That was perfectly clear – and, for once, entirely in accordance with reality.

In attempting to rectify this situation, on July 29 the Environment Ministry issued Order 628, enjoining MMA and World Fuel to clean up the damage at their own expense – an attempt that was most realistically doomed to failure, and perhaps just naive, but nevertheless politically advantageous. "We had to try something," said Minister Blanchet in an interview.

Oddly, however, the only two Canadian companies involved in the tragedy – CP, the carrier, and Irving Oil, the purchaser – were not mentioned in Order 628. Paradoxically, they were the only two companies under Canadian jurisdiction and, therefore, the only ones potentially subject to coercion. The other Canadian company, MMA-Québec, was insolvent.

World Fuel, truculently, refused to bow to Order 628. On August 6, Ira Birns and R. Alexander Lake, World Fuel's Floridian vice-presidents, flew to Québec for a meeting with the executive committee of the Québec government. World Fuel's letter announcing the arrival of the two men indicated imperiously to the Québec government that it must consider the possibility of amending the order to include CP, and that its understanding was that the ministry would not proceed with sending an opinion under section 113 of the Environment Quality Act before August 7. This had apparently been promised to World Fuel, and Québec complied, on both points, for it was not until August 7 that the ministry issued a second order amending the first, the only change being the inclusion of CP.

However, this amenable approach failed to produce the hoped-for effect of winning over World Fuel, which knew that it was invulnerable. An email sent by the Ministry of the Environment's lawyer on September 5 expressed his client's disappointment that World Fuel and its subsidiaries had not reaffirmed their "commitment to execute at least part of the ministerial order."[128]

THE SECOND DEVASTATION

CP's lawyer, the colourful Maître Durocher, has always claimed that the sole objective of World Fuel in seeking the inclusion of CP was to target a wealthy company which, being Canadian, was susceptible to legal constraint.

He is partially correct. "To have any chance of success, if it is to lead to negotiation, and for political purposes," Blanchet told the executive committee of the Québec government, "the addition of the Canadian company CP, which is solvent and implicated, is highly desirable. It's a better catch than an invulnerable American company."[129]

In this situation, where the objective was to include solvent Canadian companies, it is difficult to understand how Irving Oil, another wealthy Canadian company, was miraculously spared any legal consequences.* "I remember that Irving was a target from the first week," said Blanchet.[130]

Irving would later contribute $75 million to the victims' class action fund. However, all that this payment did, though so generous in appearance, was to extinguish any intention on the part of the victims to sue Irving. The Canadian government would follow Irving's example, secretly contributing $75 million to the same legal fund. Smart move!

As for CP, it was enraged to find itself included in the order. Christian Picard, chief of staff at the Québec Ministry of the Environment, recalls a meeting at which "eight lawyers from the biggest law firm in Canada turned up in bullying mode; they told us they had the best lawyers in North America, so if we wanted to fight that war, we would see ... What incredible arrogance ..." A triumphant arrogance, however, for we remind the reader that 2020 came without CP paying a cent, except to its lawyers.

Furthermore, the lenient treatment of World Fuel by Québec governments, both Parti Québécois and Liberal, was surprising to say the least. Could it have been the case that the government in Québec City wanted to remain in the good books of World Fuel, the all-powerful broker of North American shale oil, the very oil that Québec was so

---

* Except in one case, as we saw in the second part of the book, by virtue of the Transportation of Dangerous Goods Act, which would result in an offence and a sanction less damaging than any possible claim for damages by the victims.

eager to exploit? The answer remains buried somewhere in the offices of then-Premier Pauline Marois and her successor, Philippe Couillard.

In any case, all these ministerial orders would remain without effect. Companies would lose no time in challenging them before the Administrative Tribunal of Québec. In 2020 the case is still languishing in an extremely reassuring limbo, affording the victims no more than a few amusing anecdotes at their expense, including the moment when, in a hearing, World Fuel lawyers mentioned disdainfully the profession of the representative of the townspeople's committee, who happened to be a massage therapist, calling her a "masseuse" in a crudely suggestive tone.

As for the people of Québec and Canada, notwithstanding the orders, the "principal disadvantage" referred to by the Québec public servant (p. 200) would prevail: the costs of the spill would, indeed, be borne by us, the public, rather than by the companies responsible or the owners of the contaminants. We would be the ones to pay. And we are still paying.

✗ ✗ ✗

On the ground, and although it was no longer the paymaster, MMA continued to preside over the operations into early August. But by then, MMA's control over the site and the information was becoming unsustainable. On August 7, the Québec government, through the Ministries of Public Safety and the Environment, signed a controversial preliminary agreement with the Pomerleau company, which was to assume control of both. This agreement would be formalized on August 28. However, this initiative did not meet with the immediate success that had been hoped for, especially where access to information was concerned.

Behind the scenes, written exchanges between lawyers were intensifying. Courteous to begin with, their tone would soon become aggressive, as is shown by a World Fuel memo that ordered the ministry "to make known its position *at or before 5 p.m.*" (World Fuel's emphasis), and another, dated August 22, from a concerned ministry official, who alerted his superiors: "World Fuel wants samples taken

urgently. Their lawyer is exerting a lot of pressure" – as if the ministry was at the beck and call of private companies.

Because, in fact, Order 628 had the perverse effect of adding to the Ministry of the Environment's burden. It required MMA and World Fuel, and later CP, to produce plans for the cleanup and rehabilitation of the red zone. That amounted to a lot of plans. The ministry, which in principle was supposed to verify and arbitrate between different plans, received MMA's from Golder, and World Fuel's from Conestoga-Rovers and Associates.* This gave rise to two curious situations. First, there developed a sudden plethora of companies aspiring to take control of operations, giving rise to further disputes. Again, one has to wonder who was really in charge.

The second situation was more tragic. Everyone was fighting to obtain access to the central pollution database, originally set up by MMA and controlled by it from the outset. This was a database to which, in principle, all the entities in the field contributed and one that could potentially be very useful to companies in court when challenging ministerial orders, or in any future lawsuit. But these data were literally held hostage by MMA, as World Fuel was right to complain.

At this point an epic battle broke out between the Ministry of the Environment, the Town of Lac-Mégantic, and MMA over ownership of the data concerning the contamination. MMA had erected a wall around it. On August 22, more than a month and a half after the tragedy, Mégantic's lawyer tried to resolve the situation once and for all. He wrote a collaboration agreement with MMA, but was obliged to send it a second time, for MMA had not even deigned to answer. This document, which stressed the importance of access to all the information needed to allow the work to proceed without interruption, required MMA to cancel any confidentiality clause with its suppliers, first relieving them of any professional confidentiality, and also requiring them to refrain from invoking any laws restricting the dissemination and use of the information.

This agreement also called for MMA, which was no longer paying, yet was still the legal employer, to terminate the mandate of its suppliers as soon as possible after being requested to do so. Lastly,

---

* The services of Conestoga-Rovers as environmental consultants were retained by World Fuel after the issuance of Order 628.

it required MMA to allow free access to its properties on the site or in its immediate vicinity, and to put no obstacle in the path of this free access where any action by the competent authorities was involved.

In other words, the Town of Lac-Mégantic was obliged to beg, not only for access to critical information and the ability to employ subcontractors of its own choosing, but even to gain access to a major portion of its own downtown area. Because of MMA's numerous rail lines, branch lines, and wide footprint, the company did, indeed, own a sizable tract of land in the very heart of the disaster zone. It also owned the portion of land occupied by the former triage yard and the railway station. In short, a significant part of the contaminated area and the area that had to be rebuilt belonged to MMA. Furthermore, it was clinging stubbornly to its control.

The reason for this would emerge later, when its employees were already working to have the railway rebuilt as quickly as possible, with the collaboration of several Mégantic industrialists and the government of Québec.

On September 4, a discussion about the collaboration agreement took place. MMA was reluctant to collaborate, to say the least. The town's lawyer followed up with Pierre Legault of Gowling WLG, the law company that was also MMA's lobbyist. Maître Legault was not happy to be challenged and responded sharply: "I remind you that our client [MMA] has respected each and every one of its commitments arising from the post-order meeting. I am not sure that the same can be said of the town" – as if the town owed MMA anything! Legault concluded his reply arrogantly, addressing a final admonition to the town's lawyer, suggesting that the two of them should "exert efforts in a constructive direction."

September 12 came and went without anything being signed, without any breakthrough. The data had still not been made accessible. The ministry's lawyer again intervened with MMA, since "despite several requests to that effect, ECRC [had] never submitted the raw data [in its records] to the ministry."

In fact, MMA was playing fast and loose with the draft agreement, making additions and modifications. Finally it submitted a new proposal.

"Your proposal," said the town's lawyer, "was deemed unacceptable by all concerned."

Politely put. But what had MMA proposed?

"Requesting the restoration of the railway at the town's expense and in accordance with the wishes of MMA engineers (as if the town were to blame for the disaster …) is quite … a striking demand," added Mégantic's gobsmacked lawyer. Indeed, MMA, the owner of the lethal train, was asking, coolly and cynically, no less than that the railway be rebuilt at the town's expense and in accordance with the wishes of the company's engineers. Yet, as we shall see, and incredible as it may seem, CMQR, MMA's successor, would get its way.

Nuances, Evidence

Despite all this, on site, not everything was bleak. Over time, approximately 126,300 cubic metres of contaminated soil was excavated and removed from the red zone. This soil was initially stored on land near the Tafisa plant, awaiting a proper decontamination method. But no solution was forthcoming. According to the SVP's Daniel Green, the intense heat had, so to speak, baked in the contamination, rendering all the known processes useless. The soil would eventually be transported – at least according to reports – to Thetford Mines and Asbestos, Québec, two places already heavily contaminated by asbestos. Did they really need more?

As for the river, the steps taken to protect the safety of drinking water intakes had proved to be effective. However, the results of monitoring the effects of contamination, including the expert reports, remained redacted or were to be kept secret at the Ministry of the Environment until at least 2018. The ministry is a strongbox that even the Access to Information Act cannot pry open.

On August 7, 2013, Pomerleau, to whom the ministries of the Environment and Public Safety had entrusted the management of the fifteen companies involved on the site and the three hundred employees working there, resumed work in the red zone. Pomerleau was entrusted especially with managing all the invoices, reviewing them, and awarding contracts – in short, it was given financial control

of all of one of the largest worksites in Québec in 2013, a pay-out of $5 million a week to be reimbursed by the Québec government.

The declaration of a state of emergency on July 11, followed by Bill 57, which was introduced in September, temporarily removed the constraints on the tendering and awarding of contracts until December 2013. According to a compilation by *La Presse*,[131] almost $50 million worth of contracts were awarded very hastily, without any government oversight. Under the circumstances, no one in Mégantic was surprised to see UPAC, the Québec anti-corruption unit, move in.

On the site itself, harmony was difficult to achieve. Workers reported in the first place to the supervisors of the company that had hired them. These then referred them to Pomerleau for direction and decisions. In principle, Pomerleau reported to the Ministry of the Environment, the Town of Lac-Mégantic, and a few other organizations. This convoluted arrangement gave rise to a few mishaps.

For many workers, especially those from Mégantic who wanted to restore their downtown as efficiently and well as possible, the situation was deteriorating and anger was building. The complicated chain of command, which often included decision-makers far from Mégantic, was wasting precious time on fruitless decisions – ones that, according to many, had more to do with fraudulent billing for unnecessary hours of work than with cleaning up the living environment. "We were kept busy changing the plastic on the fences. But I was there to help," complained one worker.

That said, and despite everything, some private companies from outside were effective. One was Golder, which, according to Daniel Green, produced several very valid, comprehensive reports. Golder's sudden unexplained departure from the scene would therefore create further cause for concern.

The fact remains that there were often reasons for indignation at the way the great cleanup was being carried out. There were several shocking aspects – enough to create alarm about government's ability to respond to environmental crises. Clearly, before allowing our elected representatives to involve us in any future ventures endangering our water supply, air, and soil, it is essential that certain fundamental features of the environmental response system be corrected.

The Omnipresence of the Private Sector on Site

From the outset, private companies (sometimes even those connected with the oil companies, like ECRC) would play a central role on the disaster site, both controlling operations and managing information. But control and decision-making should reside exclusively with the public sector. The interest of private companies differs from that of the public: the only raison d'être of the former, their very essence, is profit-making. Nor should private companies be the chief source of information on the ground, for that involves them in a fundamental conflict of interest. The private sector must be overseen and governed by a public service able to supply the relevant expertise, and by elected representatives prepared to denounce the slightest misstep, unconstrained by political or other considerations. ("I was much more under compulsion than I expected; I would never accept that again," said ex-minister Blanchet.)[132]

The creation of ECRC, for example, was a consequence of the federal government's lax approach, which stripped ministries of their expertise and diminished their responsibilities by asking the oil companies themselves to clean up, at their own expense, the damage they caused. Such an approach must be rejected.

The example of Mégantic demonstrates, on the other hand, how effective a well-funded, professional organization can be – something similar to the Red Cross, for instance, in its ability to call on the services of well-trained experts and volunteers. An intervention by well-trained units would have mitigated the impact on the river much more effectively than ECRC's sorbent booms. While the oil companies should not be entitled to exercise any oversight, their money should be used to finance such an intervention.

As for the state, it is incumbent on it to provide adequate financing for the training and retention of government experts. Otherwise the public will always be at the mercy of polluters.

The Pitfalls of "Polluter Pays"

The "polluter pays" principle almost always turns out to be a delusion, as too many past examples have demonstrated. In the case of the

Mégantic disaster, it was unacceptable that the guilty party itself was entrusted with the control of emergency operations and the choice and hiring of consultants and subcontractors, as well as control over access to the site and to information about it. This system granted the polluter primacy over official authorities, who found themselves begging for access and information, like petitioners.

Such deferential treatment of those who deceive us – politicians, polluters, and their lobbies – directly harms victims and survivors. Polluters never pay for all the destruction they wreak, and often, as in the case of Mégantic, not even for part of it. It should not be up to them to repair the damage, but to pay for it. That would teach them to prevent it.

The so-called legal tools intended to constrain polluters, which are incessantly contested in court, merely supply the legal profession with billable hours. Instead, direct aim should be taken at the core activities of the guilty company, for instance by seizing property, freezing assets or goods, and keeping them until the bills are paid in full – preventive seizures, held in trust, to guarantee their compliance, like those relentlessly imposed on even modest taxpayers by our federal and provincial revenue agencies.

In the case of Mégantic, CP, with adjusted earnings of $1.6 billion in 2015, owned obvious assets in Canada. World Fuel Services, the owner of the oil being transported, also owned assets in Canada through its subsidiary World Fuel Canada, ULC – a Canadian subsidiary based in Calgary which, in a single year, between September 29, 2016, and September 15, 2017, was awarded Canada government contracts worth $3,972,499. $4 million – our little contribution to the $932 million profit made by World Fuel in 2017.[133]

Deficiencies in the Public Service, Take One: Selection of Information

How can one explain that a whistleblower from within the public service like Joëlle Généreux-Godbout, who sounded the alarm, and rightly so (see p. 189), was silenced, while others, apparently more in tune with what the powerful preferred to hear, were listened to?

Was it merely a lapse, or did it amount to systemic censorship by the bureaucracy?

The vast majority of public service employees did an admirable job. We need only remember how Généreux-Godbout, as early as July 10, recognized the risk that oil deposits would build up in the river and tried to counteract ECRC's inefficiency. Yet her voice went unheard by those in charge. On the other hand, a specialist in aquatic fauna *was* listened to, initially by the minister, resulting in a highly significant instance of disinformation. "In the Chaudière River, all the oil will be eliminated the next time the river is in spate," wrote one environmental monitoring official in a memo dated July 9, 2013. That was simply wrong, for the oil resurfaced the following spring and still sat on the river bottom throughout the summer of 2014.

"Light oil products do not seem likely to accumulate in fish," said the same official.

Yet we would learn three years later that the fish had suffered an unprecedented increase (in the order of 35 to 47 percent) of tumours, lesions, deformities, and other consequences, and that the fish population in the Chaudière River had declined by 66 percent – an impact that can be attributed with absolute certainty to the oil spill. So the same question arises again: Was it a flaw in the system, or was it, in fact, a manipulation of the information?

Deficiencies in the Public Service, Take Two: Questionable Loyalty to the Public of Some Members of the Bureaucracy

"Are they protecting themselves?" wondered the minister. As a result of the various steps taken by the SVP, especially within the framework of Canada's Access to Information Act, doubts had arisen about the devotion of some (senior) public servants to the public interest – doubts that cannot be detailed here, for lack of proper evidence. But in the heat of the moment, and privately, Yves-François Blanchet, the minister of the environment at the time of the tragedy, had himself come to share these doubts. So we must dig deeper.

Blanchet's answer, subjective though it is, deserves to be heard:

The minister is not the boss of the most senior officials. The [bureaucratic] machine, the deputy ministers, may answer to persons other than the minister. When the information didn't come via the general secretariat, I trusted it, though not entirely. The truth exists, and I shouldn't be given two possibly incompatible versions ...

There were "games," power struggles, special relationships, people who'd send us information saying: "Check this, it doesn't make sense." There's the very structure of the regional offices, there's duplication of functions there, there are kings and bosses in the regions ... And in Québec City too there are empire builders who put their own interests first ... We need a good housecleaning.

Yes, a good housecleaning is badly needed.

Being a "civil servant" means serving the public good, the people. Elected representatives and ministers must be made to answer for their actions to those who elected them. They must set limits, denounce unacceptable behaviour, and call certain actors to order. We expect no less of them. Furthermore, and above all, they need to restore funding to one area in which they continue to make irresponsible cuts: the Ministry of the Environment. Twenty-first century issues, for many people, are environmental in nature, and impact public health directly.

✗ ✗ ✗

The public figure driven into a corner by the SVP was Yves-François Blanchet, the minister of the environment. Admittedly, Blanchet was asking the right questions and would try to see through the fog, as the documents prove. That is why I acknowledge his efforts now, though I failed to recognize them at the time.

The former minister still harbours some animosity toward the SVP. For its part the SVP was very distrustful of the former minister. But if only everyone had spoken to one another. In a crisis, collaboration is essential, despite the political leanings, social status, or prestige of a group or individual. Too often, factitious antagonisms and bias stand

in the way of collaboration. Animosity and mistrust should have no place among those whose mission it is to help.

The SVP had expertise in a specific area that was useful to the victims. But above all it possessed a major asset: its credibility. *Some* civil society organizations, sometimes smaller, grassroots ones that are able to maintain their complete independence from private interests, have credibility and are therefore believed. Trust was what the people of Mégantic sorely lacked in the upheaval. But in that respect, what the future held would be even more dramatic.

THE SHOCK DOCTRINE

> It was people from outside who came to put up fences,
> and we the people were ignored, dismissed, disregarded.
>
> —Gilles Fluet, a resident of Mégantic

> It wasn't our fault that the train ended up here and
> destroyed everything. But we're still suffering ... Like the
> people in Fatima, they've suffered because of that, and
> the folk in the downtown too. And they've received no
> compensation, nothing. I find that disgusting.
>
> —Another resident of Mégantic[134]

STARTING FROM THE STILL-SMOKING DEBRIS OF THE DISASTER,
what was about to happen in the red zone in the coming months
would lead to Mégantic's second great loss, to underhand dealings,
and further devastation. It all began in the neighbourhood of Fatima.

Fatima

The Mégantic town council included a fairy tale in its Bylaw 1613 –
a rather unprecedented innovation in the rather boring realm of
municipal regulations. It was a real fairy tale, one that might very
well have begun with the ritual words "Once upon a time ..." It was
a way for the elected officials and their outside consultants to show
what life would be like in the new Fatima neighbourhood that they
were already conceiving on September 9, 2013. It went like this (the
emphases are mine):

> On this beautiful July morning Vicky and Sébastien are
> in a hurry. The twins' swim lessons start in less than an
> hour, and the two kids are still in their pyjamas. The
> Sports Complex pool may be just on the other side of

the Chaudière River, but it still takes about ten minutes to get there by bike.

The young family loves *its new condo near the centre of town, on the site of the old Billots Select sawmill.* Since they moved there, they've rarely used their car. Sébastien works at the Metro grocery store on rue Salaberry, while Vicky is a development officer at CLD,[135] whose offices are kitty-corner from the town hall ...

As she crosses the new bridge, Vicky notices *a recently installed sign with the words:* "Solidarity Bridge." "What a well-chosen name!" she thinks. In 2013, the mayor of Lac-Mégantic announced that this bridge would be much more than an edifice of concrete and steel. It was to symbolize *Lac-Mégantic's renewal* and the establishment of a town centre encompassing both banks of the Chaudière River. The bridge was to link two neighbourhoods and smooth out the differences that existed between them historically. The "Granite Lady" [the nickname of Madame Roy-Laroche, who was mayor in 2013] had never uttered a truer word. *The Fatima neighbourhood has been changed dramatically and become "in" among the younger generation. Now rue Salaberry is a busy, tree-lined shopping street* where people can enjoy strolling past the façades of the *new commercial buildings with their beautiful windows and very modern architecture.*[136]

So Idyllic, So Perfect, So Shiny

So, after its projected transformation, the Fatima neighbourhood was destined to become a district of new condos, splendid shop windows, and clean lines, without any unsightly factory – Fatima which, let us not forget, was left untouched by the fire and pollution, Fatima, which possibly would have preferred, given the nearby chaos, to be left just as it was, with its familiar landmarks preserved.

Yet this fairy tale, with its modern vision, was an integral part of Lac-Mégantic's Bylaw 1613, which changed the zoning and adopted a special urban plan (the "Plan") with a new post-disaster look. The

bylaw was adopted on September 9, 2013, about two months after the tragedy.

September 9, 2013: a date to remember. It held out the promise of an idyllic future. But at what cost?

✖ ✖ ✖

I was at Baie-des-Sables when it happened; I dashed back to our home in Fatima. We thought we'd been lucky, that we'd escaped any loss.

Then, on September 30, at ten to four, they called to say they'd be coming at four o'clock, and by ten past four they were gone.

I never thought I'd lose my home. But they repeated over and over: "You must sign, and do it right away."

It was two guys from Metro, I think, but we didn't even know who they were. They told us, "We're here to buy your home, and you have no choice. Either you sign right away and get the assessment plus 15 percent, or you wait and get the assessment less 15 percent, or you don't sign and you're expropriated, and then you'll get 90 percent of the evaluation – 90 percent and two weeks to get out of your place, taking nothing with you. The key goes in the door, and out you go."

This was all Bill 57, they told us, and we had no choice. Everyone on the street was really upset.

It was all lovely wood – pine – I had a pool, it had all been renovated, brand new. It was my father's house; I ran my business there for twenty-seven years. Our house was lovely, all renovated, just the way I wanted it, all the floors with lovely pine boards, new window frames. The kitchen counter was new.

Afterwards, it was some man from the town hall who came to see us to say that we had no choice but to sign. We had no choice, it was Bill 57, and it was finished for us. It went so fast, we signed inside two weeks. So we wouldn't lose everything. It was a man from the town

hall who took care of sending the forms to the firm. We didn't even know where. I don't know what that man did in the town hall.

It happened so quickly, we didn't even have time to think, much less call a lawyer. We didn't even think about a lawyer. We didn't even know it was Jean Coutu that bought us out, not Metro. It was Jean Coutu's notary that brought us the money. I cried, and even he was sad. He told me: "Usually I bring happiness, but here it's unhappiness …"

They wanted us out by January 1. I said, "Wow, in the middle of winter, where can we go?" It was lucky we had the Red Cross to help us. Because I'd just lost my house, my parents' house, my business. My home and my livelihood. I lost everything. And so fast.

I managed to stretch it out until March 14, and then we left. To raise a little money for the move, we sold all we could of my lovely home, bit by bit. The new window frames for $10 or $25, the boards from that lovely pine floor, the beautiful kitchen counter … All of it for $5, $10, $15. The whole house went, bit by bit. There was nothing left, nothing … I saw it all go, all of it stripped …

The worst thing is that after we signed, the house belonged to the town hall. In the winter, my pellet stove stopped working. I called the man from the town hall to have it fixed. They came once, but it wasn't fixed. I called the town hall for the men to come back, and he told me to deal with my own problems. We froze all winter, using blankets and heaters.

They paid me a pittance. I've never been able to buy a house. Now I'm renting. Once I had a lovely home and my own business, but now I'm renting. And there wasn't a thing I could do about it.

They offered me $25,000 for my business if I was prepared to move to Promenade Papineau. I didn't take their money. I couldn't. My business was in my home, it cost me nothing. Papineau made no sense. Everything

was expensive, I could never have afforded it. Electricity, heating, rent, everything. I worked in my own business for twenty-seven years, twenty-seven years as an owner. And then I lost everything. The lot. I've never been able to work again like before.

When I go into the Jean Coutu drugstore today, I can tell you where my whole house was, my kitchen, my new armchair ... It hurts so much when I go there, it's crazy.

I don't want to talk about it, it seems we're not able to talk. We're afraid, we're always scared of everything ... I don't know why we're always scared ... Maybe it's because of what happened.

—Madame M., a former homeowner
in Fatima, Lac-Mégantic

✕ ✕ ✕

The sudden, brutal eviction of Madame M., her neighbours, and the shops along one side of the main street of Fatima was the huge price to be paid for the new, fairy-tale Mégantic that was to be created in Fatima. Twenty-one days passed between the adoption of Bylaw 1613 by the town council (enabled by Bill 57) and Madame M.'s eviction on September 30. For a town plunged into such distress, this operation was carried out with astonishing alacrity.

✕ ✕ ✕

"Naomi Klein ... She describes exactly what's happening to us ... that's exactly what they're doing to us now ... In *The Shock Doctrine*, she describes everything they're doing to us," Gilles Fluet said to me a few months after the tragedy, in a voice strained by anxiety. Gilles, honest and clear-sighted behind his round glasses, had grasped it all instinctively.

"While we wept, while we trembled, while we danced," [following] an unusual disaster, explains Klein, the disaster capitalists put their shock doctrine into effect. The objective? To bring about "structural

adjustments" that will allow the forces of development, of wholesale "economic progress," to flourish. [137]

The shock doctrine is well named, since it works in places that have suffered powerful, sudden, devastating shocks – it is a strategy that unfolds on the ruins of our world. In Chile after the coup in 1973, in Thailand after the tsunami of 2004, and in New Orleans after Hurricane Katrina in 2005, the recipe was perfectly mastered and applied. But surely not here in Canada? Yes. Here too.

In phase one, speed is the key, according to Milton Friedman, the apostle of unbridled capitalism, theorist of the shock doctrine, and winner of the Nobel Prize for Economics. For him, everything depends on the speed of execution. You have to take advantage of the fact that the population is still in a daze. Then it won't be in any state to resist what you wish to impose on it.

In August and September 2013, the traumatized people of Mégantic were trying to recover and reorganize their lives. They attended an endless succession of funerals. Shows organized by the town and the Musi-Café provided some distraction and comfort. "The council lulled us to sleep with their shows so that we wouldn't see what was happening in the town," said some. And indeed, people didn't see what was in store.

While they wept, trembled, or danced, they failed to see the changes being quietly planned, or the laws and bylaws that were being adopted. Anyone who did read those laws didn't necessarily understand what they meant, "because when you read all that stuff, it's like a foreign language, you can't understand a thing," said one Mégantic woman. In less than eighty days after the initial trauma, starting on September 30, the axe began to fall on the first citizens of Mégantic to be evicted – those living in the Fatima neighbourhood. This measure was enabled by the prior adoption of municipal bylaws and a draconian law, Bill 57, which was required if the "Plan" was to be put into effect.

Without any need to read Milton Friedman, Mégantic's elected representatives and their associates obeyed his advice to the letter: they did act with maximum speed. And they would follow the next two phases of his formula just as faithfully. Here, we are not trying to show that some sinister conspiracy was afoot, but simply to note, wryly, that Friedman wasn't such a genius after all, that the winner of

the prestigious Nobel Prize was merely describing the usual behaviour of human beings when exacerbated by a crisis, the human factor as in the "law of the jungle," and "to the strongest the spoils."

And he was also describing the illusionist trick performed by the conmen and scammers – all outsiders – for the good of the still-traumatized "locals" – "locals" who would swallow the deception and lead their community into a catastrophic trap ... And in the end, he was describing the well-organized large predators who would carry off the major portion of the aid available to the distressed town.

Mégantic's second disaster was, in a way, more disturbing than the first. This was because it was artificially created by "our own people, our own fellow citizens, people we trusted" – a widely expressed reaction. That loss is still felt today, like a stain that never fades.

The Method

Starting in the first days and weeks after the original disaster, unbeknownst to almost everyone, regulatory actions and legal changes were taking place that would completely transform the Mégantic that its residents had always known. The operation required three preliminary steps.

Step One: Barely a few weeks after the cataclysmic events, a zoning regulation was introduced prohibiting any commercial development between Nantes and Mégantic,[138] where the shopping centre, the Canadian Tire, Walmart, etc. were already located – the familiar sort of commercial zone surrounded by a sea of parking lots so characteristic of every small North American town. The Jean Coutu pharmacy and the Metro grocery store had already reserved their sites near the Walmart store, a logical move to be close to the supermarkets that already attracted a substantial clientele from round about. For smaller businesses, many of which were still standing intact in the red zone, the idea was to set them up in trailers on the shopping centre parking lot until the downtown area was decontaminated – a temporary solution to allow them some income in the meantime.

But in the summer of 2013, this zoning freeze came into effect, preventing businesses from relocating. Small businesses, deprived of their incomes, were put at risk.

THE SECOND DEVASTATION

Step Two: A redefinition of the site. Lac-Mégantic town council adopted Bylaw 1613 on September 9, 2013, and again on the following October 14. This was the celebrated bylaw on which the idyllic story recounted above was based. Among other things, it radically changed the concept of the "town centre." The mandate of the plan comprising a special urban renewal program now covered a substantial portion of the Fatima district, as well as a site close to the Sports Complex which would bear the name Papineau, after the street of the same name.

In this way, the bylaw took advantage of a confusion in the minds of the citizens. For them the town centre had never meant anything except the actual historic downtown that had been hit by the disaster. In September 2013, very few people were in any shape to read the bylaw and realize that their neighbourhood had been chosen for "redevelopment." Only large businesses and manufacturers, apparently, were given the opportunity, after August 8, to acquaint themselves with the new plan and provide input.

The expansion of the downtown area was considered crucial. It was the first step necessary to allow Bill 57 (which the government in Québec City would pass eleven days later) to fulfill some of its major objectives (expropriation, demolition, etc.) over a much greater area than the townspeople suspected.

Step Three: The third and last preliminary move was the passing of Bill 57 by the Québec government on September 20, 2013. This legislation faithfully reflected the program outlined in the September 9 plan, particularly with regard to the acquisition, expropriation, and demolition of buildings. It allowed the municipality almost unlimited power over the fate of the townspeople, property owners, and small businesses within a very large area. The government was also to provide $60 million to help implement the planned reconstruction.

So by September 20, 2013, the laws and bylaws that would disrupt what remained of Mégantic were in place. The people, with their minds on other things, remained almost entirely unaware of what was going on. Between the decision of September 9 and its direct consequence, the eviction of Madame M. on September 30, only three weeks had gone by. It was speedy action, as recommended by Friedman.

Bill 57 ... or, for the Inhabitants, Another War Measures Act

Bill 57 was a piece of legislation concocted by Mégantic's elected representatives and local businesspeople (some of whom would later band together, calling themselves "Action Mégantic"), outside consultants, the Québec Ministry of Economic Development, and the Ministry of Municipal Affairs. They were well organized in dealing with the still shattered population. The bill, which had a lifetime of five years, fulfilled several objectives. First, it removed the obligation to issue calls for tenders for demolition and construction contracts as well as in another lucrative field, the provision of professional services. The law also postponed the municipal elections, lengthening by two years the terms of the elected officials then in office, under the leadership of Mayor Roy-Laroche.

Specifically, the law ratified the September 9 bylaw and allowed the town to "erect any building for the purpose of selling or renting it" – a provision that turned the town council into a real-estate developer, forcing merchants to set up shop wherever the town decided.

And at the heart of the bill lay the fateful section 15: "The town may proceed to the demolition of any building located within the zone defined as a containment perimeter in the special planning program referred to in section 13 and *deemed, according to an expert report, unsuitable for habitation or for the continuation of the activities previously exercised there because of the contaminated state of the ground on which it is located*" (my emphasis; I shall return to this point).

To ensure its stranglehold, the bill rescinded all previous provisions protecting the rights of expropriated individuals and the recourses normally allowed them under the Expropriation Act. Under Bill 57, those expropriated could no longer challenge the expropriation before the Superior Court. Every deadline that gave them some advantage over the expropriator was reduced to a few days or completely abolished.

A short while later, on at least two occasions, attempts were made to warn elected representatives of the damage this bill would inflict.

First, the SVP alerted Sylvain Gaudreault, the former minister of municipal affairs, and Amir Khadir, a member of the opposition. After making his best effort, Khadir admitted his inability to alert anyone because of the impregnable position given Mégantic's town council and mayor, Colette Roy-Laroche. Réjean Hébert, the former minister of health, would also try to warn his colleagues, with no greater success.

The Rationale

We are aware that many townspeople have had to live through and are still experiencing many disruptions because of the difficult choices we have had to make in order to recreate a vibrant economic and commercial hub [in Fatima]. The town council has always been eager to accompany residents throughout this transition. Our desire is to revitalize your neighbourhood.

—Colette Roy-Laroche, mayor
of Lac-Mégantic[139]

In Fatima ... they threw everyone out, saying, "Find yourself a house," but they didn't foresee the impact it would have from a community perspective ... It's another case of the town not considering the human factor.

—A resident of Mégantic

Why take aim at Fatima, an oasis of stability amid the chaos? What exactly did they have against Fatima – and, as we will see, the historic town centre – that could not be reconciled with the new vision? Why was it impossible to allow what already existed perfectly well to survive – the little shops, the modest but tidy houses, some of them very charming, like one stone house, a real fairy-tale cottage out of "Snow White"?

It was, explained the September 9 bylaw, because of "the poor quality of the neighbourhood's physical environment and the socio-economic characteristics of its disadvantaged population" – just official equivocation. But in short, for the authors of those rules and

the elected officials of the municipal council, the houses and shops of Fatima were unattractive, ugly, or at least not to their taste. Nor were they "in," as the bylaw itself put it. And, added the bylaw, mincing words, in Fatima, the population was "not wealthy." Two false notes in the fairy tale of the new Mégantic.

Henceforth, the elected councillors wanted what was trendy and modern. The objective was gentrification. This applied to Fatima, of course, but the same approach would apply to the reconstruction of all of the new town centre. But, one may well ask, given that half of the town centre had been devastated, why destroy what remained intact? Unfortunately, the answer was very simple: "The Fatima neighbourhood has important assets in terms of its strategic location (its immediate proximity to downtown and as a gateway to the town from the Beauce and the Québec City region) and the availability of sites for potential urban redevelopment."[140] In other words, Fatima had splendid locations to offer prospective developers of condos, pretty shops, and businesses which it was hoped would inject new life into a region that had been over-reliant on lumber. There were splendid possibilities for "potential urban redevelopment" – on condition a clean sweep was made.

But all the same, the town of Mégantic had suffered a disaster, there had been many deaths ...

There is nothing new under the sun. This was not the first attempt to revitalize a neighbourhood using expropriation as a tool. Everywhere, cities level and obliterate the vestiges of modest lives in order to provide "new" space to the developers of condominiums and office towers. In 2012 the town council had already proposed such a plan, but it had been rejected by the citizens. In 2013, with the town in a state of shock, it could be resurrected and successfully put into effect. Did the Fatima neighbourhood really lack "vitality"? Upon close examination, no, it didn't. The signs of a moribund community, according to the official definition, are the loss of accessible services – a school, a grocery store, a gas station, a restaurant, a convenience store, a post office, a credit union. The Fatima of 2013 was nothing like that, for, while it is true that the church had been closed, all the other services still existed, including a gym and a tanning salon. For everything else the town centre was just across the river, only a ten-minute walk away,

as Bylaw 1613 acknowledged from the outset when it spoke of Fatima's "strategic location (its proximity to the town centre)."

In short, Fatima was, indeed, a less well-heeled neighbourhood, but was it dying, according to the accepted criteria? Far from it! That was merely a pretext concocted to make more land available for redevelopment. To the residents of Fatima I have met over the years, saying that their neighbourhood was dying sounded like using the danger of rabies as an excuse to put down your dog. But, unfortunately, some of them felt guilty in some way: "It's true we weren't that well off," said several, as if that was a sin. "But before, everyone walked, everyone talked together, everyone came together, it was liveable, it was nice. The people from Sainte-Agnès came down, and we went up, you always met people ... It was great," said Richard Poirier, born and bred in Fatima.*

The bylaw adopted on September 9 stated: "Rue Salaberry is a link between properties that lend themselves to redevelopment but that present certain obstacles (requiring the demolition of buildings, the relocation of businesses, the acquisition of private buildings, *a relocation that a municipal intervention could smooth out, if necessary*" (my emphasis). Now equipped with powerful legal tools, the town was able to "smooth out" Madame M.'s and her neighbours' houses to facilitate "urban redevelopment."

✕ ✕ ✕

"The young family loves its new condo near the centre of town, on the site of the old Billots Select sawmill," read the town council's fairy tale. When it was named in the September 2013 bylaw, the Billots Select sawmill in Fatima was still in operation. It employed about fifty workers directly and created a number of jobs indirectly. The sawmill was situated on the riverbank, just off rue Salaberry, Fatima's main thoroughfare. Houses had been built all around it, creating an organic cell.

A sawmill close to homes is both ideal and irritating. You can walk

---

* It was Richard Poirier who organized the first citizen's march to re-establish a direct, easy link, via the bridge, between Fatima and the rest of Mégantic. His efforts were successful.

to work, but you have to tolerate the ceaseless noise. At the time of the disaster, the council had been trying for several years to expropriate the sawmill. It finally managed to force the company out in a process extending over 2014 and 2015. The owner, after seeking in vain to move to the industrial park, closed it down. Fifty employees lost their jobs. The owner sued the Town of Lac-Mégantic successfully. It was ordered to pay him $8 million.

In the fall of 2017, at a council meeting, it was learned that the financially strapped town was asking the Québec government to pay the $8 million on its behalf. Five years later, the consequences of this expropriation were devastating. The town was left with a debt of more than $8 million, jobs were lost, and abandoned buildings stood empty in the very centre of town.

✖ ✖ ✖

That a devastated town should dream of rebuilding itself on a human scale deserves universal praise. But what model of town planning will serve as its inspiration? Shouldn't it be up to the citizens together to dream about it, and to their elected representatives to put the result into effect? Surely there should be no need to debate that.

The disturbing thing, starting with the treatment of Fatima, was less the substance (though we will return to that) than the tactics adopted by the town council of the day. Its approach, as it affected almost all the victims, took the form of a power-grab, a denial of justice, a relationship of predator to prey. For instance, to this day it isn't clear who turned up at Madame M.'s door: it seems to have been representatives of real-estate subsidiaries of Metro, the big supermarket chain, or Jean Coutu, the pharmacy chain, rather than of the town itself. The small businesswoman was allotted a mere ten minutes to deal with two trained and informed representatives from outside the community, without anyone to advise her. It was highly confusing. Madame M. wondered if it was the town that wanted to buy her out, or private developers. That remained a mystery. What was certain was that she had little opportunity to call on outside assistance in the form of a lawyer or adviser. On the contrary, care was taken to isolate her. She was rushed into a decision.

Why did the town use private companies as go-betweens? Because it really didn't have a choice. If it wanted to demolish the buildings as soon as possible, it could do so, according to Bill 57, but only if the building was contaminated and unfit for human habitation. This did not apply in Fatima, meaning that the town had to obtain the property owner's consent. But some property owners on rue Salaberry might well have dug in their heels. Or perhaps some might have wanted to take a careful look at the wording of the government legislation being used to evict them and might have discovered that the threat of expropriation under the bill was hollow.

So the homeowners in Fatima were lied to – let us call a spade a spade. Intimidation and harassment were used – again, we cannot mince words. The panic-stricken owners were held at bay, allowed no way out, no time to reflect. It was simply intimidation by the two representatives of the purchasers, people the homeowners thought were official representatives of the town.

But there was worse. For residents of rue Salaberry, the writing had been on the wall for much longer than they suspected, as is revealed by an illustration contained in the bylaw adopted on September 9. Dated August 29, 2013, an entire month before Madame M.'s eviction, a drawing depicted the future Jean Coutu store, exactly like the one that exists today, standing precisely where her house had been. As of August 2013, Madame M.'s home was doomed to be replaced. And she was left completely in the dark about it. Today her swimming pool and yard are a parking lot – just like the Fatima church, which has been replaced by parking for the Metro supermarket.

✕ ✕ ✕

In what was an extremely stressful time for Madame M., the Red Cross helped her to pay her high rent and moving expenses. The Red Cross, according to general opinion, did a remarkable job, paying for the needs of many of the victims and evacuees. Donations from outside given by thousands to help disaster victims like Madame M., amounting to almost $4 million, were incorporated into the Fonds Avenir Lac-Mégantic, intended to fund the town's future. Madame M. received $992 from this fund as compensation for her suffering

and to cover her expenses. In 2015, the Jean Coutu Group, which evicted Madame M., received a grant of $241,000 from the assistance fund – in other words, from donations intended to support victims of the disaster.

Downtown – the Red Zone

Plunged into a tragedy beyond their understanding, a few Mégantic residents in positions of authority were groping in the dark and losing their way. In the years following the tragedy there would be major lessons to be learned from the tragic sequence of events, and from this second great, enduring devastation. But to think that we have anything to teach those who had lived through the tragedy of Mégantic is to play the armchair critic; everyone, or almost everyone was acting in good faith, if not always wisely.

But that having been said ...

The Surviving Buildings

> When it happened, this business, they put a big black screen around the town centre. You weren't allowed to see what was going on because they were looking for bodies. You could accept that ... But when people woke up, they realized that by the time that black screen had been put around the downtown, plans had already been made – plans to rebuild the town. And those plans weren't to everyone's liking.
>
> —A citizen of Mégantic

As the dust settled, half of the town centre emerged from the ashes. Mégantic was tough; it had survived, it would continue to survive. Thirty-nine buildings remained miraculously untouched by the cataclysm: the beautiful, recently enlarged L'Eau Berge, a few houses, the Knights of Columbus Hall, the barbershop, the stationery store, the hairdressing salon ... all relics of an earlier life. For the next eighteen months, the glimpse of the buildings left standing, seen through the gaps in the plastic screens, would remain as a sign of hope for all – a hope that, despite everything, life would be restored as it once had

been. *Despite everything*. Thirty-nine buildings, each like a shot of adrenaline for the small business owners and residents. Thirty-nine buildings had been left standing, symbols of life. But within eighteen months they would become symbols of distress and anger.

The Scar

From the outset, MMA lobbied fiercely for the rail line to be rebuilt. Mégantic's large manufacturers also wanted this. Yes, jobs did depend on it. But it was not what the citizens wanted. After all, this was the second accident of the kind, for in April 1918 a runaway train had caused two deaths in Mégantic. On July 13, 2013, regional doctors presented a petition calling for a bypass line. The town council expressed the same desire. Even the local manufacturers were mostly in favour: "We were promised that the restoration [of the former line] would be temporary," said one of them, Béland Audet.

Nevertheless, the former line would indeed be rebuilt. As soon as MMA was ousted, the municipal government and various ministries took over and played an active part in restoring the railway. In fact, it would be rebuilt so rapidly that it now included an eight-degree curve – much more dangerous than the four-degree one it had replaced, as the BAPE confirmed in the fall of 2017. And it still passed within just a few hundred metres of the new Musi-Café.

The first train was back on December 12, 2013, 132 days after the tragedy. "We're going to need a special communications strategy for the return of the train," advised one individual in a position of responsibility. "The first time after the disaster that I had to stop my car in the town centre to let a train go by," said one survivor of the disaster, "I collapsed on the steering wheel and sobbed my heart out."

Communications strategy or no, the return of the train was an excellent deal for CMQR, the company that had acquired MMA. After the takeover was finalized in July 2014, CMQR declared an increase of 20 percent in its profits for 2016,[141] thanks to growth in the transportation of oil, propane, chemicals, and fertilizers – all along the same route as that followed by train MMA-002 to Mégantic on July 6, 2013. And this left a fresh scar that remained a

challenge for the redevelopment of the town centre – for who would want to move in next to a railway line that had now been made more dangerous than ever?

✘ ✘ ✘

At the end of August 2013, the cleanup workers, many of them from Mégantic or the surrounding area, were suddenly transferred out of the red zone and sent to work some distance away, near the town limit. Their assignment was to construct, as quickly as possible, the new commercial centre, soon to become the famous Promenade Papineau.

This was a vital decision, the very crux of the reconstruction, for the devastated centre of town had been just that: a town centre. The shops there had been the heart of the town, the centre of its life. But already in September 2013, the municipal government, using its zoning bylaws, sent some stores to Fatima. Others, it decided, would have to move to Papineau – in other words, outside the historic town centre. One worker would testify to the sentiments shared by many of his friends:

> We already had plenty of guys who were keen to rebuild the tracks, so suddenly we were told to drop everything we were doing in the downtown and go to build the commercial condos on the Promenade Papineau. Nobody knew exactly what plan was being followed, nobody wanted any of those condos, but that was that. If they'd left us alone, we'd have finished the cleanup and the infrastructure in the red zone a lot faster and then been able to go back home. To our own homes.

The workers weren't wrong. For, when tackled energetically, jobs tend to make rapid progress. By October 18, for instance, the excavation of the contaminated soil along the route of the railway tracks was already complete. By October 30, Pomerleau's progress report was expressing concern about the fact that "work needs to advance faster. The deadline for the tracks was November 15." New workers

were brought in, and the reconstruction would eventually meet its deadline. It was the same on the Promenade Papineau, where work was progressing at a rapid pace.

By November 15, 2013, as a result of council decisions, the entire heart of Mégantic was already almost completely dismantled. Yet the population had not been consulted or even properly informed. The decision-making process remained covert and obscure.

The Commercial Condos on rue Papineau

The town had to move quickly to relocate the storekeepers. The smaller businesses, who were barred from carrying on their trade in temporary trailers near the mall, felt they were being pressured to rent one of the commercial condos that the town was building for them. Except that two factors militated against the town.

Time was one of these. Businesses couldn't afford to wait too long before reopening their doors. Some would never reopen. A few others would move, either into their homes or some other less expensive premises, for instance on a street with more traffic, like at the top of rue Laval. Rue Laval, an extension of the destroyed downtown, was in any case part of people's DNA. They were used to strolling there, shopping and meeting their friends.

The second drawback was the additional expense, which some thought exorbitant. "We went from $8 a square foot in the downtown area to $20. And that's not counting the other overheads ..."* This made it difficult, if not impossible, to turn a profit. After all, there were just six thousand residents, and a few tourists for a few weeks in the year.

Finally, a factor which was far from negligible for a town encouraging tourism, Papineau is quite far from the lake. There is no view of the water from there; the view from Promenade Papineau is, in fact, of the Sports Complex parking lot on one side and the railway tracks on the other. It is difficult to imagine tourists wanting to spend much time there. The planners had made an inexplicable choice.

But, blind to the signs of its imminent mistake, the town, now the

---

* Lawyer Daniel Larochelle, among others.

proprietor of the condos – which were paid for by the Québec government – persevered with its plans. By November 5, 2013, work was in progress and the grass seed was already sprouting on the Promenade Papineau, according to one report.[142] Yet four months later, on February 20, 2014, *L'Écho de Frontenac* reported:

> We find that in the commercial condos of the "new downtown," discouragement is setting in. Some prospective tenants are tired of seeing completion dates pushed back month by month.
>
> The town handed them the buildings on a silver platter – to revive the economy quickly! Mid-November came, then mid-December, then January, then February, then March, April, and May. The merchants were tearing their hair out, as were their suppliers. Orders would be placed and then cancelled. Should deliveries be made, or not? Was it better to install chic or cheap furnishings? Most would lose an entire year's business before they could welcome customers again.

In the spring of 2014, as soon as the snow melted, residents strolled along rue Papineau, their new downtown. They were appalled. The place had a model: the impersonal Quartier DIX30 "lifestyle centre" in Brossard, Québec. Its architectural model was provided by the well-known "smart centres" that had been proliferating for the previous decade: all on one level, flat-roofed, with a modern, uncluttered design – not at all reminiscent of the bustling, booming shopping street of the old town centre. No living accommodation had been incorporated, so that once the shops closed at 6 p.m. the street became deserted, except for a few popular spots like the Citron Vert restaurant, which had been forced to exchange its terrace overlooking the lake for a view over a parking lot.

The merchants who agreed to move to Promenade Papineau were assured that they would be eligible for financial assistance. But the cheques, which were supposed to come from the Québec government, never arrived. "We saw businesspeople in tears at the town council, at the end of their tether: 'Help us ... Do something.' But

THE SECOND DEVASTATION

the mayor said, 'I'm waiting for a cheque too ... Tell Couillard to do something.'"[143]

The provincial government had changed during the year, resulting in disruptions, and for the new Liberal government, Mégantic was a thorn in the side. Cooperation with various ministries became minimal, or even non-existent. "Everything came to a stop overnight," confirmed Béland Audet. Without financial support, several merchants were unable to open their shops. As a result, in the summer of 2014, for the benefit of a handful of passersby, the new store windows would be lined with posters saying: "Waiting for the cheque."

The New Musi-Café, Promenade Papineau

Yannick Gagné owned the Musi-Café, the symbol of the tragedy: thirty of the forty-seven victims were there on the evening of July 6. The former café, owned by this well-known individual, served as a theatre and social centre. Renovations to the café had been completed the day before the disaster. In 2013 no one doubted that the Musi-Café would survive. Supported by family, friends, and acquaintances, Gagné began to construct a new establishment on the Promenade Papineau. He, too, would have preferred to move to somewhere else, closer to the lake. But things being as they were, he was left no choice in the matter: the municipal government was sending him to Papineau, so he got on with it. "My partners got behind the project. The guys from the granite companies, for the roof, the glass, the terraces. It's because of their contributions that it's so lovely today," said Gagné. He is right. It is lovely, modern, and bright.

Still, rebuilding isn't cheap. Of course, since Gagné's former premises burned down in the disaster, he was compensated by his insurance. He was also granted a five-year holiday from paying property tax. But his new building was large, in line with the new standards. Materials had to be found. "Without my big buddy Dumas, there'd be no Musi-Café," says Gagné. "For example, the cellar should have cost between $25,000 and $35,000. But Dumas told me: 'Wait, I've got pine in my garage.' So I moved in here and trimmed pine. During the weekend, I created something in my head. In the end it cost $5,000, with the glass. It's been like that all over the restaurant."

Despite the assistance of his friends, it was still a difficult experience for Gagné. The bureaucratic maze he had to navigate to obtain financial assistance from Québec City was frustrating. The municipal government provided no assistance. "I understand that in government there are several levels, so it takes time to get through. But with the Town of Mégantic, I don't get it. It makes no sense to have to fight like that with the government and with the Town of Lac-Mégantic. It was a huge disappointment. I hope the anger and rage will fade, with time. It's been very hard, and it's not settled yet. I'd never do it again," he said in a December 2014 interview with Radio-Canada.[144]

Gagné had, for example, chosen an extremely durable, aesthetically pleasing exterior cladding that came highly recommended by several municipalities, since it was eligible for LEED certification.* It was a much more costly investment than simple wood cladding, but very long-lasting. And Gagné, who takes pride in his premises, intended to be there for the long term. But there was a problem: the ecologically approved cladding didn't comply with the new standards laid down in the town plan – standards which were still almost unknown to everyone. Gagné fought with the town and lost. He was forced to rip off the new cladding and pay for what the town required.

In December 2014, Yannick Gagné opened the new Musi-Café. Even today, the mere act of crossing its threshold is more emotional than one might have expected. Since March 2018, he has been trying to sell business. This is understandable. It was inhuman to have to carry the symbol of Mégantic's survival and rebirth on his shoulders. And then, as he explained to me bitterly in the summer of 2018, tourists would ask him where the old Musi-Café used to stand … and then where they could have a drink while admiring the lake. But there's nowhere like that anymore, unless you travel four kilometres from town.

And then there were the very high overheads for businesses that had relocated: the mortgage or rent, electricity, taxes. Often, the former premises were old and had been partly paid for. The cost of

---

* LEED, or Leadership in Energy and Environmental Design, is a widely used certification process that "provides independent, third-party verification that a building, home or community was designed and built using strategies aimed at achieving high performance in key areas of human and environmental health." See www.cagbc.org/CAGBC/Programs/LEED/LEED_Certification_Process.aspx.

THE SECOND DEVASTATION

rebuilding according to the new standards was staggering – far above what was covered by the insurance. It is difficult to make ends meet. Several other businesses face the same challenges as the Musi-Café.

The town hasn't shown much restraint where costs are concerned. It dreamed big, and big is costly. For instance, what sense did it make to upgrade the electrical network of the Promenade Papineau to carry industrial-level power – a type of current that now costs merchants a fortune each month? What was planned that would require that amount of energy? And what plans are we talking about, anyway? In early 2014, no one had yet set eyes on any plans, certainly not officially.

Reconstruction Plans? What Plans?

It would be learned on May 24, 2014, at a press conference given by Mégantic businesspeople, who had banded together in a group named Action Mégantic, that it was thought, following the examples of "disaster tourism" developed in Hiroshima and New York, that "tourism opportunities could be centred on the tragedy that has made Mégantic known all over the world."[145]

The *Journal de Montréal* provided a glimpse of this vision:

> A bold tourism product focusing on the tragedy of July 6, 2013, in Lac-Mégantic could generate economic benefits exceeding $500 million, according to the man behind Action Mégantic, David Sepulchre.
>
> With a light show by Moment Factory featuring tank cars left from the accident, several hotels, and a 3D cinema: the Montréal businessman was thinking big. "People are absolutely without hope and see no future, apart from this project ... I have the backing of the whole business community of Mégantic. The mayor no longer has any choice," says David Sepulchre.
>
> He has met with Mayor Colette Roy-Laroche more than ten times to present Action Mégantic's vision. He has also introduced her to the people at Moment Factory during a trip to Montréal.

"Everything has to be rebuilt," believes Mr. Sepulchre. "We could salvage a few tank cars and make quite an impressive show with a 'Cirque du Soleil'-style effect and music ..." According to the businessman, the economic spinoff could amount to over $500 million. "That is data provided by the marketing firm DentsuBos," he explained. The firm estimated that more than half a million tourists would visit the site each year ... "Look at Chernobyl, it's still contaminated, but they still expect a million visitors each year. In all these places, tourism keeps the hotels busy."[146]

And so that the picture might be clear to everyone, the renowned Sepulchre and the businesspeople of Mégantic produced a slick video showing the new town centre as they envisioned it. In this splendid model one could admire, to the accompaniment of lyrical music, the scorched tankers arranged in a kind of montage that was to be lit up by a *son et lumière* spectacle based on the theme of the disaster and its victims – a video that would turn the stomachs of many, especially some of those close to the victims.

Sepulchre gave himself a lot of credit for his vision of the new Mégantic. But in fact, the Mégantic businesspeople who joined the Action Mégantic lobby group had already set to work shortly after the tragedy, even before he came on the scene. "We all got together to work out a new plan for Mégantic," Béland Audet would say later, referring to the group. "A grandiose vision ... of an institute of transportation safety, for instance. And of tourism especially, for today Mégantic is known all over the world. Yes, it's true, it's disaster tourism ... but a lot of tourists visit Ground Zero in New York or Chernobyl ... If we can take advantage of that to get back on track ... There's no harm in thinking, in dreaming big."[147]

By November 25, 2013, not quite five months after the tragedy, this vision had already been espoused by the mayor, Madame Roy-Laroche. "Already, with the town council," she explained to Gérald Fillion of the Radio-Canada program *RDI économie*, "and with groups of residents, we've been thinking about where we could go

with the reconstruction in the medium and long term ... My dream, whether it's of a place where people come to learn, or whether it's about the environment, transportation safety, or hazardous materials ... [is of] a place where we come to remember, where we come to be entertained."[148]

One clue about the influence exerted on the elected officials of Mégantic was the mayor's reference to the flagship project that was dear to one of the leading members of Action Mégantic, namely the proposal for an institute of transportation safety. From the very outset, the plan was largely established (although some elements would never be put into effect). And again, this was prior to any public consultation.

Amid these backstage manoeuvres, Sepulchre, who landed in his private helicopter in the middle of a devastated Mégantic, made quite an impression. Rumour had it that Guy Laliberté, owner of Cirque du Soleil, had accompanied him on the flight. Said Daniel Larochelle, the lawyer who initiated the class action suit on behalf of Mégantic's victims:

> And then we talked a lot about Moment Factory as an investment; after all it wasn't a trifling matter. I was asking questions and they were telling me, "Wait, there's something very big in the works for the town centre." So I waited before I invested, I lost a year that way. It was when I saw the drawing of the 150-room hotel that I understood it made no sense. Mégantic is magnificent but few people come, you have to go out of your way to get here. I knew a plan like that made no sense.

Sepulchre and others who rushed to Mégantic were nevertheless fanning the flames of ambition. As a result, no one would ask who exactly this Sepulchre was, with his great flights, oratorical and literal. Nor would anyone, it seems, ask to see the data from the analyses carried out by DentsuBos, the company that was forecasting spinoffs worth $500 million. In the end, DentsuBos turned out to be merely a marketing agency with offices located in Sepulchre's buildings in Montréal.

The town council and local businesspeople may have been obsessed with and bewildered by the seductions and attention surrounding them – and overwhelmed by the enormous, too enormous, disaster that they had to deal with. And, as in the case of the Promenade Papineau, warnings that the splendiferous plan might be headed for disaster were overlooked in the confusion.

Because in fact, by 2014, apart from the government, major outside investors had yet to make an appearance. Yet the investments required surpassed local capacity: a convention centre, a 150-room hotel, an institute of transportation safety. "'It'll be a fabulous project here one day,' Sepulchre told me," said lawyer Larochelle. "'You've got to invest!' 'So what about you?' I asked him, 'How much are you putting in?' 'Not a penny,' Sepulchre told me."

What the town councillors and businesspeople found even more bewildering was the amount of funding being showered on the little town by the Québec government – which was insisting, quite properly, on helping its recovery. Money was plentiful, especially from the point of view of local elected officials accustomed to snatching up even the tiniest subsidy. The availability of funding can induce a dangerous euphoria, even when intentions are laudable. For instance, the shopkeepers who moved to Papineau were eligible to receive aid to develop their premises. This would prove very costly, even disproportionately so in certain cases, one example being a personal care business that was said to have spent as much as $150,000 on its new quarters. The euphoria inspired by such largesse concealed the harsh reality that would inevitably strike after five years, when the financial assistance would end.

And it was precisely this plethora of funding that allowed the municipal government, which already owned some of the business premises in the downtown area, to launch the second phase of its plan, the likes of which had not been seen before: the acquisition of the entire town centre. To achieve its objective, the town would adopt the same modus operandi that had been used six months earlier to gut Fatima – in other words, harassment, especially of the more

vulnerable property owners, using the spectre of expropriation under Bill 57, with pollution as an additional bogeyman.

It was now early 2014. The town had prepared the houses and buildings still standing within the red zone for the winter, to prevent further damage. Yet the owners were not entitled to set foot there. They had to wait to learn their fate.

✕ ✕ ✕

They've got this plan in their heads and they want us to think it's all out in the open, that it'll be rebuilt, but this plan of theirs was already settled in advance.

"It doesn't seem like a town council. They're behaving as if they own the town. Then the citizen involved feels excluded, humiliated, unjustly treated, abandoned."

—Statements collected during the
INSPQ inquiry into the disaster

"The man from the ministry had told me already: 'Your house isn't polluted.' I was happy. I'd just renovated everything, and I had the most beautiful view of the village, right in front of the Veterans' Park and the lake," said Hélène Rodrigue, a recently retired nurse who was living in what had once been her parents' home. After surviving the night of July 6, she had been living in temporary accommodation, a rented house.

"Then, out of the blue, I got an evaluation for my house. They said it was worth almost nothing and that I had to sell it to the town for that amount or I'd be expropriated. At first I refused to sell. I wanted to go back to our family home. But above all, I was terribly angry. How could they enter our house without telling me, value my house without me being there, and confront me with a *fait accompli*? Mind you, it's not as if I didn't suspect something. Already in November 2013, I'd seen on TV the map of the new downtown that the mayor was talking about, and in place of my house there were bistros and restaurants."

"It's true," Daniel Larochelle confirmed, "I saw the plans very early in the fall of 2013. I requested copies. The authorities refused. I took

photos with my phone. Everything was there, the hotel, the Convention Centre ... It was nothing like what was there before."

At the end of the summer of 2013, representatives of the town, accompanied by people from the Ministries of Economic Affairs and Municipal Affairs, descended on the fenced-in area. Illegally, without the owners being present and without their knowledge, they valued properties with a view to purchasing or maybe just expropriating them. The municipality had decided to take possession of the entire historic downtown site. As a result, it would become the uncontested, undisputed master of every decision relating to the reconstruction and reallocation of the lands it had acquired. By acting in this way, the town council was endorsing the offensive that some Action Mégantic members were promoting. "The Québec government has just granted us $60 million. We must buy the land and the houses ... Two years from now, the government's offer may no longer be available. It's better to sell now," advised Michel Duval, manager of the Desjardins caisse populaire* in the Mégantic Region.

Duval, who would become the main promoter to reluctant owners of the idea that they should consider selling, was speaking as manager of the caisse, and in many cases as the mortgage holder of the properties in question. But in October 2014, alerted by Jonathan Santerre, the founder of Le Carré Bleu Lac-Mégantic, a citizen's group pushing for more transparency surrounding the reconstruction efforts[149] and the creator of an online forum for the people of Mégantic,[150] Radio-Canada would reveal that Duval belonged to Action Mégantic, whose members had their eye on the town centre site. They would be sanctioned for illegal lobbying.[151]

The town orchestrated the repurchase mechanism in a rather simple way. If your property had burned down, you would receive compensation from your insurance and the town would buy your land "for a dollar." "I framed it!" Daniel Larochelle, whose building and office did burn down, said sarcastically. According to victims' testimonies, representatives of the town and the provincial government who met privately with the owners offered them a choice between giving in ... and giving up – of surrendering their property right away,

---

* A caisse populaire is the Québec equivalent of a credit union.

or a little later. They were assured that there were only advantages to signing over their property. (Possibly this was temporarily the case, for the duration of the cleanup.) They also dangled before them a right of first refusal that would turn out to be a sham.

If, on the other hand, your building or home was intact, the town offered a purchase price based on a ridiculously low valuation. But in this case there was an added incentive: the government would reimburse up to the replacement value of your insurance if you rebuilt within five years. For instance, if the town offered you $100,000 for your home but the insured replacement value was $150,000, you would be eligible for the additional $50,000, though you would not be able to receive this sum until you had rebuilt your home – or relocated – in Mégantic. Otherwise, this compensation would be forfeited. This incentive would turn out to be an unfathomable puzzle that many couldn't afford, or even a decoy prejudicial to owners.

Nevertheless, as of 2013 the town council had everything in place to implement its plan, namely the acquisition of all the lots and the still-surviving buildings in the town centre. To do so, it had a weapon: the notorious, deadly Bill 57, which allowed it to demolish any contaminated building.

× × ×

Friedman's shock doctrine, phase two: take advantage of the necessary cleanup and decontamination, excluding the population from the scene of the tragedy and ensuring a clean sweep of the old world, leaving people nothing to hold on to and making it impossible to backtrack.

× × ×

The Spectre of Pollution

> Decontamination was used against Mégantic as a weapon of mass destruction.
>
> —Daniel Green, SVP

"With such danger of residual pollution, ownership is a big risk. Who will be willing to finance it, and who will want to insure it? You see how many problems there are," insisted Michel Duval, addressing the owners and the media. It was a message repeated ad nauseam by the mayor and councillors. Roughly speaking, what they told the owners was that there was no future for them in the town centre because of the actual, or potential, pollution. It was in their best interest to sell, right away. Even at a very bad price.

Duval's statement to Radio-Canada that the pollution would prevent owners from insuring or financing their home was immediately contradicted by the Insurance Bureau of Canada, whose spokesperson explained that several policies had already been renewed since the disaster. Mortgage experts concurred: "There is nothing to contraindicate mortgage financing or mortgage renewal for people in the sector," said Julien Chaumont, a mortgage broker.[152]

It is true that under normal circumstances pollution can be an obstacle to mortgage financing or insurance. But it seems that Mégantic enjoyed a special status. After all, tons of contaminated soil were still being excavated. But that was not even relevant, for the experts' reports, based on results from drilling and analysis, found that most of the houses and other buildings had escaped contamination. Yes, they had actually escaped contamination.

✕ ✕ ✕

Even today most citizens of Mégantic remain unaware of this fundamental fact, or merely have their suspicions. The town has never published or explained the official reports Golder produced about the extent of the pollution of Mégantic's soil and buildings – reports whose results have also been confirmed by witnesses in the field.

A few of us, including Daniel Green, did peruse the reports submitted by the Golder company, which were obtained by the SVP and Jonathan Santerre under the Access to Information Act. (It was already inexcusable that the Access to Information Act had to be used to obtain such information, which should automatically be public property. After all, it provided a foundation upon which informed decisions could be based.) But there was also the reality. And people

working in the red zone knew and talked about the reality of the pollution. After all, it concerned them, their neighbours, and their friends. Concealing information only served to further undermine the already fragile trust between the town authorities and the victims.

So the majority of the buildings left standing in the town centre had escaped contamination, something the authorities learned very early. As early as July 22, Mégantic firefighters visited the surviving buildings (which stood on a lower level than the derailment site) and discovered that the basements of six out of thirty-nine were contaminated by oil. Only these six buildings, which included the pretty lakeside restaurant, the Citron Vert, would need to be demolished. In September 16, 2013, Golder's assessment of the buildings showed that only ten buildings out of forty-one in the red zone were contaminated, and four of these were already polluted before the disaster. The majority of the buildings were not affected and could possibly be repaired.

Reoccupying the premises, according to Golder, would depend on how long it would take to excavate the soil and replace the damaged underground pipes and other infrastructure. But most of the colourful buildings were redeemable. Among the pollution-free buildings was L'Eau Berge, the elegant, recently renovated Victorian inn and one of the town's loveliest buildings. Its owner, who had patiently forged his success, was well known in the community. In fact, L'Eau Berge was so free of contamination that it would provide accommodation for the first workers immediately after the disaster.

In early 2014, however, the risk of pollution spoken of by the town council and some other prominent figures did influence homeowners: "Because they told us it was on account of an environmental problem. [They were using] the fear that oil might turn up later on those lots or in the uncontaminated houses ... But no one from the Ministry of the Environment confirmed that," said one stricken property owner.

In addition to the threat of contamination, the property owners, especially the most vulnerable, would also be subjected to the same intimidation tactics as were used in Fatima. "When I went to the meeting about buying my house," said Hélène Rodrigue, "there were seven of them sitting across from me, Gilles Bertrand, the town manager, the deputy minister for municipal affairs, a man called Arseneault ...

Seven against me! I asked what they would do if I didn't sell. That was the only time Gilles Bertrand looked at me. He said to me straight out: 'Then we'll expropriate you!' It was intimidation, no doubt about it."

Several other residents confirmed that the threat of pollution was used as an intimidation tactic. "They got people by wearing them down ... It was like being questioned by the police: maybe you're innocent, but they'll question you for forty-eight hours and you'll end up saying, 'Yes, I did it.' You're so tired of it all," said another citizen. "Well it was the same thing going on. People ended up saying, 'Give me my cheque, even if I lose a million, I've had enough.' And that's not right."

Was it just ineptitude on the part of the town that it failed to be transparent about the pollution risk or to explain the contents of the expert reports to the property owners? That is doubtful. Because if they were going to move forward with the plan concocted behind the scenes, it was essential that the exact content of the reports and information about the pollution risk be withheld. Bill 57 was categorical in saying that the municipal government might demolish "any building ... judged, according to an expert report, unfit for habitation or for the pursuit of the activities that were carried on in it previously because of the contaminated condition of the site on which it is located." In other words, if there was no contamination, demolition was not allowed. Yet, despite this, the town would later manage to render the buildings unfit for occupation.

An Example: the Société des Alcools du Québec (SAQ)

"On Saturday, August 31, 2013, the trench in the SAQ sector was filled in. No materials were present," says one of the Railway Committee minutes. This finding was confirmed by the Golder report and reconfirmed by a worker: "I was there, I dug the trenches, and I could see, there was no oil in the SAQ. The building was clean."

In 2013, the SAQ building, located quite close to the river, belonged to a Mégantic couple. They had made it their "retirement nest egg," like several major downtown property owners. The building was perfectly functional, and the owners had signed a long-term lease with the SAQ. Everything was going well – until disaster struck. Yet the building, located a fair distance from the site of the derailment,

was spared. It had escaped contamination. In theory, it was possible for it to resume its normal existence without endangering the owners' life savings. Unfortunately, using the false pretext of contamination, the municipal government expropriated the building, and it was demolished.

Of course, the town and the SAQ could have made a little effort to preserve the lease agreement between the SAQ and the owners of the building. But that was not to happen. There would first be a temporary relocation to Promenade Papineau, and the lease would be renegotiated between the SAQ and the town, as the owner of the new commercial condo. The couple would be out of the picture. In fact, the fate of the owners of the SAQ building had already been sealed, unbeknownst to them, in the fall of 2013. The SAQ sat in on the negotiations between the town and Metro's real-estate subsidiary. The SAQ was to be situated in an annex of the new Metro building in Fatima. "The picture is still in my mind," said lawyer Larochelle. "It was at the Sports Complex, where I was hanging about at the time trying to find out what they had in store for us. I can still see them arrive. They walked in a V formation, with the local owner of the Metro store in the lead, followed by a whole troop of lawyers from Metro Québec Immobilier.[*] They were going off to negotiate with the mayor and one or two people from Mégantic. I told myself that Mégantic's elected councillors never had a chance."

The SAQ is now located in a building in Fatima owned by Metro Québec Immobilier. So the "pension plan" of the owners of the former SAQ building has doubtless passed into the hands of the already very wealthy financial group. In other words, the income of two individuals was literally stolen from them, with the active complicity of the town, to benefit the wealthy real-estate subsidiary of a large chain.

How much did Metro Québec Immobilier ask from the town – and therefore from the government and the taxpayers – in return for agreeing to occupy premises where they had had no desire to go? (Metro already had its premises in the commercial zone of Laval

---

[*] The real-estate subsidiary of the Metro Richelieu grocery chain. According to Corporations Canada's registry, Metro Québec Immobilier Inc., shares the address of Metro Richelieu's headquarters. See also: opencorporates .com/companies/ca/7254911.

North.) That remains a mystery. However we do know that as of August 31, 2015, the very profitable Metro subsidiary was granted almost $500,000 from the Fonds Avenir Lac-Mégantic in the form of a property tax holiday – money, in other words, that was donated by the public. By how much would Metro have benefited overall from that program by its scheduled termination in 2018?

The two expropriated owners would, it is true, have "benefited" from a certain financial "incentive" if they had decided to rebuild. Except that to date, and despite all their efforts, they have been unable to rebuild or purchase anything, largely due to financial constraints. Before long, they may well have lost a small fortune. In any case, according to someone close to them, they have lost heart.

✖ ✖ ✖

"Of course, it's the same with everything," said Gilles Fluet. "Some people didn't want to go back and got a good deal when they sold. But for most ..." "This business of pollution, together with the deadlines certainly got everyone worked up," continued the lawyer Daniel Larochelle, "How long did we have to wait before we could return to our offices, our homes? We had no means of support, landlords were without tenants, and therefore without an income. Others needed their offices and couldn't wait." But what if, in the interim, the municipal government – using the Avenir Mégantic fund, for instance – had provided financial support to the owners?

Gilles Fluet was categorical: "There's no doubt that would have been the best option ... And that's what should have happened. A lot of owners were proud of their newly renovated, well-maintained buildings ... But that's not what the money was used for ..."

✖ ✖ ✖

As of August 31, 2015, the Jean Coutu Group had received $241,047 from the Fonds Avenir Lac-Mégantic in property tax credits and other tax relief, to finance its relocation to Fatima. As for Metro Québec Immobilier, it received $493,800 for its new building, of which the SAQ store was part. The Jean Coutu Group reported profits of $45

million in 2017, while Metro reported profits of $608 million for the same year. Dollarama, meanwhile, preferred to rent premises in Promenade Papineau instead of rebuilding. The money to support its relocation came from the Québec government's aid package of $60 million. The grant amount to Dollarama, therefore, remains unknown.

Very reliable sources indicate, however, that the negotiations with Dollarama were extremely tough, for the company's demands were astonishing. The same sources indicate that the Town of Lac-Mégantic was obliged to pay for everything, down to the garbage cans. Dollarama is a star on the Québec Stock Exchange and according to *Le Journal de Montréal*, "since 2009, the stock's growth has exceeded 1,500 percent … *A mere detail: the total market capitalization of Dollarama is over $17 billion, 10 billion more than Bombardier!*"[153]

Metro Québec Immobilier, today one of Fatima's major real estate holders, together with the Jean Coutu Group, benefited from almost a quarter of the donations contributed by the public to help the victims, to the tune of at least $750,000. In addition to this amount, undisclosed sums were granted to them as well as to Dollarama. These three financial groups can, therefore, be estimated to have benefited from well over $1 million of the funds associated with the Mégantic tragedy. (It should be pointed out that this money benefited the financial groups, not the employees, managers, etc., of their stores.) The evicted homeowners whose cases are described here received less than $1,000 each from the Fonds Avenir Lac-Mégantic – in other words, from the money donated by the public.

Today, it is imperative that Metro Inc., the Jean Coutu Group,* and Dollarama reimburse the sums they received from public donations and government assistance. That money was solely intended to support the victims of one of the worst disasters in the history of Québec. How can one not question the ethical sense of the top officials in those three companies who helped themselves to money intended for the victims, and the moral turpitude of our elected officials who enabled them to plunder the victims' aid in such a way? For two years now, all my appeals in the media, together with the many emails

---

* It is worth noting that in October 2017 these two groups (Metro and Jean Coutu) merged, giving birth to a Québec giant that is expected to generate revenues of $16 billion annually.

from disgusted members of the public to the Metro Group and Jean Coutu calling for them to reimburse these monies to the Mégantic community have been met with deafening silence.

✕ ✕ ✕

"Reinventing the Town"

Finally, on March 26, 2014, the Town of Lac-Mégantic launched its first official consultation session with residents, a "citizen participation approach," with "Réinventer la ville" (Reinventing the Town) as its theme. The aim of this approach, said the announcement, was to "collectively define the redevelopment plan for the town centre [using] a participatory approach, inviting the stakeholders on all levels and the citizens to become informed, express themselves, and exchange views about their new town centre."

Thus there began a process of consultation with the townspeople that would last over a year, following which, in May 2015, the mayor would produce a plan supposed not only to represent a synthesis of the citizens' wishes but, most importantly, to implement their wishes – the implicit purpose of the whole procedure. However, when the consultation began on March 26, 2014, the actual state of affairs in Mégantic was as follows:

- The businesses that constituted the heart of the old downtown area on rue Frontenac had already been dismantled and relocated to two different sites, namely Fatima and Promenade Papineau. Other businesses had been dispersed to the shopping centre and rue Laval.

- The Fatima district had been deprived of its main thoroughfare, which had been half demolished, and the property owners driven out. The Billots Select sawmill had been expropriated and closed, leaving the buildings and adjacent land vacant.

- Metro Québec Immobilier now owned most of the land in

THE SECOND DEVASTATION

the expropriated centre of Fatima. The remainder belonged to the Jean Coutu Group.

- The municipal government was in the process of finalizing the buyout of all the downtown property owners. It would become the sole proprietor of the entire town centre, with total control over the redevelopment and, most importantly, the allocation of land to whomever it liked.

- Zoning changes had been approved on the sly, preventing former owners from moving back to their former sites. The old town centre had been, de facto, already irreversibly changed, unless the various measures that had been adopted were amended.

- The architectural choices had already been made, as was shown by the losing battle Yannick Gagné had to fight for the exterior cladding of the Musi-Café.

In short, as townspeople settled down to define their new downtown core collectively, a plan had already been determined and substantially put into effect. However, there was still a vestige of hope for everyone in the form of the still-intact buildings that had survived in the old town centre. The entire half of the street that was still standing and visible behind the fences had become, for the community, a symbol of rebirth, of a renewed existence.

About the "Consultants"

The elected Mégantic town council ultimately retained control over the decisions, of course. It appears, however, that the councillors were subjected to a great deal of pressure – from developers, of course, but also from government bodies that were not always sensitive to the local reality. Obviously, the councillors had difficult dilemmas to resolve. In addition, a rumour was circulating that they had rejected the offers of town planning assistance made by various government

ministries. The councillors preferred to keep control and felt that they had a team around them. And so they did, for in the first days following the disaster several consultants and other highly paid advisers lost no time in arriving from outside. Some, while working in the shadow of the town council, would be allowed a great deal of scope. A few are listed here.

From the outset, the town hired the IBI/DAA Group, an urban planning company. It was this company that quickly prepared the notorious September 9, 2013 plan showing that everything, or nearly everything, had already been decided. Shortly before the disaster, on May 2, 2013, the daily newspaper *Le Soleil* had revealed a possible case of fraudulent electoral financing, a report that turned out to be true. The IBI/DAA Group was sentenced in March 2014 for illegally financing the electoral team of Mayor Régis Labeaume of Québec City. The case was likely to deprive IBI/DAA of its ability to tender for public contracts. Yet while this was going on, the company and its VP were the main actors involved in the process of "reinventing the town."

IBI/DAA, like many other firms, had developed a strategy: one-third of the contracts it was awarded came in below the $25,000 level, allowing municipal governments to avoid having to go to tender. IBI/DAA had been awarded thirty-two such contracts by Québec City, with a total value of almost $500,000. Although the case was publicized in the press, IBI/DAA would repeat the same strategy in Mégantic. Some contracts, a copy of which Jonathan Santerre managed to obtain after an epic battle with the town, showed that in a single year, between August 28, 2013, and October 14, 2014, IBI/DAA, using the same approach, had been awarded contracts amounting to at least $295,000. All contracts awarded after December 2013, when the normal bidding process resumed, were broken down into amounts below the $25,000 threshold. IBI/DAA would become firmly established in Mégantic, where its senior partner and executive vice-president, Marc Perreault, became the town's official planner for the redevelopment.

"Who was the planner behind the Promenade Papineau, the 'reinvention' of Fatima, and the future downtown?" wondered Jonathan Santerre in early 2014. "Just as we were learning that at a cost of $35,000 the islands of greenery in the condo area on Papineau were

to be done away with, a lot of people were wondering who came up with these plans." It was Marc Perreault. He had played a leading role in the reconstruction process from early on and was appointed a member of CAMEO, the municipal committee in charge of reconstruction, chaired by Stéphane Lavallée, a former publisher of the business newspaper *Les Affaires*.

In May 2014, when "Réinventer la ville" was in progress, Marc Perreault had his moment of fame. He was the designer of the notorious underground parking garage at the McGill University Health Centre super-hospital in Montréal, an "underground" parking garage whose eight floors nevertheless rise proudly above ground. But Perreault was able to convince the district that the outdoor parking *was* underground. "Even Perreault admits that that defies common sense," explained André Noël, the journalist and investigator for the Charbonneau Commission who would uncover the case. "It took a lot of creativity," added Noël with a smile.

It was indeed creative and also highly rewarding. The incredible ploy of reducing the estimate by $25 million allowed SNC-Lavalin (Perreault's employer at the time) to edge out a rival consortium and win the hospital's lucrative tender. Remarkably, Perreault was both working for SNC-Lavalin and acting as a consultant for the hospital; in other words he both awarded and benefited from the contracts.

Perreault repeated the same scenario in Mégantic. Appointed a member of CAMEO, which planned initiatives and awarded contracts, he was not at all shy about proposing contracts for tender with one hand and pocketing them with the other. "The Advisory Committee of Lac-Mégantic's CAMEO has recommended the organization of a 'design charrette'* ... We therefore offer our services ... within a budgetary envelope of $19,800," Perreault wrote in a letter to town council. The same would apply to several other contracts.

Another personage who became a fixture in Mégantic was the famous David Sepulchre, the man in the helicopter. Sepulchre wasn't unknown in the area; he was already known as the developer of a hotel project in Coaticook. There, too, he set local politicians dreaming

---

* A kind of collaborative brainstorming session allowing members of a team to collaborate and sketch out plans, sharing and testing various design ideas.

for a moment. The project would collapse in 2016 when Sepulchre abruptly picked up and went off to invest elsewhere.

According to the Québec Business Register, Sepulchre, through his holding companies, owned the Château Saint-Ambroise in the Saint-Henri district of Montréal. Curiously, one of his companies owns the Château's parking lots. Why bother with parking lots? Because they attract a lot of people! Three different sources confirmed this unreservedly. One individual told me, "There are cars in there like I've never seen. Cars of incredible luxury. And incredible parties in a space equipped with lights and so on. I'd never seen anything like it."

Sepulchre, who, on August 27, 2013, registered with the Québec register of lobbyists as a lobbyist in connection with Mégantic, would lose no time in forming an alliance with the Action Mégantic group. This was the same Sepulchre who would later tell the lawyer Larochelle that he didn't intend to invest a penny in the "fabulous project" under way in Mégantic. It was also Sepulchre who had contacts with the prestigious Québec company Moment Factory, really impressing the people of Mégantic. Sepulchre, as is widely recognized, had the ear of the town council, and especially of Madame Roy-Laroche. But the time came when he would depart the scene to invest, as he said, under other skies.

Finally, because Mégantic had become a gold mine, construction companies flocked into the town. And the results were very mixed. Rémi Tremblay, of *L'Écho de Frontenac*, related that Hexagone, a new construction company formed in the spring of 2013 as an offshoot of Tony Accurso's fallen empire,[*] announced that it had been awarded the contract to construct a bridge over the Chaudière River (the pont de la Solidarité) linking the sectors of the town – a project on which the town council planned to spend $5 million in 2014[154] – a bridge that, two years later, would undergo repairs because of its poor construction.

✖ ✖ ✖

In April and May 2014, more than 250 townspeople participated in the

---

[*] Accurso, a Québec "construction mogul," has a history of legal tangles. See "Tony Accurso Timeline," *Montreal Gazette*, September 2, 2014, montreal-gazette.com/local/tony-accurso-timeline.

THE SECOND DEVASTATION

"Réinventer la ville" workshops in order to express their views about the "commercial and institutional components," as the notice of the meeting put it. This was a smokescreen, for the merchants from the old downtown had already been relocated, as the council wanted. Far from being deceived, the citizens knew this perfectly well. "Whatever we say won't really be used, or they'll just use it to fill up a report saying 'Yes, yes, we did consult the public.' But at the end of the day it's all decided ahead of time," said one.

Vacillating between scepticism and hope, more than five hundred townspeople nevertheless attended the initial meeting on March 26, 2014. "To start with," said one of the participants, "I thought it was great to allow the citizens a say." But things got off on the wrong foot. At the very first workshop, Geneviève Boulanger and Miroslav Chum, the owners of one of the most beautiful Victorian lakeside houses, which had been destroyed in the fire, stared in disbelief at the plan of the downtown that was on display, for it failed to recognize the existence of their piece of land, although they had not yet agreed to give it up: on it, the entire disaster area was shown as an area for redevelopment. "I was shaking with anger," said Boulanger.[155]

Following a series of workshops, the town council invited the townspeople to a "public meeting" on June 17, 2014, to present the "preferred scenario for development, its basis and objectives." Some 350 citizens attended to find out about the synthesis that had emerged from their suggestions and wishes. The town and its consultants were there to present their interim report. It was full of splendid ideals: "sustainable development," a "lived-in, vibrant environment," "green spaces," the creation of "attractive, comfortable, safe links between zones of activity" – in other words, the epitome of a humanistic, reassuring vision. At first glance, it was difficult to disagree with this virtuous proposal. On closer inspection, however, some clues were revealing, to say the least.

First, the report staked everything on tourism as the means to set the town on the road to financial prosperity. This corresponded precisely with the scenario advocated by Action Mégantic. But since the new hotels and entertainments for vacationers had to go somewhere, the best place, said the report, was in the historic downtown, facing the lake.

Except that for that to be possible, space was required. Because on June 17, 2014, that space was still occupied by the buildings spared by the disaster, which, for the most part, still belonged to their original owners. But the town gave the residents a gentle warning: "The downtown development concept has to offer some flexibility in order to adjust the availability of commercial space to an increased demand, particularly considering Lac-Mégantic's tourism ambitions, which should generate an increase in business." It was a nice choice of words. "What you are being shown on this plan," people were told, "is subject to change, because we are about to enjoy a successful tourism industry," making it necessary to "encourage the emergence of a critical mass of businesses and services." And that was extremely opportune, since the Action Mégantic group and the developer David Sepulchre, who was still active in the wings, had just proposed a 150-room hotel with a conference centre, a Sound and Light show, etc. But the "Réinventer la ville" report made no official mention of these covert influences and proposals, nor of the fact that a clean sweep was necessary if this new tourism initiative was to get off the ground.

The rosy future proposed for Mégantic, based on tourism, nevertheless concealed a substantial note of caution, coyly hidden away in the small print of a footnote: "At the moment," it said, "Lac-Mégantic's tourist office has recorded an increase in the number of visitors from 6,470 in 2007 to 10,399 in 2011." A far from overwhelming number …

The area is beautiful. The Appalachians, which extend from Newfoundland and Labrador to Alabama, unfold their slopes up to the edge of large lakes, the natural environment is gentle, the air is fragrant with the smell of balsam fir. But the large urban centres are a long way off and, furthermore, there is a winding drive of an hour and twenty minutes from the closest city, Sherbrooke, to Mégantic, on a road where deer may often be encountered. It may be picturesque, but it deters a lot of people.

One citizen pointed this out. "It seems that some people can only dream about tourism for Mégantic. That's no way to revive the town … Tourists just pass through. A 140-room motel will be empty maybe 60 percent of the time. They're kidding themselves." Another comment was even more scathing: "That's the bubble [the elected municipal officials] have gotten themselves into, for I think they've lost touch

with everyday reality, or else they've forgotten how to put themselves in the place of the townspeople they're supposed to represent. It's as if they're completely out of touch."

Cynical, disbelieving, or trusting, those participating in "Réinventer la ville" were still conscientiously doing their homework at the tables to which they had been invited. And during the discussions, on June 17, 2014, with a single voice they made two strong demands about the "reinvention" of their town. The first was to get the railway out of the town centre. Even the members of Action Mégantic agreed with that.

The second, and most urgent demand, was that what remained of the downtown area not be demolished and the surviving structures be retained. From all those workshops and public consultations, a tragic paradox would emerge: the citizens of Mégantic *had absolutely no desire* to "reinvent their town." They wanted to find it again as it was, or at least those vestiges that fate had left them as landmarks. And in June 2014, they still believed this was possible.

✕ ✕ ✕

"I won't beat about the bush," declared Mayor Colette Roy-Laroche. "I'm letting you know that your elected council intends to ask for the complete demolition of the buildings within the fenced-off area." This announcement was followed by "twenty-five-seconds of total silence in the gym of the Sports Complex, which held about four hundred people at the fifth public meeting of 'Réinventer la ville,'" on October 29, 2014.[156]

A resident would sum up the widespread sentiment: "The way [the mayor] announced it, that the buildings were going to be demolished. I was shocked, and if I'd spoken up what I'd have said wouldn't have been nice to hear. We'd have needed to stand up, fifty of us would have had to stand up and say, 'We understand you've reached that decision, but we can't accept it. Either give us a different explanation or bring in competent people so that we can really understand.' But then it was as if we were bowled over, we were in shock, so it was hard to react that night."[157]

The mayor's announcement caused great distress, which was

expressed by many. "First, the destruction of July 6, and then all the other destruction in Fatima, and now here. It's as if the destruction never ended." "It's back: the discouragement, the sadness. It's as if we were just turning the knife in the wound." The INSPQ report confirmed this: "The announcement of the destruction of the downtown buildings marked once again a turning point in people's perceptions, this time concerning the primacy of administrative control over human factors."

✗ ✗ ✗

Friedman's shock doctrine, phase three: Friedman concluded that in dealing with a public whose shock has been exacerbated by the obliteration of all their landmarks and habits, "we" have an opportunity to carry out the reconstruction, or "reinvention," which will then be welcomed with resigned acceptance of our proposals. (By "we" he presumably meant the forces of economic progress.)

Demolition Derby: the Justification

"One more loss to be suffered, this time for environmental reasons," said the mayor on October 14, 2014, on announcing the demolition. "The measures used to measure pollution are recognized as reliable by international standards, but they will never provide a 100 percent degree of certainty," explained the mayor, who also cited economic reasons to justify the municipal officials' decision. "There's no point in keeping buildings if nobody will be willing to finance or insure them."[158] Pollution was being used as a justification, as a weapon of mass destruction.

On November 3, 2014, three months before the demolition, an email exchange between Jonathan Santerre and an official with the Ministry of the Environment confirmed that the decision to demolish for environmental reasons lacked any foundation, and that the decision had originated with the town, not with the Environment Ministry:

Several scenarios could be envisaged concerning the buildings that had escaped the fire but were within the disaster area. According to the results of the characterization studies of the properties, these scenarios could be restricted to the rehabilitation of the ground surrounding the buildings, to raising the buildings to carry out decontamination underneath them, or to demolishing the buildings, excavating their foundations, and rehabilitating the contaminated soil. Following the process of acquiring the buildings in Zone One ... the scenario chosen by the local authorities requires demolishing the buildings.

I trust this is to your satisfaction and remain, Yours truly ...

✖ ✖ ✖

Technically, Bill 57 did not allow those buildings to be demolished, since, contrary to what the authorities claimed, they were pollution-free and fit for use. By the end of 2014, however, they had become unfit for use. Even before the demolition was announced, the town council had decided not to winterize the spared buildings. With doors and windows gaping throughout the winter and the heating and electricity cut off, the surviving downtown buildings were at the mercy of the elements. "They made sure we couldn't go back, that the buildings were done for," said several townspeople.

✖ ✖ ✖

"Will we be able to go back to rue Frontenac one last time to mourn the downtown?" wondered Dominique Bilodeau when the demolition was announced.

Some 2,150 people marched in the old downtown on that cold December Saturday. It was the first time since the tragedy and the last time in an area that in a way was about to disappear with the demolition of almost all the

buildings ... Inside the closed-off area, made accessible for a few hours, children and adults peered into the shop windows, touched for the last time the structures that were condemned to demolition, storing up visually what remained – or not – inside ... On Frontenac, Thibodeau, and boulevard des Vétérans, many memories emerged: here a former workplace, there a building belonging to a relative.[159]

× × ×

The Nagging Question of Why

> The decisions about redeveloping the town were taken as fast as that train reached the town. We hadn't even finished burying our dead ... We needed a little time to breathe.
>
> —Johanne Tousignant, joint leader of a
> group of rental property owners in the
> downtown, speaking on the program
> *RDI économie*, November 25, 2013,
> just four months after the tragedy

It is a brutal act to knock down buildings that are the heart of a town. It is a terrible thing to be robbed of one's bearings, one's home, and one's memories. It is so traumatic that in some countries it is used as a weapon of war. The victims of floods and wildfires can also confirm this. Obviously, when such a measure is undertaken, tact and extreme care are essential. So why were they dispensed with in this case?

To this day, three questions continue to haunt the people of Mégantic: Who took the decision to buy up all the properties in the town centre, leaving the town as sole master of the place and ruining any prospect the former occupants had of returning to their homes? Who decided to demolish the town centre? And above all, why?

Ultimately, the three phases of the process that began in the first weeks following the disaster were quite simple and revealing. First, the town bought everything, then it changed the zoning to prevent former occupants from returning, and finally it knocked everything

THE SECOND DEVASTATION

down to make way for new construction. And now the municipality, as sole owner, could distribute the land made available in this way to whoever it chose – or to whoever was sufficiently well placed to stake a claim.

My theory about this, which is supported by a number of facts (including the initial plan), is as follows: even before the "Réinventer la ville" consultation, the town council had begun to take possession of the land and was promising it to people other than those who had occupied it before the disaster. So it seems that the previous owners' property was expropriated so that it could be given to others – a hypothesis which also explains what almost everyone felt and expressed confusedly: that "Réinventer la ville" was nothing but a sham and a smokescreen.

But all this was to what purpose? For profit, of course – profit for some. Or to obtain a superior building site on the shores of a magnificent lake. For others, finally – including no doubt the elected councillors – there was the irrepressible desire to plan a visionary town, starting from a perfectly blank page, and so leave a prestigious personal legacy. But this dream was not shared by the people destined to live in the "reinvented" town. There may be other scenarios to explain what happened. But for now they're in no hurry to emerge.*

So up to the end of 2019, until it became obvious that no projects would materialize, the vacant lots in the town centre were reserved for some – but not for their former owners. As of now, except for one family, no former owners managed to go back to their previous locations, and they were definitely excluded from the downtown area.

✕ ✕ ✕

"It was terrible, because you saw everything abandoned ... The Knights of Columbus, for example, had all the trophies, the signed photos ... For us, it was hard to watch ... Before the demolition, the contractors, the workers, and others could take away anything they wanted:

---

* I asked the former mayor, Colette Roy-Laroche, for an interview, but received no reply. Similarly, after an initial discussion with Béland Audet, a member of Action Mégantic, he was unable to complete his testimony because of demands on his time.

new windows, plumbing, electric appliances, washing machines … anything they wanted. The buildings were literally gutted before the demolition, but not by their owners," said one worker in the red zone.

"The last time I was able to go home, I took a few things quickly. Later, I got a notice saying that they were reducing the purchase price of my house because I had removed some hand-built cabinets … Why would it bother them that I was taking a few memories with me?" relates Hélène Rodrigue. "They were mine, and anyway, they were going to demolish it!"

✖ ✖ ✖

On a chilly week toward the end of February 2015, excavators and bulldozers set about demolishing the town centre. The last building to fall would be the legendary L'Eau Berge, a building that had recently been enlarged and that had completely escaped contamination.

✖ ✖ ✖

The fire of July 6 had levelled forty-one buildings. The town levelled a greater number: almost sixty, including those in Fatima, the neighbourhood adjoining the scene of the tragedy. Over a hundred buildings in a small town of just over six thousand inhabitants.

✖ ✖ ✖

On May 11, 2015, before 250 townspeople, the municipality presented its final plan, purportedly decided upon after the participatory "Réinventer la ville" consultations. The public was given seven days to comment. But on what? "That project … was supposed to be a collective one, according to what we were told. We found that we had no say, none," is how one resident summed it up.

Even Mégantic's historical boomtown look would be consigned to the past. The town had already retained the well-known Pierre Thibault architecture firm to design the new modern buildings in Mégantic with their clean lines. "Boxes," some townspeople call them. But it's a matter of taste. Or of soul.

A semi-detached house in the new downtown area by the railway line now sells for $675,000 – out of reach for most Mégantic residents.

✗ ✗ ✗

> Once upon a time, people were happy
> And it was all so simple and wonderful
> There was the sky, there was the earth ...
> Talk to those who remember ...
> The world is beautiful
>
> > —Stéphane Venne,
> >   "Il était une fois des gens heureux," *Les Plouffe*

> I'd park my car right in front of the post office to go and get my letter, and I'd go quickly to the pharmacy and to the Korvette.* There I'd meet an acquaintance, and then sometimes we'd go to have a little coffee in the Brûlerie† or beside the lake. After that I'd dash to the Metro and by the time I got home, I'd have done all my shopping and caught up on all the news.
>
> > —Robert Bellefleur, resident of Mégantic

Amid Mégantic's endless tragedies, it must never be forgotten that the first, true culprits in this tragedy remain the Ackmans and Harrisons with their sorry contingent of complicit shareholders, the elected officials and ministers who made the disaster possible, and the other officials and policy-makers who turned a blind eye – and who still do so – to the risks taken in the pursuit of profits. The people of Mégantic, whether at fault or not, were dragged into a storm that was born elsewhere. We must resist the temptation to make scapegoats of those in charge of Mégantic and try instead to rebuild bridges between all, to stand together.

---

* A family-owned chain of bargain department stores.

† A café-bistro, now located in the Promenade Papineau.

EPILOGUE

BEING ... HUMAN

> The second blast from the tanker cars was so powerful that I thought my hair had melted, and because of the fright it's what caused my depression ...
>
> —Yves Faucher, a resident of Mégantic

ONE ICY FEBRUARY NIGHT, A LOT OF PEOPLE WERE UNABLE TO sleep, their rest stolen by pain and fear. Images roiled in their heads, repeated endlessly. Whatever the hour of the day or night, Jonathan Santerre always replied to the ones who described their distress on Facebook. He had created his webpage for that very purpose. "I know it's tough, but the sun will rise again tomorrow. In the meantime, call this number now. To everyone reading this tonight, call this number if things aren't going well. Someone will answer you. Don't stay alone."

Early in the morning, when Santerre returned to his keyboard, he wrote the banal but comforting words: "Today, sunny and not as cold. It's going to be a beautiful day. I'll find out the news and then I'll get back to you." It was early in 2014. Jonathan Santerre, like everyone else, felt helpless when the tragedy struck. He had to help, he wanted to help – but how? Then he had a stroke of genius: the Facebook page he set up, which immediately became a public forum. It was a sort of twenty-four-hour radio program, providing information and reassurance. It created a community. Over the months, Santerre assumed the role of intermediary, asking the authorities questions on behalf of the victims. To begin with, he was trusting. Then, relentlessly, when answers were redacted and when the silences became louder than the information provided, he continued to probe, pursue, and denounce.

Santerre's website was an exemplary initiative, one that should be remembered when, sooner or later, inevitably, other tragedies occur: it was a forum where victims could describe their anger, distress, or simple concerns to someone who would answer at any hour, and could do so feeling sure that they would not be judged – judged for

making mistakes, for instance, because sometimes the spelling was phonetic. "And that's what was so difficult," said Daniel Larochelle, the lawyer who launched the class action on behalf of the Mégantic victims. "Because when you had to fill out forms, it was complicated; it reopened wounds sometimes impossible to face. And also, how could people for whom writing was so intimidating be expected to write documents for the court? We lost a lot of people because of that."

Yes, like one young woman who never recovered after her house was brushed by the death-train, but who couldn't, and still can't, find the strength to fill out all those forms. Or like Yves Faucher, the author of the lines quoted above, who chose Facebook as a confidant. Faucher, a hero of Mégantic, was already a fragile individual before the tragedy; despite this, he plunged into the flames to rescue elderly people from a seniors' home. He was frightened, of course, for it was really terrifying. A few years later, Yves Faucher and his brother Gilles both fell victim to fentanyl overdoses. "Every time he spoke about the disaster," said his sister Lucy, "he'd tremble. He cried a lot."[160]

And then there was Yvon Ricard, the musician from the Musi-Café, who went on Facebook to explain how he couldn't continue living and to say a final goodbye. Of course, the Department of Public Health was there to help these tormented souls, and its workers on the ground were humane and supportive. But over the years a feeling of malaise set in – the malaise of "resilience." Barely perceptible at first, it was eventually like a stealthy infection that spread. "Resilience" became a watchword that the authorities, the town council, and the Department of Public Health had gradually appropriated and were trotting out at will. Resilience workshops, resilience seminars, conferences, books ... "Be resilient, become resilient, we are all resilient ... and get on with living!"

But resilience isn't for everyone. Not everyone has an equal capacity for it – nor can it be bought, or produced on order. When the lethal train struck, some people were living happily and enjoying perfect health, but others not so much – because of illness, difficulties in love, depression, or aging.

Resilience is capricious, as capricious as the oil on the river in its ability to envelop even the healthy in a deadly fog. And for all those who succumbed after July 6, for all those who still succumb,

the model of resilience that is held up to them makes them see them-selves as incapable, weak, or culpable. Their pain, which never leaves them, becomes a blemish on the public image of strength. Alone and ashamed, they retreat into silence. Resilience can be a dangerous word.

In 2017, BAPE hearings were held in Mégantic, with a chairperson, commissioners, experts, everyone. The purpose was to ascertain whether the region wanted a bypass railway line. While the towns-people's testimonies provided little hard data, they did contribute many personal stories, which mounted like a tide impossible to resist. "I attended a dozen funerals in succession, sir, me personally ..." Throughout three nights of hearings, more people than ever were unable to finish their testimonies and cut them short when overcome by emotion. One evening I saw a man reduced to tears – and he was a tragedy-hardened first responder.

Over the years, the Department of Public Health has collected statistics on the psychological state of the population. It did a fol-low-up, for that is its role. The Director of Public Health, Dr. Mélissa Généreux, discussed these statistics during a public relations cam-paign. In a spread across two pages of *Le Journal de Montréal*,[161] she explained that her department had used Mégantic as a model, a sort of template for disaster intervention. She announced that she was now travelling around the world, rushing to disaster scenes to apply her model, for she now knew what had to be done. Reading this Depart-ment of Public Health publicity leaves a bitter taste, as though the algorithm developed by health experts had been enough to siphon off the pain and distress of the people of Mégantic, transforming it into beautiful, coloured graphics that can be carted around from country to country, from conference to conference.

When Robert Bellefleur, a former worker in the Québec health network, asked publicly to see the graphics and model in order to find out what was being said around the world about his hometown, he came up against Dr. Généreux. She had him served a formal notice, demanding an immediate apology. (Bellefleur was well accustomed to this sort of thing, having previously received a similar admonition from the Order of Engineers for publishing photos of the damaged railway track behind his house.)

The most striking thing is that the work of the Department of

Public Health is far from over in Mégantic. Some of the survivors are still suffering, not receiving adequate support. Perhaps it is socially beneficial to share the model that was developed in the wake of the Mégantic disaster. But surely it is most important to continue reaching out to those townspeople who still find it difficult to cope and finally offer them the support they need.

✖ ✖ ✖

Pretty colours can be a temptation, whether in graphics or in photographs ...

One photographer took some striking pictures of the tragedy and assembled a remarkable exhibition of them. The cost of the huge prints was covered by a major Québec environmental group. (Here, a confession: the SVP asked the same group to pay for the printing of a leaflet to explain the pollution to the population of the town. That request was rejected.) On a spring morning, people from Mégantic came to Montréal for a media event, having been falsely led to believe that there would be a discussion of the disaster. With their minds elsewhere, they listened to a presentation of the summer programs of some environmental groups.

Facing them was an entire wall covered with enormous photographs of the most beautiful iridescent pink and blue oil on the surface of their river – pictures as lovely as Monet's. But how can a disaster be beautiful? How is it possible to approach it from an aesthetic angle? It turns out it's entirely possible: it all depends on the point of view one chooses, what side one is on. On the victims' side, for instance, there is heroism, generosity, and solidarity ... but no aestheticism. Disasters are hard, raw things.

✖ ✖ ✖

"'Well,' I told them, 'this has to stop, this foolishness.' I think there were others with unhealthy thoughts too." Jean Clusiault's voice rises. "We'd gone out to have a smoke on the porch of the funeral home. This young guy, I knew him, he was my nephew's buddy. Still young. What do you expect? Those young people had lost their friends in

the fire. And then they'd started down a slippery slope. You know, suicide, once it gets started ..."

Jean Clusiault was mourning the loss of his daughter Kathy, aged twenty-five, a beautiful young woman. Clusiault cherishes the last photos he has of her, in which her cousin captured her singing and dancing for the camera just a few months before the tragedy. Every day, Jean followed the trial of the three Mégantic accused, Thomas Harding, Richard Labrie, and their boss, Jean Demaître. Every day, for four months, including the interminable nine days before the verdict was delivered, he was there in court, listening.

"Why, Jean?"

"Because I wanted to learn the truth. Because until we know the truth, we'll never be able to find closure. We can't find closure until we feel justice has been done."

✖ ✖ ✖

"It must have been about 6 a.m. We'd spent part of the night being questioned in the Parthenais prison, and then they took us across to the south shore, to a cell in a police station. Around six o'clock, they told us: 'Get in. We're going to your trial in Mégantic.' Then our hearts failed us."

On May 12, 2014, Richard Labrie and Jean Demaître were summoned to the Parthenais Detention Centre, headquarters of the Sûreté du Québec, in Montréal. They went there eagerly. They had always insisted that they would collaborate with the investigation. It was a Monday morning. On the previous Friday, May 9, at 4 p.m., Mathieu Bouchard, in charge of the police investigation of the Mégantic disaster, was instructed by the Directeur des poursuites criminelles et pénales[162] that Harding was to be arrested. Over the weekend Bouchard, taken by surprise and running out of time, asked a judge for a warrant allowing him to enter a residence to make an arrest.

On the following Monday, May 12, Harding and his son were in the backyard of their home, repairing Harding's boat. Harding's lawyer, Thomas Walsh, was on vacation, but before his departure he had informed the SQ that if Harding was needed, they just had to "let him know" and he would come to their office. The arrest came

brutally, with no warning. The SWAT team, the anti-terrorist unit of the SQ, in combat dress and armed to the teeth, battered down the door. Rushing in, they found Harding behind the house and screamed at him and his son to lie down, hands behind their heads. It was an ugly picture: guns pointing at the two men lying prone on the ground, cuffs being placed on Harding's hands and ankles.

"Why did you decide to arrest Harding that day? What suddenly made it so urgent?" one of Harding's lawyers later asked Bouchard during the criminal trial. Bouchard cast a quick glance toward the crown attorneys seated in front of him.

"It wasn't my decision ... it was theirs."

Bouchard was visibly ill at ease.

"And why the SWAT team?"

"I was the one decided that. I was told that Harding had a gun and might be suicidal."

Harding, an enthusiastic hunter, had once owned some guns. However, he no longer had any in his possession, having turned them in to the SQ at the beginning of the proceedings.

No one could explain how or why, but on May 12 the media had been informed that Harding was to be arrested. They were ready and waiting when the SWAT team arrived, so that all of Québec would see the endlessly repeated image of a dangerous criminal being held on the ground and handcuffed, with guns pointing at his head. Someone, somewhere, wanted to offer the public an image of "Justice" arresting *the* culprit.

Even before the trial began, the guilty parties had been chosen. And the police investigation of the tragedy, as well as the conditions of the trial, were set up in such a way that only those three individuals, Harding, Labrie, and Demaître, could be considered.

✖ ✖ ✖

In the police van, on the way to Mégantic, we were suffocating. One of us threw up. When we stopped, when we understood we'd arrived, it was one of the worst moments in our lives. We could hear the crowd shouting outside, through the steel sides of the truck. Anyway,

that's what we imagined. We were going to have to face the families of the people our train had killed. And, quite rightly, they'd show us their pain and anger.

The three men agreed on the order in which they'd get out of the van. One of them was afraid, so the others would protect him. Harding got out first. The men's hands and feet were chained, making it difficult to step down. Again the image of the three men, dishevelled after a night's questioning and detention, would travel across Québec.

"And then suddenly, coming from the crowd, which was much less noisy than we thought, we heard people shouting: 'It's not them. They're not the guilty ones!'"

The show of force – the heavy-handed arrest and public exposure of the chained defendants – had been a big mistake on the part of the Québec and Canadian judicial apparatuses, which had focused entirely on those three individuals and no one else. The people had failed to react in the way the authorities had hoped.

✕ ✕ ✕

The criminal trial began on October 2, 2017. Fourteen men and women were chosen to be jurors. Twelve of them were expected to reach a unanimous verdict for each of the three men on forty-seven counts of criminal negligence causing death. From the start, limits had been imposed on the investigation. The only events allowed to be considered were those that transpired between noon on July 5 and 1:15 a.m. on July 6, 2013, and within those thirteen hours only – thirteen hours within which only the actions of the three accused could be scrutinized and included in the evidence. From the outset, any opportunity to demonstrate the responsibility of the entire system, involving MMA, CP, Transport Canada, and the regulatory system, was eliminated by this time frame. Those three were to be in the dock, and no one else.

The trial reflected the police investigation. Harding's lawyers claimed that the investigating officer, Sergeant Bouchard, who had tried to carry out a broader investigation, had been constantly reined in by his superiors. Finally, Bouchard had even been abruptly replaced

as the head of the investigation. The same happened to Steve Callaghan, a former TSB investigator and the SQ's expert. His mandate was steadily reduced until it, too, applied almost exclusively to the precise duration of the derailment.

Of course, no American, no MMA boss, would appear to testify. Most of the top bosses, safely tucked away behind the U.S. border, refused even to meet with Bouchard and his team when, after obtaining the various prior authorizations, they were able to travel to the U.S. Several police officers gave evidence at the trial of the three accused. That allowed some details of the investigation to emerge:

- On the morning of July 6, the MMA supervisors were the first to locate the locomotives, including the defective locomotive 5017. They had ample time, while alone in the cabin, to remove or tamper with the evidence, make copies of the black box, etc.
- During a search at MMA, computer specialists from the SQ, seeking to retrieve data, emails, and conversations, had to ask the MMA bosses in Maine for the password. They obtained one. But when they used it, the computer's cursor, to the stupefaction of the police, suddenly began to move across the screen by itself, erasing and/or modifying data on the hard drive.
- When they went to the United States to conduct their interrogations, the SQ investigators did not ask any questions about the polymer repairs to locomotive 5017, nor about the malfunctioning emergency brake systems, nor, especially, about the incriminating email from a superior instructing Harding not to apply the automatic brakes as a backup.
- There has never been an SQ investigation into the false labelling of the oil.
- Transport Canada representatives were always present as the investigation proceeded, as we have seen, and were allowed access to the train engineers' written statements.
- The written statements of the MMA locomotive engineers changed over time. At the request of his bosses, one of the

American supervisors from MMA met with all the drivers *before* they made their official statements to the police. "Some guys didn't answer well during the first interrogations," wrote one of the bosses. Therefore, before their next encounter with the police, the American Randy Stahl once again reminded drivers what they were supposed to say about the handbrake effectiveness tests.

Several times during the trial, counsel for one or other of the accused would ask for a stay of the proceedings against their client, arguing that there was insufficient evidence to convict. But the prosecution systematically refused to withdraw the charges, even when Judge Dumas declared, in a moment of impatience, that the evidence was very weak. "We have almost reached the end of the trial," Judge Dumas would even say, "and the jurors still do not know what may have caused the fire on locomotive 5017, in Nantes, preceding the derailment." But the hunt went on. Those three individuals were the quarry.

There were several worrying aspects about the conduct of the investigation. First, on too many occasions, people from MMA were allowed plenty of time to tamper with the data, with the evidence. Second, there was a concerning proximity of representatives of Transport Canada to the investigation; they were always on the scene, always informed of the evidence and about the documents related to the investigation, even though they themselves were directly involved in the tragedy – a notable example being the inspector Alain Richer. Finally, there was the obvious desire to avoid investigating anything apart from the actions of the three accused within that thirteen-hour time frame.

Is it possible that, in the corridors of power, in Québec City as in Ottawa, the investigators' independence was deliberately restricted? Were they purposefully denied the resources to carry out a criminal investigation on a scale appropriate to the forty-seven violent deaths? One thing is beyond doubt, as Charles Shearson, one of Thomas Harding's lawyers, asserted: the investigation had been conducted in a way that made it impossible to lay any charges against MMA. And in April 2018, the Crown abandoned any case against the company, citing a lack of evidence.

A lack of evidence, perhaps. But could it also be that some authorities, or indeed some individuals, feared that certain incriminating facts might come to light should MMA be put on trial? For instance, might the public have learned more about Burkhardt's and the railway lobby's contacts with the highest levels of the Ministry of Transport, perhaps even with the minister himself, about the use of single-person crews or any of the other issues, such as poorly maintained tracks, overloaded, overly long trains, and the mislabelling of dangerous goods? The investigation into Mégantic's tragedy leaves the strange impression that a lid had been clapped on a foul-smelling cesspool.

✕ ✕ ✕

Sometimes unusual visitors would be seen in the courtroom – for instance the employees of the Exceldor chicken-processing plant, members of the Teamsters Union, who took a day off from work at their own expense and, wanting to support Harding and Labrie, workers like themselves, hand-drew them a postcard saying: "You are not the ones responsible."

This was one clue among many that should have alerted the judicial and political authorities. The people were not deceived by the spectacle staged for their benefit.

✕ ✕ ✕

December 2017

In a room in the Sherbrooke courthouse that day, a storm was brewing – an indoor storm. For several hours, the silent courtroom listened to the recordings, one after the other, of the disaster as it was captured by the MMA recorders between July 5 and 6, 2013, recordings of Harding, Labrie, and the police.

Harding, as always, maintained an inscrutable mask. People who knew him a little better knew that the ordeal was putting his health under strain. At the back of the courtroom sat his brother, who never missed a session during the two years. Labrie, staring directly ahead, made sure that his gaze never came to rest on anyone, not on the

jurors, nor on the spectators. At the front was his daughter, providing unwavering support.

Also in the courtroom were relatives of victims, including Jean Clusiault, who listened, minute by minute, to the events that had led to the death of his beloved Kathy. As the telephone conversations continued, some of us, in our concern, would cast him a sidelong glance to make sure he was okay.

The judge decreed a recess, perhaps because this barrage of phone calls was difficult to listen to. The tragedy paused for a few minutes. Then what seemed an infinite moment occurred in the courtroom. The accused looked anxiously toward the victims' family members. Whether or not they were guilty in the eyes of the law, in that moment they felt guilty. Everyone, the accused and the spectators, was paralyzed. Then, suddenly Jean Clusiault got up and went over to Harding. He led him out of the courtroom into the harsh light of the media cameras outside. Then the father reached out to the accused man and shook his hand. This image would be captured on camera and shown all over the media: the bereaved father shaking hands with the man accused of his daughter's death.

"I consider this man my friend. He's no different from us, he was just trying to earn his living," said Jean Clusiault.

✕ ✕ ✕

The jury's deliberations lasted nine days, nine difficult days. "My client is done for," murmured one lawyer. "I'm very worried about Tom and Richard," Jean Clusiault kept repeating as the days of waiting passed one by one.

The verdict finally came on Friday, January 19, 2018, in the afternoon: "not guilty" for all three accused. "Forty-seven dead and no one to blame," read the headline in Le Journal de Montréal. Like the authorities, Le Journal de Montréal failed to understand the feelings of the general population at the time. Even in Mégantic the verdict brought relief, but also a surge of anger – though the anger was directed at the system rather than at the acquittal of the three men.

"They take us for idiots. For halfwits," said Jean Clusiault, expressing what many people were thinking. "From the very start they've

been trying to make us swallow the idea that those three were the only ones to blame. That's not so. We can't accept that. And one day the truth will have to come out, if justice is to be done – really be done."

"So you didn't get answers to your questions, Jean, during the trial?" I asked.

"No, I didn't."

× × ×

The lawyers for the prosecution and criminal investigation officers met with the victims' families after the acquittal. They explained to them, or attempted to, that the sole cause of their tragedy was the fact that one man, Harding, failed to apply enough brakes – Harding, who had recognized his responsibility and whose only public statement would be an apology to the families and friends of the victims.

The fact remains that the spectacles of the SWAT team and the learned legal deliberations would fail to overcome people's feelings. Even in Mégantic, people would not be satisfied by the offer of a few scapegoats instead of the real culprits. To this day, the real culprits remain invisible.

REBIRTH

Death doesn't win. Death won't win.

—Father Steve Lemay, parish priest of
Mégantic at the time of the tragedy

HOW IS IT POSSIBLE TO PICK UP THE THREAD OF LIFE AGAIN when everything has been destroyed? Is it possible ever to be as carefree as before? How can one look for rebirth?

First, we must never forget those we have lost. Each year in Mégantic, they have tried to pay tribute to the victims. Of course it is impossible to thwart death, but we can try to remember life, their lives, in a hundred ways – with candles, wind chimes, Masses, fir trees, and sculptures. In 2017, it was stuffed toys: forty-seven of them placed symbolically on the railway track – it was Gilles Fluet's idea, but he finally found it so painful that one November evening he got rid of them.

But life goes on. Five years later, Gilles, Jean and the others have different ideas. First among them is that bypass line which, from the very first morning, everyone was calling for – the doctors, the parish priest, the businesspeople, the town council, and of course the townspeople: "In the end, it can't go on. How can you recover when the train keeps on going through, loaded with propane? When I was reading the funeral service, at the burials of the last victims, the train whistled, it even interrupted my prayers. That's intolerable," Father Lemay exclaimed emotionally.

In terms of railway safety nothing, or almost nothing, has changed since the disaster, not in Mégantic, nor elsewhere, as is shown by the fatal incident above Field, British Columbia, on February 4, 2019. In 2020, it is still up to townspeople and Canadians everywhere to keep watch over the operations of the trains, some of them as lethal as bombs, that travel through their communities.

Since the beginning, Robert, Gilles, Gilbert, Richard, Jacques,

and the others have formed a coalition of citizens to fight for rail safety in Mégantic and have fought with remarkable persistence to finally obtain those fifteen kilometres of railway line that are so long overdue. They have harried and challenged Transport Canada. They have met all the premiers and the foremost elected officials – without exception. Working to serve their fellow citizens, they have refused to throw in the towel. The railway bypass around Mégantic did finally materialize, though in a way that was far from ideal – indeed it was catastrophic, a further disaster in two respects, namely the choice of route and the funding.

Where the route was concerned, Transport Canada – at whose request? CMQR's? – chose a path that required the expropriation of several dozen properties, as if the people of the town had not already undergone enough expropriations and demolitions of houses. And although the adopted route made little sense, any alternative suggestions that would have limited the impact were rejected out of hand by Minister Garneau. The considerations underlying his refusal remain mysterious to this day.

The funding and planning of the bypass line were definitely related to the upcoming Québec election on October 1, 2018, and to the need for the major Canadian political parties to facilitate the conveyance of oil from Western Canada. Huge quantities of crude remain trapped in Alberta, the price of oil has collapsed, taking the Alberta economy with it. Since the opposition to pipelines and other conveyance of petroleum is so ferocious in British Columbia, the only fast route to seaports is to the east, through Québec. But Québec has only two train lines leading to the coast, by way of Mégantic or along the lower Saint Lawrence. It was therefore necessary, before oil trains could again travel through Mégantic, to offer the citizens a few "goodies."

Nothing could be clearer than the announcement made on May 11, 2018. According to the Transport Canada website, the federal government was to cover 60 percent of the $133 million cost, while the other 40 percent would come from the government of Québec. And it was announced that the project would be under the direction of CMQR, which would own the bypass.* If MMA had wanted the railway to be

---

* CMQR, we remember, was owned by Fortress Investment Group LLC, which had $70 billion under its management in 2016.

rebuilt at the expense of the town, its successor, CMQR, had achieved this, in spades!

And even better was to come, for in the fall of 2019, it was learned that CMQR was offering to sell its line, which it had bought for $17 million, for $100 million – including, of course, the brand-new bypass line, built to measure to the company's specifications. It has just been acquired for an undisclosed sum by CP – which has so far failed to acknowledge any responsibility whatsoever for the Mégantic disaster.

But perhaps there is also another – more sinister – reason for the sudden haste with which the railway bypass was announced. The people of Mégantic had been clamouring for a much-needed commission of inquiry into the tragedy to finally shed light on the role of Transport Canada and the rail lobbies, as well as to review the current state of the laws and regulations. And that was not to everyone's liking. In Ottawa, Marc Garneau firmly closed the door on any such inquiry. He announced that surveillance cameras would be installed in the driver's cabins, thus acquiescing to an insistent demand from the rail lobby, which wanted to monitor its employees. Garneau added that all the necessary investigations into the tragedy had been carried out, and that the people of Mégantic were going to get their bypass line. A commission of inquiry, he insisted, would serve no further purpose.

The minister, the authorities, and the lobbies have seriously underestimated the people of Mégantic. For them, their fight to bring the whole truth into the light of day is essential to their healing and their rebirth. Furthermore, they have assumed the responsibility of ensuring that as few people as possible die in Canada as a result of inadequate safety precautions on our railways. Their fight will succeed because they are stoic, determined – and stubborn. Stubbornness in such matters is a guarantee of success, as was demonstrated by the unshakeable determination of the coalition demanding a rail bypass.

Further proof is the fact that the only people who succeeded in recovering their land in Mégantic and rebuilding on the shores of the large lake were Geneviève Boulanger and Miroslav Chum, who fought on every front. "They never let city hall off the hook, never.

And they won," one person in Mégantic told me, wearing an undeniable smile of pride.

× × ×

Fighting against an enemy influenced by rapacious lobbies and defeating the immoral forces of greed is one thing – but fighting in your home, in your own community, too? That is a difficult, heartbreaking undertaking. What occurred in Mégantic itself – the reconstruction that brought harm to so many people – is a chapter of the tragedy that no one wants to write. People would rather simply bury it with as little fuss as possible, as if it had never happened. But something more needs to be said to prevent similar mistakes from being repeated elsewhere.

Even more importantly, shining a harsh light on these events might help the people of Mégantic to find peace, renew their bonds, and rebuild together. And maybe it is the role of an outsider, of someone who can see, make revelations, and then depart the scene, to bear the odious burden of making certain revelations. When a catastrophe of such terrible magnitude strikes, the local elected officials, trapped in the maelstrom like everyone else, hear contradictory messages. Their citizens, who expect a great deal from them, may want quick fixes on the one hand, but on the other hand they want every action to be carefully considered before it is taken. Because of this dilemma, mistakes are made. Vultures move in. The desire to move on leads to an irremediable disaster.

The highest authorities, national governments, do have a supportive role to play. However, they cannot replace the local leaders, who must rebuild a home that is truly a home, not a factitious imposition of the vision of others. But apart from the obvious obligation to supply logistical and financial support, how can a community immersed in an overwhelming disaster best be supported? Perhaps – and this applies to everyone – by admitting the human factor, how human beings behave when brutally confronted by an unimaginable reality.

First, it is necessary for the local elected representatives to recognize their own vulnerability, for they are no less overwhelmed than those who elected them. It is a vulnerability that prevents them from

bringing a cool head to their deliberations and leaves them feeling overcome in the face of adversity. This feeling, intensified by the urgency of the decisions they must make, drives them to retrench, to defend themselves, to erect a wall of secrecy, and to open the door only to individuals who seem to provide a reassuring presence and are therefore enlisted as advisers, but who actually put their own interests first.

Might there be a way, in such circumstances, to avoid this trap by automatically appointing, subject to the approval of the community itself, one or two wise persons, elder statespersons for example, with unimpeachable records and experience? While not themselves acting as decision-makers, these sages could help to recognize and reject the inevitable predators. They could follow the reconstruction effort, acting as the much-needed advisers required by the elected officials. Thanks to their detachment, they could bring indispensable, impartial, and perhaps even technical expertise to dealing with a crisis, while leaving the elected officials to carry out their proper duties and make the ultimate decisions.

When someone is in shock – after a diagnosis of cancer, for instance – the brain mobilizes its own defence mechanisms. It fails to follow instructions, to take the logical steps that are required, to adhere to the proper order of things. A more detached guide is able, gently and tactfully, to restore order to the disorder. Maybe it could work the same way for an organism as alive as a community in a state of shock. Anyone who got to know the people of Mégantic – and the reports of the INSPQ are eloquent in this respect – could see that the frustration of the townspeople had gelled around the "Réinventer la ville" consultations. They felt, essentially, that they were being duped by a process that had been hijacked to suit the special interests of a few individuals. The townspeople repeated tirelessly that everything had been settled in advance. They felt their town was being stolen from them – quite a shattering admission of the failure of citizen involvement in what was a (perhaps overly) well-funded and well-organized initiative.

This brings us back to the essential problem: the problem of trust, for it is all a matter of trust. And, in the case of Mégantic, the process was clearly perverted by a lack of neutrality. When that happens, the

only solution may be to entrust such a public consultation exercise to some outside agency recognized both for its objectivity (an absolute priority) and for its expertise. This agency – which cannot be just any organization, however well intentioned – must be able to demonstrate clearly that things have not been decided in advance. In addition, it must have the authority to call to order anyone who breaks the rules. Finally, it must accept responsibility for its decisions and actions. It could be a retired judge, or an organization devoted to consulting the public in the public's own interest.

Finally, there remains the thorny issue of the expropriations and demolitions, the massive destruction. Again, it is essential to recognize the nature of the beast. The bulldozing of a neighbourhood inevitably creates incurable wounds. The demolition of houses and a community's landmark buildings should be, it must be emphasized, a tool of last resort. When a government grants a municipality – especially one in a state of shock – a weapon as powerful as Bill 57, it must be accompanied by watchdogs from outside the community. The destiny of vulnerable townspeople cannot be entrusted to a few local elected officials, nor can the latter be granted the power of life or death over large parts of their community. The risk of serious missteps is evident.

But we must go further. It must never be forgotten that the vulnerable townspeople of Mégantic lacked any process for an appeal or for arbitration. They were isolated and kept in ignorance. To remedy such vulnerability, surely any procedure of the kind should include a formal obligation to ensure that anyone facing expropriation has the benefit of independent legal advice. Such a measure was included – albeit imperfectly – in the new Québec law governing mining activities, ensuring that anyone facing expropriation is entitled to free legal advice completely devoted to that person's best interests – a fundamental principle lacking which myriad abuses will continue to occur.

✖ ✖ ✖

Years later, the sight of the former town centre was still heartbreaking, with only a few scattered buildings remaining in a place where the vibrant heart of a greatly beloved town once beat, with a few buildings overly modern in style and lacking any real character. All this is so

gloomy, distressing, and destabilizing ... It is possible to find something positive to say? May we ask Monsieur le Curé if a happy ending is possible to what seems a never-ending tragedy?

> In Mégantic, in Sainte-Agnès Church, interminably, month after month, day after day, there were funerals. The funerals of disaster victims, but normal funerals too, of people in the community ... and occasionally a baptism, but always funerals ... endlessly ...
>
> The choir, the members of the choir, would arrive early in the morning. At noon I would have sandwiches brought up to them where they were, so they hardly needed to leave. They sang and sang, were always present ... They showed strength, incredible determination, they found a way, their own way, to support their people. Everyone needed them. And they needed everyone. In that way, completely bonded together, we were able to get through.
>
> The people of Mégantic will soon come together again, unite again, be as one again. They built this town and it is the loveliest, with its big lake. They'll rediscover their strengths and reinvent their town, reinvent their lives.
>
> Death will not win. Nor will despair.
>
> —Father Steve Lemay

✕ ✕ ✕

At every memorial event I have witnessed for the past five years, at the very moment when the church bells are tolling and everyone is afraid of breaking down, I still get the overwhelming feeling that for once, I am finally among genuine human beings, among hearts that are as one, without any protective shell. The strong support the weak, knowing that one day it will be the other way round. And when I think about it, the years I have spent with the people of Mégantic have afforded me those rare moments when life is worthwhile, truly worth living. They have also proved to me that human beings are

more than predators who infest the planet, and that humanity is stronger than evil.

On the day of the verdict, Richard Labrie stroked the photograph of a two-year-old boy, his grandson. Jean Clusiault held up a photo of a tiny person, just a few hours old, his first granddaughter, another symbol of a victory beyond price. And today noisy youngsters emerge, rowdy and full of uproarious laughter, from Montignac high school, where just a few years ago everyone was prostrate with grief.

Kathy Clusiault believed in life. Just before the tragedy, she and her sister wrote this in their last birthday card to their father:

> You taught me this:
>
>> To do my best
>> To follow my dreams
>> To overcome my fears
>> To believe in the future, in life
>> To believe in myself, and most importantly,
>> Learn to forgive myself
>
> Thank you, Dad

I know that some people will continue to suffer for a long time. But for once, atheist though I am, I want to believe the priest. Death will not win.

AFTERWORD

> You give us purpose to pursue justice and accountability for you. I want to assure all families and all Canadians we will not rest until there are answers.
>
> > —Justin Trudeau, Prime Minister of Canada, speaking at the ceremony in memory of the victims of the Ukrainian International Airlines Flight 752 crash of January 12, 2020, when he stated his intention of exerting pressure on the Iranian authorities

THE BOMBS THAT BRUSH PAST OUR HOUSES AND VILLAGES ALL across Canada at eighty kilometres per hour have continued to increase in number since 2013. So the question arises: Seven years after Mégantic, have we learned anything? Are the tracks safe? Has anything actually changed on the part of the predators and the government?

"Yes," repeats ad nauseam the Minister of Transport, Marc Garneau, for whom all the lessons of Mégantic have been learned, the DOT-111 tank cars are being replaced by the allegedly much stronger DOT-117s, and "Railway safety has always been my priority."[163]

Really?

Where the predators, hedge-fund managers, shareholders, and companies are concerned, we might as well give up all hope, as Peter A. DeFazio, the U.S. House Committee on Transportation and Infrastructure chairman, pointed out, the United States railway system has fallen into the hands of "the jackals on Wall Street ... Only if there's an absolutely catastrophic accident that bankrupts a railroad will they care about it, but short of that, they don't give a damn."[164]

If this is so, then the role of governments must be to protect the public, to prevent the inevitable deaths, and to seek explanations and justice when they occur. But do they? There is no need to cite the history of the seven years following the Mégantic disaster to answer

that question. An account of recent events within four short months, between December 2019 and March 2020, will suffice.

On **December 9, 2019**, near Guernsey, Saskatchewan, on Treaty 6 Indigenous Lands,* a CP train derails; thirty-three tank cars of crude oil derail, pile up, and are breached, setting alight one of the by-now-emblematic columns of fire and smoke visible from kilometres around. The choking residents of the nearby town are evacuated in haste. The fire would burn for over twenty-four hours. Nineteen of the new and supposedly stronger DOT-117s had been breached,† and one and a half million litres of crude petroleum had flowed into the fields. Later, CP would reassure farmers that the company would "implement a soil-remediation plan based on the tests being done by its environmental experts."[165] The accident had blocked other rail traffic carrying petroleum and grain, so CP was in a hurry to reopen the lines.

@MarcGarneau assured the public that he was following the situation closely: he had, he said, designated a "ministerial observer" and would continue to prioritize safety.

On **February 6, 2020**, near Guernsey, Saskatchewan (again!), thirty-two tank cars out of 104 derailed and caught fire. Another evacuation was necessary; 1.2 million litres of crude escaped, and the fire burned for several days. "That's strange," people wondered, since before these two derailments, railway employees had spent six months repairing the track.

@MarcGarneau again reassured the public that he was "following [the incident] closely." "I cannot compromise on safety and will not hesitate to take further action as is necessary ... Rail safety remains my top priority,"‡ he repeated.

---

* the Treaty 6 First Nations on this spot are: Niitsítapi ᑏᑊᒍᐧᑐ (a.k.a. Blackfoot), Métis, nēhiyaw ᑐ�"ᐃᐞᐤ (Plains Cree), Očhéthi Šakówiŋ (Sioux), and Anishinaabe ᐊᓂᔑᐋᐧᐯᐧ (Ojibwe).

† The "new" DOT-117s are often merely "retrofitted DOT-111s," and are not strong enough to take the weight and speed of present-day trains. In Canada, as in the United States, the latest derailments have shown their fragility.

‡ Marc Garneau (@MarcGarneau), "I've asked my officials to examine all issues related to these accidents to determine if additional safety measures will be required," Twitter, February 6, 2020, 12:25 p.m., twitter.com/MarcGarneau/status/1225516002781417474.

Marilyn Bieber, who lives less than five hundred metres from the accident site, exclaimed, "Another derailment and so close to Guernsey! ... What the heck is going on?"[166]

On **February 6**, the day of the derailment, Minister Garneau issued a ministerial order: trains carrying hazardous goods had to travel more slowly. Trains hauling more than twenty tank cars containing dangerous goods, which normally travelled at sixty-four kilometres per hour in metropolitan areas and eighty kilometres per hour elsewhere, were required to reduce their speed by half. These reductions were supposed to be applied for one month, according to the same ministerial order. However, on **February 17, 2020**, just ten days later, Minister Garneau backtracked: the former speed limits were restored, including those applying to trains hauling dangerous goods. "The department said it made the changes *after ... consulting industry*," confirmed Sean Finn, CN Rail's executive vice-president of corporate services. "The company has been in discussions with the federal government since the initial order was made on February 6. *We* were capable of explaining to the official Transport Canada [*sic*] why *we* felt our railway was safe with our signal technology and *we* thought that was the right outcome," Finn explained[167] (my emphases).

On **February 19, 2020**, scarcely two days after the ministerial U-turn, yet another train carrying petroleum was derailed, this time close to Emo, Ontario, on Treaty 3 Territory near the Ojibwe Rainy River First Nation. "The train that derailed and spilled crude oil [was] travelling at a speed that would have been prohibited just two days earlier."[168] Nor was this the first derailment in the region: "Fort Frances town council earlier this week passed a resolution, expressing concern about the number of derailment incidents in the Rainy River District and calling on provincial and federal officials to investigate the frequency of derailments."[169] In fact, this derailment was the sixth to occur in the region since 2013. @MarcGarneau did not comment on this derailment.

Since **February 12, 2020**, demonstrators from First Nations such as the Kanien'kehá:ka (Mohawk) Nation on the East Coast and the Wet'suwet'en Nation on the West Coast have been blocking railway lines across the country, attracting a great deal of media attention. The entire government and judicial system was mobilized against the

demonstrators in order to end an interruption of railway service that threatened the economy. "I am calling for all Canadians to respect the Railway Safety Act," declared Minister Garneau.[170] Ironically, however, it was under the provisions of that very law that, all in the space of six years, in Mégantic and elsewhere, fifty-two deaths have occurred, twenty-nine children have been orphaned, and a little town has been destroyed.

In these circumstances, the derailment of February 19, in Emo, Ontario, went almost unremarked. "How many derailments are going to happen in the same forty kilometres of track ... before governments start asking CN some serious questions about safety?" wondered Emo town councillor Douglas Judson. "I'm asking for some public engagement on the topic of rail safety, and some inquiry from governments into the pattern of events or at least the frequency of them."[171] The citizens of Emo are asking for "some inquiry," like those of Mégantic, who for the past seven years have been calling for an independent, credible commission of inquiry to investigate the causes of their tragedy.

In early **February 2020**, a similar request, demanding that some light be cast on their drama, was formulated by the parents of the three victims of the February 4, 2019 accident at Field, BC. But this time the request – a heartbreaking one – took a special turn when a call for witnesses to come forward under the protection of anonymity, in order to forestall any possible reprisals against the employees, was issued by the parents of the accident victims. "One year after a Canadian Pacific Rail derailment in Field, BC, that killed three men, families of two of the victims are asking CP employees who may have information about what happened to speak out ... 'I want to say to those who are afraid to come forward, it *may be possible to do it anonymously*'" (my emphases), urged the mother of one of the victims.[172]

A year after the loss of their children, father, and partners, the families were, in fact, losing any faith in the possibility of an official, independent, exhaustive inquiry. A report by the CBC program *The Fifth Estate*, televised at the end of January 2020, had just revealed that CP itself had carried out the inquiry into this disaster involving CP itself – and that the same CP had concluded that there were no grounds to lay any charges against ... CP.[173]

"How can a company investigate themselves?" asked Albert

Bulmer, father of one of the victims. How can they be allowed to find no one was at fault, when the train ended up as a heap of metal, when it had been parked at the top of a much steeper gradient than at Mégantic, with no handbrake applied, when the weather and conditions were terrible?

There is a simple explanation: "I was ordered to stop investigating," said Mark Tataryn, one of three officers from the CP Police assigned to inquire into the derailment. This is what he told CBC's *The Fifth Estate*, adding that his employers prevented him from obtaining access to key witnesses, audio recordings, and other resources. "I would say it was some type of cover-up. I believe it's an injustice," he confided to the journalists. Tataryn became suspicious when files began to disappear from the computer system of the CP Police.* "Those files were removed. I replaced them on two occasions. On yet the third occasion, I went back to look, they were gone," Tataryn said. "I was suspicious … and sort of took other steps to safeguard information, because I knew that it would likely not be available in the future."

Tataryn, today an RCMP officer, submitted his information to the RCMP and the TSB, and in early February made a public demand for an independent inquiry conducted by the RCMP. This demand was immediately supported by Don Crawford, chief of the TSB investigation into the Field disaster, who also stated publicly that the RCMP should step in to investigate potential negligence by the railway company. "There is enough to suspect there's negligence here, and it needs to be investigated by the proper authority."[174]

On **February 4, 2020**, the very day that he called for this intervention by the RCMP, Don Crawford was punished: "The Transportation Safety Board of Canada has demoted its lead investigator in the probe of the crash, stripping him of his title as investigator in charge, after deciding his comments to CBC News about the case were 'completely inappropriate,'" reported the CBC. According to CBC News, Crawford would no longer be in charge of the Field investigation.[175]

---

* The investigation described by Tataryn bears some striking similarities to the one into the Mégantic disaster conducted by the SQ: the disappearance of computer files, an order not to investigate anything apart from the conduct of the three employees and not that of the company or the authorities, the manipulation of key witnesses by the company, the non-involvement of the RCMP, and so on.

On **March 6, 2020**, a further CBC investigation[176] revealed that only the private police of CN and CP conduct investigations into derailments and fatalities, and that this has been the case for at least twenty years. Public police forces, such as the RCMP, are not involved.* This included the uninvestigated deaths of Jamie Jijian, an employee killed in 2012 in a CP marshalling yard in Regina, Saskatchewan, and of Kevin Timmerman, killed three years later in a CN marshalling yard in Saskatoon, Saskatchewan. "If it was a traffic accident or a murder or anything like that, the RCMP within Canada would investigate it, and there's reports, and there is accountability to everybody, right?" asked Lori Desrochers, Timmerman's former spouse. "Here you've got a police force that's paid by a company. Well of course they're not going to call out their employer," she said. "When it comes to fatalities, the RCMP should be involved."[177] To the best of my knowledge, no blame – not for criminal or any other kind of negligence, or anything else – has been attributed in the past decade to a railway company for a death or for environmental damage.

Minister Garneau did not respond to the CBC journalists' request for an interview on this matter. But this determination to stifle any investigation did have the merit of opening our eyes. It made us wonder what the companies and governments were so eager to hide. An individual error? Some failure by an employee? No. To arouse such a need for a smokescreen, the truth had to be much more serious, much more crucial.

Only very little investigation was required to discover that railway safety laws and regulations are entirely at the mercy of the companies; they are left free to do whatever they like and are monitored only by themselves: the legislative and political system is broken. But there is worse: the equipment itself is broken. Rails, wagons, locomotives, and tank cars are unfit for the use that companies now make of them in order to maximize profits. The new unit trains transporting dangerous goods – sometimes as much as five kilometres long in the United

* In Mégantic, the SQ carried out an investigation, since MMA was a small independent company with no private police, unlike CN and CP. The SQ investigation, which was partially exposed during the employees' trial, was perplexing in many respects. The RCMP was never seen in Mégantic. According to one source, its investigators, who came on the scene shortly after the accident, were recalled almost immediately.

States – are too heavy for our railway tracks, and travel too fast for them. This is even more the case in the context of extreme climatic events that modify the terrain.

The simple truth is that the tracks and wagons are inadequate for the job they have to do. The tank cars are too fragile to convey explosive products in huge quantities. They can be repaired, patched up, the ballasts replaced, etc., but the more strongly welded tank cars still rupture. And the rail system's foundation – the tracks – remains the same. And those tracks date from the last century. The companies have "let go" the majority of the well-trained inspection and repair workforce; train drivers have been replaced by technology. But all the technology in the world – the magic credo and lure of an industry that dreams of running its trains and carrying out inspections via high tech, with no employees – doesn't seem to be enough. More and more, the basic machinery goes off the rails.

So it is also this fundamental error of using equipment in ways that are dangerous and beyond its capabilities which has to be concealed from the public. This explains the reluctance to hold a public inquiry; the mechanical, legislative, and regulatory inadequacies have to remain hidden from the public. Yet the new strategy to increase shareholder profit relies precisely on the principle of longer, heavier, faster, while cutting all that can possibly be dispensed with: training, repairs, staff. Here is a classic conflict of interest: Which should come first, safety or profits? Government, at least for the time being, seems to have chosen; profits are all-important.

In its defence, there is no denying that the economy has been built (by the very people who profit from it) in such a way that the slightest delay in deliveries can lead an industry to collapse. Elected officials feel they are in a Catch-22 situation. Unless they bow to the needs of large companies, the economic wheels will stop turning, they think. Are casualties and other kinds of damage to communities merely the price to be paid for our "just-in-time" economy?

But deaths caused by runaway trains are not inevitable. Yet one might even think that, unofficially, they are actually sanctioned. How can a train of 104 cars, with malfunctioning brakes, hold at the top of a 2.2 percent slope at −30 °C without a handbrake being applied? The answer is simple: it can't. Elected officials must put the protection of

human lives above all else, and do so by concrete action, not merely profess to do so.

Because there *are* solutions, as long as there is a willingness to consider and apply them. The application of handbrakes on gradients is an obvious one, even if it means a company must accept that a few hours will be spent walking through snow to apply them. And that, perhaps, an additional crew member will be required. And that yes, profits will be a little lower.

Furthermore, isn't it the bearing capacity of the track that should determine the weight of the trains, rather than the reverse? Isn't it also obvious that speeds must be reduced? (Indeed Minister Garneau did reduce them, but then backed down.) Shouldn't the length, weight, and speed of trains be compatible with the technical capacity of the rails? And should that capacity not be calculated by extremely competent and independent government engineers, free of any input or influence from the railway lobby? Three trains of fifty tank cars, well inspected, will deliver the same amount of petroleum or sulphuric acid as a unit train of 150 cars. Of course it is true that dividend to shareholders might be affected ...

But it is also a fact that the deaths, pollution, and destruction will continue until the day when our elected representatives choose safety and human lives over the profitability of companies. It is a matter of moral choice. The rest is incidental. The rest, including the economy, will adjust and adapt.

Can ordinary citizens, who tirelessly demand changes and responses, finally make their voices heard, and influence decisions? It is true that after six years of struggle, letters, petitions, demonstrations, interventions, simply asking for a commission of inquiry to be held, without any result, hope fades. Is it possible for us to have even minimal control over our safety? To have the ear of our elected officials on matters that are far from revolutionary? Is there no one who will just listen to us anymore? Who will see us? It is true we are gifted with a stubborn persistence in combat. Yes, we are trying to build a more powerful citizenry with greater electoral weight than that of the companies that suffocate us. Solidarity, action, activism are the key words here. The solution is political, and will always be political.

But elected officials must consider the possible consequences of

their rigid positions, of the deaf ear they turn to the fears, questions, and suffering of their citizens. If citizens always come up against a blank wall when voicing their most basic demands concerning what is most precious to them, namely the protection and well-being of their family, what alternative remains for them to finally make themselves heard? Our patience is being worn down.

✗ ✗ ✗

I close with some news of Mégantic.

After the initial shock, followed by the razing of their town centre, the townspeople's pains were not over. Firstly, the bypass, a token of healing, caused a lot of anger: the route chosen by Transport Canada, applying the criteria of the railway company, travels through the heart of populated areas, forcing further expropriations. A very similar route, just five hundred metres farther on, would have gone through the forest, causing minimal disturbance. No official explanation has been provided.

Secondly, Hydro-Québec planned the passage of a huge 735-kilovolt line through the very heart of one small part of town that remained intact.[178] Hydro-Québec withdrew its project after some stupefied, angry members of the public discovered this by chance.

Then citizens learned, again by chance, that the air they breathe is contaminated with arsenic emitted by Mégantic's biggest employer, Tafisa, a multinational company. And, yet again by chance, it was learned that one solution proposed by the authorities was the creation of a hazardous waste incinerator in Mégantic. This incinerator, like its peers, will only be profitable if it imports hazardous waste from elsewhere: Mégantic as the trash can of others.

In 2019, we also learned that the drinking water was contaminated with benzene[179] – information based on a simple laboratory error, according to city officials, who have provided no evidence in support of this claim.

The old town centre, still scarred by the railroad tracks, remains quite deserted, for none of the major projects have yet materialized, including that of a sensible hotel project to replace L'Eau Berge, the uncontaminated Victorian gem bulldozed after the disaster.

In the summer of 2019, on the terrace of the Musi-Café, citizens would demonstrate some bitter humour to visitors: "Breathe the fresh air of Mégantic, savour a Scotch with crystal-clear water, and admire from your – future – hotel room, the oil-unit petroleum train heading down the slope toward you ..."[180]

Robert Bellefleur continues his unrelenting struggle. He has become an ace in activist documentation, has bought himself a drone, checks the state of his lake when diving, and harasses all the ministers responsible with his smiling persistence.

In the fall of 2019, Jean Clusiault walked one thousand kilometres of the pilgrimage route to Santiago de Compostela, fulfilling a promise to his daughter Kathy. He now plays the loving granddad to his beloved granddaughter.

Richard Labrie has returned to work in a completely different field. He has been able to recover a measure of serenity. He and Jean Clusiault have become close friends.

In the fall of 2019, Thomas Harding was finally absolved of all charges against him, allowing him the opportunity to recover a little from his trauma.

Gilles Fluet has found a smile. He continues the fight: it gives him a reason to live, he says.

Lawyer Daniel Larochelle fights fiercely against CP to try to make them pay for what they did to his fellow citizens.

Yannick Gagné and his Musi-Café warmly await you on the sun-drenched terrace on which extraordinary musicians perform, as they always have.

—ANNE-MARIE SAINT-CERNY
March 2020

ABBREVIATIONS

AAR   Association of American Railroads

BAPE   Bureau d'audiences publiques sur l'environnement (an independent panel established by government to study projects liable to have a major impact on the environment or any other question related to the quality of the environment)

BLEVE   Boiling Liquid Expanding Vapour Explosion

CAMEO   Comité d'aménagement et de mise en œuvre (the committee in charge of Lac-Mégantic's reconstruction, planning initiatives and awarding contacts)

CAW   Canadian Auto Workers (CAW, merged with the Communications, Energy and Paperworkers Union of Canada in 2013 to form Unifor)

CMQR   Central Maine and Quebec Railway

CN   Canadian National Railway

CP   Canadian Pacific Railway

ECRC   Eastern Canada Response Corporation (a private management company, owned by several of the major Canadian oil companies, whose role is to provide marine oil spill response services, when requested, "to the 'responsible party,' the Canadian Coast Guard, or to any other Government Lead Agency")

INSPQ   Institut national de santé publique du Québec (the Québec Institute of Public Health)

MDDEP   Ministère du Développement durable, de l'Environnement et des Parcs (the Ministry of Sustainable Development, the Environment, and Parks; later called the Ministry of Sustainable Development, Environment, and Fight against Climate Change)

MMA   Montreal, Maine and Atlantic Railway

SAQ   Société des alcools du Québec (the provincial Crown

corporation responsible for the sale of alcoholic beverages in Québec)

SMS   Safety Management Systems

SQ   Sûreté du Québec (the Québec provincial police)

SVP   Société pour vaincre la pollution (an NGO devoted to combating pollution)

TAQ   Tribunal administratif du Québec (the Administrative Tribunal of Québec, which hears appeals resulting from administrative decisions made by government departments, government bodies, commissions, municipalities, and health and social services establishments, and whose decisions cannot generally be appealed to another court)

TC   Transport Canada

TSB   Transportation Safety Board of Canada

UPAC   Unité permanente anti-corruption (the Québec anti-corruption unit)

ENDNOTES

1 Anne-Marie Saint-Cerny, *Mégantic, un démo* (2017), 11 min., vimeo.com /189057742.

2 Boucar Diouf, "Des hyènes et des hommes" [Of hyenas and humans], *La Presse*, September 13, 2014, www.lapresse.ca/debats/nos-collaborateurs /boucar-diouf/201409/12/01-4799736-des-hyenes-et-des-hommes.php.

3 Naomi Klein, *The Shock Doctrine: The Rise of Disaster Capitalism* (Toronto, ON: Vintage Canada, 2008).

4 Regional Office of the Centre de contrôle environnemental de l'Estrie et de la Montérégie; Ministère du Développement durable, de l'Environnement, de la Faune et des Parcs.

5 *Gagné v. Rail World, Inc.*, 2014 QCCS 32 (CanLii) (Fourth Amended Motion for Authorization), www.clg.org/pdf/9/2/7/Fourth%20Amended%20 Motion%20for%20Authorization.pdf.

6 Andrew Ross Sorkin, "The Short-Seller Stands Tall," *New York Times Magazine*, October 4, 2013, www.nytimes.com/2013/10/06/magazine/william-ackman-you-need-a-thick-skin-to-be-in-this-business.html.

7 Deborah Hardoon, *An Economy for the 99%: It's Time to Build a Human Economy That Benefits Everyone, Not Just the Privileged Few* (Oxfam Briefing Paper, January 16, 2017), oxfam.org/en/research/economy-99.

8 Fred Frailey, "Bill Ackman's Plan to Transform Canadian Pacific," *Trains*, February 7, 2012, cs.trains.com/trn/b/fred-frailey/archive/2012/02/07/bill -ackman-s-plan-to-transform-canadian-pacific.aspx.

9 "War of Words: The E-Mails that Touched Off a Battle at CP," *Globe and Mail*, January 16, 2012, updated May 9, 2018, www.theglobeandmail.com /globe-investor/war-of-words-the-e-mails-that-touched-off-a-battle-at-cp /article1358767/.

10 Interview by the author.

11 Pershing Square Foundation, "The Pershing Square Foundation Supports Global Human Rights with $10 Million Grant to Human Rights Watch," May 24, 2012, www.prnewswire.com/news-releases/the-pershing -square-foundation-supports-global-human-rights-with-10-million-grant -to-human-rights-watch-153680445.html.

12 This is elegantly described in the book by the journalist and writer Michael Lewis, *The Big Short: Inside the Doomsday Machine* (New York, NY: W.W. Norton, 2010).

13 Tomi Kilgore and Ciara Linnane, "Bill Ackman Is Losing Billions as Valeant's Stock Tumbles," *MarketWatch*, March 2, 2016, www.marketwatch .com/story/bill-ackman-is-losing-billions-on-his-valeant-stock-2016-03-01.

14 On the events surrounding this battle, see Jacquie McNish and Brent Jang, "The Giant Killer: Inside CP's Overthrow," *Globe and Mail*, May 19, 2012, updated May 1, 2018, www.theglobeandmail.com/globe-investor/the

-giant-killer-inside-cps-overthrow/article4186956/; and Scott Deveau, "Corporate Culture Shift Underway in Canada after CP Rail Proxy Fight," *Financial Post*, May 11, 2012, business.financialpost.com/investing/shift -underway-for-canadas-clubby-corporate-culture-after-cp-rail-proxy-fight.

15 See Canadian Pacific Corporation, *Change: Canadian Pacific 2012 Annual Report*, n.d., s21.q4cdn.com/736796105/files/doc_financials/Annual-Report /cp-ar-2012.pdf.

16 Frailey, "Bill Ackman's Plan."

17 "Our Mandate," CPP Investments, www.cppinvestments.com/about-us /our-mandate.

18 Richard Blackwell and Guy Dixon, "Swimming in Profits, Ackman to Sell Down CP Stake," *Globe and Mail*, June 3, 2013 , updated March 26, 2017, www.theglobeandmail.com/report-on-business/swimming-in-profits -ackman-to-sell-down-cp-stake/article12316671/.

19 Gordon Pitts, "Turnaround Ace: Inside the Hunter Harrison Era at CP Railway," *Globe and Mail*, April 24, 2014, updated December 16, 2017, www .theglobeandmail.com/report-on-business/rob-magazine/hunter-harrison -cp-report-on-business-magazine/article18190120/.

20 Saint-Cerny, *Mégantic, un démo*.

21 Saint-Cerny, *Mégantic, un démo*.

22 Transportation Safety Board of Canada, "Railway Investigation Report R04Q0040: Main-Track Derailment, Canadian National Train U-781-21-17 Mile 3.87, Lévis Subdivision, Saint-Henri-de-Lévis, Québec, August 17, 2004" (Minister of Public Works and Government Services Canada, 2007), www .bst-tsb.gc.ca/eng/rapports-reports/rail/2004/r04q0040/r04q0040.pdf.

23 Transportation Safety Board, "Safety Issues Investigation Report SII R05 -01: Analysis of Secondary Main-Line Derailments and the Relationship to Bulk Tonnage Traffic" (Minister of Public Works and Government Services Canada, 2006), www.bst-tsb.gc.ca/eng/rapports-reports/rail /etudes-studies/siir0501/siir0501.asp.

24 Scott Deveau, "'Get Ready to Deal with Fear': CP Rail Chief Harrison Fires Back at Union Critics over Safety Concerns," *Financial Post*, May 22, 2013, business.financialpost.com/transportation/get-ready-to-deal-with-fear-cp -rail-chief-harrison-fires-back-at-union-critics-over-safety-concerns.

25 Transportation Safety Board, "Railway Investigation Report R13D0054: Runaway and Main-Track Derailment, Montreal, Maine and Atlantic Railway Freight Train MMA-002, Mile 0.23, Sherbrooke Subdivision, Lac-Mégantic, Québec, 6 July 2013" (henceforth referred to as the "TSB report"), (Minister of Public Works and Government Services Canada, 2014), www.tsb.gc .ca/eng/rapports-reports/rail/2013/r13d0054/r13d0054.pdf.

26 On August 24, 2019, there was a minor derailment on the track between Nantes and Mégantic (Alessia Simona Marata, "Small Train Derailment near Lac-Mégantic," Global News, August 24, 2019, updated August 25, 2019, globalnews.ca/news/5810321/train-derails-lac-megantic/). Two weeks before that incident, Robert Bellefleur and a coalition of citizens in Mégantic had made public the photograph Bellefleur had taken showing the precise location of the derailment, illustrating beyond all doubt that the track was broken in that spot. Furthermore, a Transport Canada report had identified almost 250 cases of broken track, including that one, and asked CMQR to repair them without delay – but to no effect.

27 Pitts, "Turnaround Ace."

28 Deveau, "'Get Ready to Deal with Fear.'"

29 Scott Deveau, "Unions Flag Safety Concerns at CP Rail as Railway Ramps Up Efficiency Efforts," *Financial Post*, May 21, 2013, business.financialpost.com/transportation/unions-flag-safety-concerns-at-cp-rail-as-railway-ramps-up-efficiency-efforts.

30 Deveau, "Get Ready to Deal with Fear."

31 "Report of the Standing Committee on Transport, Infrastructure and Communities on Rail Safety in Canada," May 2008, www.ourcommons.ca/DocumentViewer/en/39-2/TRAN/report-3.

32 Dave Seglins, "Railway Safety: TSB Discovers Companies Not Reporting All Derailments," CBC News, April 7, 2014, www.cbc.ca/news/railsafety-tsb-discovers-companies-not-reporting-all-derailments-1.2598417; Eric Atkins, "Canadian Railways Fail to Properly Report Accidents, Regulator Says," *Globe and Mail*, October 27, 2014 , updated May 12, 2018, www.theglobeandmail.com/report-on-business/canadian-railways-fail-to-report-254-accidents-over-seven-years-tsb/article21312626/; and Dave Seglins, "TSB Says CN Rail Failed to Report Hundreds of Derailments, Collisions," CBC News, December 9, 2013, www.cbc.ca/news/canada/tsb-says-cn-rail-failed-to-report-hundreds-of-derailments-collisions-1.2451186.

33 Canadian Press, "Calgary Train Derailment: Mayor Nenshi Blasts CP over Bridge Inspection," *HuffPost*, June 27, 2013, updated August 27, 2013, www.huffingtonpost.ca/2013/06/27/calgary-train-derailment-mayor-nenshi-cp_n_3512145.html.

34 Chad Beharriell, "Poor Choice for Railroader of the Year," *Windsor Star*, February 3, 2015, windsorstar.com/news/local-news/poor-choice-for-railroader-of-the-year.

35 Amanda Stephenson, "CP Rail's Hunter Harrison Tops List of Calgary's Best-Paid Executives," *Calgary Herald*, June 23, 2016, calgaryherald.com/business/local-business/cp-rails-hunter-harrison-tops-list-of-calgarys-best-paid-executives.

36 Jean-François Codère, "Mieux vaut trop investir, a appris le CN" [Better to over-invest, CN learns], *La Presse+*, April 25, 2018, www.lapresse.ca/affaires/economie/transports/201804/25/01-5162386-mieux-vaut-trop-investir-a-appris-le-cn.php.

37 Christopher Reynolds, "CN Rail Boosts Dividend 18 per Cent as It Forecasts Strong Performance in 2019," *Financial Post*, January 29, 2019, business.financialpost.com/pmn/business-pmn/oil-sales-drive-cn-rail-revenue-growth-in-fourth-quarter-full-year.

38 Ashley Halsey III, "House Committee Leader Says Railroads Have Fallen to 'Jackals on Wall Street,'" *Washington Post*, June 20, 2019, www.washingtonpost.com/local/trafficandcommuting/house-committee-leader-says-railroads-have-fallen-to-jackals-on-wall-street/2019/06/20/65d9f276-92b1-11e9-b570-6416efdc0803_story.html.

39 For further information, see Alain Deneault, *De quoi Total est-elle la somme?: Multinationales et perversion du droit* (Montréal: Écosociété; Paris: Rue de l'échiquier, 2017), especially the first chapter.

40 Mark Druskoff, "The Competitors Who Stand to Win from Denial of Keystone XL," *Forbes*, November 10, 2015, www.forbes.com/sites

/mergermarket/2015/11/10/lose-some-win-some-keystone-xl-denial-opens
-windows-of-opportunity/#72f197c3508d.

41   Marianne Lavelle, "Space View of Natural Gas Flaring Darkened by Budget
      Woes," *National Geographic*, October 10, 2013, www.nationalgeographic
      .com/news/energy/2013/10/131009-budget-woes-darken-space-view-of-gas
      -flaring/.

42   Mark D. Peterson et al., *2016 One-Year Seismic Hazard Forecast for the
      Central and Eastern United States from Induced and Natural Earth-
      quakes* (U.S. Geological Survey, June 2016), pubs.usgs.gov/of/2016/1035
      /ofr20161035ver1_1.pdf.

43   "Donald Trump's News Conference: Full Transcript and Video," *New York
      Times*, January 11, 2017, www.nytimes.com/2017/01/11/us/politics/trump
      -press-conference-transcript.html.

44   See the very eloquent photograph accompanying the article by Matta-
      thias Schwartz and Lee Fang, "Spot the Billionaires Given Special Seats
      on Donald Trump's Inaugural Platform," *The Intercept*, January 21, 2017,
      theintercept.com/2017/01/21/identify-trump-donors/.

45   *Bloomberg Business*, June 29, 2012.

46   National Energy Board, "Canadian Pipeline Transportation System –
      Energy Market Assessment," April 2014, www.neb-one.gc.ca/nrg/ntgrtd
      /trnsprttn/2014/index-eng.html.

47   Ari Altstedter, "Ackman like Buffet Buoyed by Fracking in Bakken:
      Freight," *Bloomberg*, June 29, 2012, www.bloomberg.com/news/articles
      /2012-06-29/ackman-like-buffett-buoyed-by-fracking-in-bakken-freight.

48   Murray Brewster and Benjamin Shingler, "Quebec Disaster: Oil Shipments
      by Rail Have Increased 28,000% since 2009," CTV News, July 7, 2013, www
      .ctvnews.ca/canada/quebec-disaster-oil- shipments-by-rail-have-increased
      -28-000-per-cent-since-2009-1.1357356.

49   "Our Markets," CP, www.cpr.ca/en/our-markets/oil-gas-energy/bakken
      -shale.

50   Altstedter, "Ackman like Buffet Buoyed by Fracking."

51   Altstedter, "Ackman like Buffet Buoyed by Fracking."

52   Canadian Association of Petroleum Producers, "Transporting Crude Oil
      by Rail in Canada," March 2014, www.capp.ca/~/media/capp/customer
      -portal/documents/242427.pdf.

53   Dakota Plains Holdings, "Dakota Plains Commences Construction on
      Pioneer Project, Expanding Rail Capacity in the Williston Basin," press
      release, March 15, 2013, sec.report/Document/0000897101-13-000360/.

54   "It's Simple: Canadian Pacific Annual Report, 2014," s21.q4cdn.com
      /736796105/files/doc_financials/Annual-Report/cp-ar-2014.pdf.

55   "Bill Ackman a vendu le tiers de ses actions du CP" [Bill Ackman sells a
      third of his shares in CP], *Les Affaires*, October 25, 2013, www.lesaffaires
      .com/secteurs-d-activite/transport/billackman-a-vendu-le-tiers-de-ses
      -actions-du-cp/562929.

56   TSB report, 65.

57   National Transportation Safety Board (NTSB) Railroad Report Accident,
      CHI96FR010, August 16, 1997, modified July 9, 2013, dms.ntsb.gov/pubdms
      /search/hitlist.cfm?docketID=8867&CFID=3228059&CFTOKEN=92fc-
      669fe0fb9acb-534FD7FA-C1EF-22F1-C52C300850B529A5.

58 ICI Radio-Canada,"MMA et la règle 112: des infractions à répétition, aucune sanction" [MMA and Rule 112: repeated infractions, no sanctions], February 12, 2014, ici.radio-canada.ca/nouvelle/653418/mma-infractions-sanctions-reglements-transports-canada.

59 Fred Frailey, "Maine Reaches Deal to Buy Imperiled Rail Lines," *Trains*, October 20, 2010, trn.trains.com/news/news-wire/2010/10/maine-rail-purchase.

60 François Desjardins, "La MMA a bénéficié de l'aide des gouvernements" [MMA benefited from government aid], *Le Devoir*, July 11, 2013, www.ledevoir.com/societe/382696/la-mma-a-beneficie-de-l-aide-des-gouvernements.

61 Gilles des Roberts, "Le propriétaire du train de la mort avait ses entrées à Ottawa" [Death-train owner had ear of someone in Ottawa], Droit-Inc.com, July 9, 2013, www.droit-inc.com/article10514-Le-proprietaire-du-train-de-la-mort-avait-ses-entrees-a-Ottawa&highlight=propri%C3%A9taire%20du%20train%20de%20la%20mort%20.

62 Canada Safety Council, "Report Blows the Whistle on Railway Safety," April 3, 2008, canadasafetycouncil.org/report-blows-the-whistle-on-railway-safety/.

63 Ross Marowits, "CP Rail CEO Hunter Harrison to Trudeau: 'Just Leave Us Alone,'" *HuffPost*, October 20, 2015, www.huffingtonpost.ca/2015/10/20/hunter-harrison-cp-rail-trudeau-leave-us-alone_n_8340690.html.

64 Report of the Standing Committee on Transport, Infrastructure, and Communities.

65 Canadian Safety Council, "Report Blows the Whistle."

66 Transport Canada, "About Us," www.tc.gc.ca/eng/aboutus-department-overview.htm.

67 Lecture by Brian Stevens at the "Have the Lessons of the Lac-Mégantic Rail Disaster Been Learned?" conference hosted by the faculty of law at the University of Ottawa, December 8, 2016.

68 Guillaume Bourgault-Côté, "Matières dangereuses – Hausse importante du trafic au Canada" [Dangerous goods: Significant rise in traffic in Canada], *Le Devoir*, August 16, 2013, www.ledevoir.com/politique/canada/385306/hausse-importante-du-trafic-au-canada.

69 File T-1005-16, *Canadian National Railway Company v. Attorney General of Canada and Transport Canada*. Attorney General of Canada and Transport Canada.

70 Transportation Safety Board, "Derailment and Fire of Second Canadian National Crude Oil Train near Gogama, Ontario," undated press release, updated March 26, 2019, www.tsb.gc.ca/eng/medias-media/communiques/rail/2015/r15h0021-20150317.html.

71 "Train Carrying Crude Oil Derails near Gogama, Ont.," CBC News, March 7, 2015, updated March 13, 2018, www.cbc.ca/news/canada/sudbury/train-carrying-crude-oil-derails-near-gogama-ont-1.2985703.

72 Transport Canada website, chap. 5, "Safety Management Systems," www.tc.gc.ca/fra/sstc/Examen_LSF/chapitre5-392.html. (This webpage is no longer available. However, elsewhere Transport Canada states the same in slightly different terms, including in "Enhancing Rail Safety in Canada: Working Together for Safer Communities; The 2018 *Railway Safety*

Act* Review (May 2018)," which states: "Key components of the Act that are crucial to the rail safety regime include: a) The recognition that the railway industry is responsible for managing and mitigating safety risks." www.tc.gc.ca/en/reviews/railway-safety-act-review/enhancing-rail-safety -canada-working-together-safer-communities.html.)

73   Transport Canada website, chap. 5.

74   ICI Radio-Canada, "Harper maintient sa position" [Harper maintains his position], February 2, 2007, ici.radio-canada.ca/nouvelle/339352/baird -surpris-climat.

75   National Association of Women and the Law, "Kim Rogers: Death in the Modern-Day Pauper's Prison," September 18, 2001, nawl.ca/fr/kim-rogers -death-in-the-modern-day-paupers-prison/.

76   See www.pressreader.com/canada/ottawa-citizen/20150204 /281762742673990.

77   Bruce Campbell, *Lac-Mégantic: Loose Ends and Unanswered Questions* (Ottawa, ON: Canadian Centre for Policy Alternatives, 2015), 35.

78   TSB report, 18.

79   TSB report, 65.

80   TSB report, 129.

81   Transport Canada, "Measures to Enhance Railway Safety and the Safe Transportation of Dangerous Goods," updated January 26, 2018, www.tc .gc.ca/eng/mediaroom/infosheets-menu-7564.html.

82   TSB report, 58.

83   TSB report, 21.

84   From the author's trial notes, reviewed by Richard Labrie.

85   TSB report, 86, 82, 127.

86   TSB report, 159.

87   Maury Hill and associates, Inc., "A Study of the Role of Human Factors in Railway Occurrences and Possible Mitigation Strategies," conducted in support of the Railway Safety Act Review, August 2007, www.tc.gc.ca /media/documents/railsafety/HumanFactors.pdf.

88   www.tc.gc.ca/eng/tcss/RSA_review/chapter5-392.htm. This page, which cited Reason's book *Human Error* (Cambridge: Cambridge University Press, 1990), has now been removed.

89   Mélanie Marquis, "Lac-Mégantic: Ottawa récuse l'analyse du patron du CP" [Lac-Mégantic: Ottawa rejects analysis of CP's boss], *Le Devoir*, October 4, 2014, www.ledevoir.com/politique/canada/420203/lac-megantic -ottawa-condamne-les-propos-du-patron-du-canadien-pacifique.

90   Marowits, "Harrison to Trudeau."

91   TSB report, 29.

92   TSB report, 65.

93   TSB report, 64.

94   TSB report, 65.

95   TSB report, 65.

96   TSB report, 67.

97   Privy Council Office, Canada.ca, "Commissions of Inquiry," www.canada .ca/en/privy-council/services/commissions-inquiry.html.

98   Sylvie Fournier, *Enquête*, ICI Radio-Canada Télé, January 22, 2015.

99   Cited by Fournier, *Enquête*.

100 Tribunal administratif du Québec (TAQ), document WF33.

101 Saint-Cerny, *Mégantic, un démo.*

102 Ministère de la Sécurité publique, Gouvernement du Québec, "Guide des opérations en sécurité incendie" [Fire safety operations guide], sect. V, chap. 7.1, 46, www.securitepublique.gouv.qc.ca/fileadmin /Documents/securite_incendie/publications/guide_operations/guide -operations-ssi.pdf.

103 Lisa Riordan Seville and Lisa Myers, "Danger on the Tracks: Unsafe Rail Cars Carry Oil through US Towns," NBC News, November 2, 2015, www.nbcnews.com/news/world/danger-tracks-unsafe-rail-cars-carry-oil -through-us-towns-flna8C11082948.

104 TSB report, 114.

105 Document obtained from the Tribunal administratif du Québec.

106 From the author's trial notes. All further quotes from the trial are from the same source.

107 TSB report, 30.

108 TSB report, 76.

109 Email from Transport Canada to Robert Bellefleur, private archives.

110 TSB report, 78.

111 TSB report, 7.

112 TSB report, 179.

113 Grant Robertson, "Ten-Second Procedure Might Have Averted Lac-Mégantic Disaster," *Globe and Mail*, March 7, 2016, updated May 16, 2018, www.theglobeandmail.com/news/national/new-info-shows-backup-brake -may-have-averted-lac-megantic-disaster/article29044518/.

114 Grant Robertson, "Rail Workers Dispute Lobby Group's Take on Lac-Mégantic Disaster," *Globe and Mail*, April 28, 2016, updated May 16, 2018, www.theglobeandmail.com/news/national/rail-workers-dispute-lobby -groups-take-on-lac-megantic-disaster/article29795877/.

115 Audio recording of the conversations. It, along with a transcript, can be found on the *Globe and Mail* website: www.theglobeandmail.com/news /national/dispatches-from-a-disaster/article20148699/.

116 See "Le vautour de Lac-Mégantic" [The vulture of Lac-Mégantic], *Enquête*, ICI Radio-Canada, September 14, 2017.

117 Alexandre Shields, "Environnement au Lac-Mégantic – Les séquelles seront permanentes" [Permanent consequences for the environment at Lac-Mégantic], *Le Devoir*, July 10, 2013, https://www.ledevoir.com /societe/environnement/382605/les-sequelles-environnementales-seront -permanentes.

118 In order to preserve their peace of mind, we shall not identify certain witnesses by name. Moreover, most of the unattributed comments are taken from the INSPQ report on the Mégantic tragedy, and particularly the "Opinions" section (Geneviève Brisson and Emmanuelle Bouchard-Bastien, *Opinions locales quant à la gestion des risques et du rétablissement à la suite de la tragédie ferroviaire de Lac-Mégantic* [Local opinions on risk and recovery management in the wake of the Lac-Mégantic rail

disaster], Institut national de santé publique du Québec, 2017, www
.inspq.qc.ca/sites/default/files/publications/2211_opinions_locales_
gestion_risques_retablissement_megantic_o.pdf.

119 The emails and various documents related to the Ministry of the
Environment are taken mainly from two sources: the still-pending case
at the Administrative Tribunal of Québec on Orders 928 and 928 B
(2014QCTAQ02129) and a fight, still ongoing in 2020, between Daniel Green
and the Québec Access to Information Review Board, to obtain information
held by the Ministry of the Environment on the contamination. Henceforth
these documents will be identified by the abbreviation "TAQ."

120 See the images on Vimeo: saintcerny: vimeo.com/71067944, a video
included in the "Mégantic" album: vimeo.com/manage/albums/2593835.

121 saintcerny: vimeo.com.

122 Institut national de santé publique du Québec (the Québec institute of
public health).

123 "Lac-Mégantic: Précisions sur les quantités de pétrole impliquées et
sur la suite des opérations" [Details of the quantities of crude petroleum involved and about future operations], press release, Ministère du
Développement durable, de l'Environnement, de la Faune et des Parcs,
July 24, 2013, www.environnement.gouv.qc.ca/infuseur/communique
.asp?no=2541.

124 vimeo.com/71067944, filmed by M. Laflamme and the SVP.

125 "About ECRC," ECRC/SIMEC website, www.ecrc-simec.ca/en/about/ecrc/.

126 TAQ.

127 TAQ.

128 TAQ.

129 TAQ.

130 Interview by the author.

131 Maxime Bergeron and Kathleen Lévesque, "L'UPAC enquête à Lac-
Mégantic" [UPAC inquiry in Lac-Mégantic], La Presse, May 15, 2014,
www.lapresse.ca/actualites/justice-et-affaires-criminelles/actualites-
judiciaires/201405/14/01-4766791-lupac-enquete-a-lac-megantic.php.

132 Interview by the author.

133 Public Works and Government Services Canada, "World Fuel Services
Canada, Ltd. (E60HL-160050/010/HL~000)," buyandsell.gc.ca/procure-
ment-data/contract-history/E60HL-160050-010-HL.

134 As before, anonymous testimonies are taken from the INSPQ report.

135 Centre local de développement (Local Development Centre).

136 Extract from Bylaw 1613 (October 14, 2013), replacing Bylaw No. 1613
(September 9, 2013) establishing a "special urban development plan for
Lac-Mégantic town centre," www.ville.lac-megantic.qc.ca/wp-content
/uploads/2016/07/No1613.pdf.

137 Klein, Shock Doctrine, 203.

138 Claudia Collard, "Lac-Mégantic va se relever!" [Lac-Mégantic will rise
again!], L'Écho de Frontenac, December 4, 2014.

139 Jacynthe Nadeau, "Lac-Mégantic: 12 M$ investis dans le secteur Fatima"
[Lac-Mégantic: $12 million invested in the Fatima district], La Tribune,

ENDNOTES

February 19, 2014, www.latribune.ca/archives/lac-megantic-12-m-investis
-dans-le-secteur-fatima-41aa1b55d9f647fe1e3ffa6c39456910.

140 Lac-Mégantic Bylaw 1613, Plan particulier d'urbanisme [Special Urban Development Plan], 13.

141 Darren Fishell, "Firm That Bought Bankrupt Railway after Lac-Megantic Tragedy Reports 2016 Profit," *Bangor Daily News*, February 28, 2017, updated June 2, 2017, bangordailynews.com/2017/02/28/business/firm-that-bought-bankrupt-railway-after-lac-megantic-tragedy-reports-2016-profit/.

142 TAQ, "Procès-verbal – avancement des travaux" [Work progress report], Pomerleau.

143 INSPQ report.

144 ICI Radio-Canada, "Musi-Café: une lente reconstruction parsemée d'embûches" [Musi-Café: A long reconstruction strewn with pitfalls], December 12, 2014, ici.radio-canada.ca/nouvelle/698070/musi-cafe-lente-reconstruction.

145 Pascal Ferland, "Le Groupe Action Mégantic veut 'transformer la tragédie en opportunité'" [The Action Mégantic group wants to "turn tragedy into opportunity"], *La Tribune*, May 27, 2014, www.latribune.ca/archives/le-groupe-action-meganticveut-tranformer-la-tragedie-en-opportunite-98828b631e2f969c331439fa5121f34f.

146 Nicolas Lachance, "Projet touristique audacieux" [Audacious tourism project], *Le Journal de Montréal*, July 1, 2014, www.journaldemontreal.com/2014/07/01/projet-touristique-audacieux.

147 Interview by the author.

148 Colette Roy-Laroche, interview by Gérald Fillion, *RDI économie*, November 25, 2013, youtu.be/ZAsuCxP7MxE.

149 Laura Beston and Verity Stevenson, "Two Years Later, Lac-Mégantic Struggles to Rebuild," *Globe and Mail*, July 15, 2015, updated May 15, 2018, www.theglobeandmail.com/news/national/two-years-later-lac-megantic-struggles-to-turn-the-page/article25306708/.

150 www.facebook.com/lecarrebleulacmegantic/.

151 Julie Vaillancourt, "Reconstruction de Lac-Mégantic et lobbyisme illégal" [Reconstruction of Lac-Mégantic and illegal lobbying], ICI Radio-Canada, October 19, 2014, ici.radio-canada.ca/nouvelle/689599/reconstruction-lac-megantic-lobbyisme-illegal-desjardins-michel-duval.

152 Denis-Martin Chabot, "Lac-Mégantic : des pressions pour vendre dans la zone rouge" [Lac-Mégantic: Pressure to sell in the red zone], ICI Radio-Canada, July 22, 2014, ici.radiocanada.ca/nouvelle/677075/lac-megantic-proprietaires-commerces-zonerouge-pressions-intimidation.

153 L'investisseur masqué, "Le succès de Dollarama en Bourse" [Dollarama's stock exchange success], *Le Journal de Montréal*, January 27, 2018, www.journaldemontreal.com/2018/01/27/le-succes-de-dollarama-en-bourse.

154 Rémi Tremblay, "Des avancées vers le 'nouveau' Fatima" [Steps toward the "new" Fatima], *L'Écho de Frontenac*, January 16, 2014, echodefrontenac.com/2014-01-16/2711-des-avancees-vers-le-nouveau-fatima.

155 Catherine Dubé (text) and Claude Grenier (photos), "Lac-Mégantic: des gagnants et des perdants" [Lac-Mégantic: Winners and losers], *L'actualité*, June 27, 2014, lactualite.com/societe/2014/06/27/lac-megantic-des-gagnants-et-des-perdants/.

156   Claudia Collard, "Un autre deuil, celui du centre-ville ..." [Another loss: the town centre], *L'Écho de Frontenac,* October 31, 2014, echodefrontenac .com/2014-10-31/3216-un-autre-deuil-celui-du-centre-ville.

157   INSPQ report.

158   Collard, "Un autre deuil."

159   Claudia Collard, "Une étape vers le deuil du centre-ville" [A step toward losing downtown], *L'Écho de Frontenac,* December 11, 2014, echodefron-tenac.com/2014-12-11/3274-une-etape-vers-le-deuil-du-centre-ville.

160   Maxim Deland and Félix Séguin, "Triste fin pour un héros de Lac-Mégantic" [Sad end for a hero of Lac-Mégantic], *Le Journal de Québec,* September 28, 2017, www.pressreader.com/canada/le-journal-de-quebec /20170928/281479276609794.

161   Denis Méthot, "Les leçons de Lac-Mégantic à l'aide des villes sinistrées" [Lessons from Lac-Mégantic to help disaster-struck towns], February 11, 2018, www.journaldemontreal.com/2018/02/11/les-lecons-de-lac-megantic -a-laide-des-villes-sinistrees.

162   "Director of Criminal and Penal Prosecutions," like an attorney general.

163   Transport Canada, "Transport Minister Delivers on Promise to Accelerate Removal of Legacy DOT-111 Tank Cars from Crude Oil Transport," news release, October 31, 2016, www.canada.ca/en/transport-canada/news/2016 /10/transport-minister-delivers-promise-accelerate-removal-legacy-111 -tank-cars-crude-oil-transport.html.

164   Halsey, "Jackals on Wall Street."

165   Canadian Press, "Last Tanker Cars to Be Removed from CP Rail Derail-ment Site near Guernsey, Sask.," Global News, December 19, 2019, globalnews.ca/news/6320067/train-derailment-guernsey-saskatchewan/.

166   David Shield, "Federal Transport Minister Orders Trains to Slow Down after Fiery Crash in Sask.," CBC News, February 6, 2020, www.cbc.ca /news/canada/saskatoon/sask-train-derailment-1.5453942.

167   "Government Further Revises Train Regulations, Speed Limits for Dan-gerous Goods on Canadian Railways," CBC News, February 17, 2020, www .cbc.ca/news/canada/saskatoon/updated-rail-speed-limits-permanent -safety-measures-sask-guernsey-cp-rail-oil-train-1.5466354.

168   Matt Vis, "Northwestern Ontario Train Derailment Came Days after Feds Raised Rail Speed Limit," CBC News, www.cbc.ca/news/canada/thunder -bay/emo-train-derailment-speed-1.5474893.

169   Vis, "Northwestern Ontario Train Derailment."

170   Transport Canada, "Statement by Minister of Transport on Unsafe Behav-iour around Railways," February 17, 2020, www.canada.ca/en/transport -canada/news/2020/02/statement-by-minister-of-transport-on-unsafe -behaviour-around-railways.html.

171   Gary Rinne, "Emo Derailment Raises Questions about Train Speed," TBNewsWatch.com, February 24, 2020, www.tbnewswatch.com/local -news/emo-derailment-raises-questions-about-train-speeds-3-photos -2114567.

172   Ronna Syed, "'Search Your Hearts': Families of 2 Men Killed in CP Rail Crash Urge Witnesses to Step Forward," CBC News, February 4, 2020, www.cbc.ca/news/canada/cp-rail-crash-anniversary-families-urge -witnesses-1.5448086.

173 "Runaway Train: Investigating a Fatal CP Rail Crash," *The Fifth Estate*, aired on January 26, 2020, on CBC, youtu.be/ZAsuCxP7MxE.

174 Dave Seglins and Joseph Loiero, "Train Safety Investigator Wants RCMP to Probe Fatal CP Mountain Crash," CBC News, January 27, 2020, www.cbc.ca/news/canada/cp-rail-crash-call-investigation-1.5441955.

175 Dave Seglins and Joseph Loiero, "Rail Disaster Video Surfaces on Anniversary of CP Crash Amid Controversy over Police Probe," CBC News, February 4, 2020, www.cbc.ca/news/canada/video-derailment-canadian-pacific-railway-field-1.5449758.

176 Dave Seglins and Joseph Loiero, "Police Not Probing Recent Rail Disasters, Crude Oil Derailments, Deaths for Possible Negligence," CBC News, March 6, 2020, www.cbc.ca/news/canada/rail-accidents-investigations -1.5486897.

177 Seglins and Loiero, "Police Not Probing."

178 Hydro-Québec, "Ligne d'interconnexion des Appalaches-Maine" [Appalaches–Maine interconnection], Spring 2018, www.hydroquebec.com/data /projets/interconnexion-am/pdf/2018E1455-f-appal-maine-ig-web.pdf.

179 Julie Marceau, "Des 'erreurs' dans la vérification de l'eau potable à Lac-Mégantic" ["Mistakes" in drinking-water testing at Lac-Mégantic], ICI Radio-Canada, July 12, 2019, ici.radio-canada.ca/nouvelle/1218164/benzene -analyses-tests-aqueduc-laboratoire-erreur-delais-eurofins-environex.

180 Robert Bellefleur in conversation with the author.

SOURCES

THE FACTS AND QUOTATIONS USED TO SUPPORT THIS STORY
are taken from documentary sources and from the collected testimonies of more than sixty witnesses, starting from the first days following the disaster. I have visited Mégantic frequently since the disaster, so I was privileged to witness a great deal. I also attended almost all the hearings of the three, the hearings on Orders 628 and 628 B issued by the Québec environment ministry, as well as those held by the Tribunal administratif du Québec.

Among the testimonies are several from residents of Mégantic, the majority of whom I have identified by name. In some cases, however, and at their request, I have not revealed the names. Other testimonies came from a variety of domains: railway employees, lawyers, municipal records, unions, business, etc. However, there were special cases. After several contacts and after obtaining his consent, a list of questions was sent to Gérald Gauthier, vice-president of the Railway Association of Canada. He did not reply. Béland Audet, a Mégantic businessman and member of Groupe Action Mégantic, kindly answered some questions. Exceptionally, his testimony was not recorded, but it was given before a witness who can corroborate the comments I have reported. Finally, a request for an interview was sent to Colette Roy-Laroche, mayor of Mégantic at the time of the disaster. That request also went unanswered.

Facts and data quoted from media sources are mostly identified by a single source. However, they were chosen because they tally with other reports from several other serious media sources, confirming their reliability.

My narrative is based on an abundance of documents (often partially redacted), mostly derived from three sources. First, documents, including emails, filed in connection with the above-mentioned case at the Tribunal administratif du Québec, and second, from the case (still pending at the time of writing), brought by Daniel Green to the

Access to Information Commission (Lac-Mégantic, *Daniel Green v. MDDEP*). And, in a few cases, documents coming from judicial sources related to the trials.

Finally, several testimonies, especially in the section entitled "The Shock Doctrine," are anonymous. Unless otherwise indicated, they are taken from two documents produced by the INSPQ: *Opinions locales quant à la gestion des risques et du rétablissement à la suite de la tragédie ferroviaire de Lac-Mégantic* (Local opinions on risk management and recovery in the wake of the Lac-Mégantic railway tragedy) and *Changements sociaux et risques perçus à la suite de la tragédie ferroviaire de Lac-Mégantic* (Changes and perceived risks following the Lac-Mégantic railway tragedy).

Other documents came from my own personal archives, as well as those of some of the victims' families and other residents of Lac-Mégantic.

INDEX

ACKNOWLEDGMENTS

THIS BOOK COULD NOT HAVE BEEN PUBLISHED WITHOUT THE help of many individuals. I thank all of them, but I wish especially to express my gratitude to those mentioned here.

Many of the people I encountered in Mégantic left an indelible mark on my life. Among them were Robert Bellefleur, who offered me his unshakeable support and who became an expert on railway matters; Nicole Boulé; Jean Clusiault, who infused this story with soul, pain, and hope; Jonathan Santerre, whose tenacity and dedication are remarkable; Monsieur and Madame R. and their paradise on the Chaudière River – the trout will return, it's a promise!; and Gilles Fluet, one of the first people I encountered, who always had his place in the forefront of the fight.

Gilbert Carette and Richard Poirier were also a continual presence; André Blais was always discreet, but his financial help was extremely useful; Jacques Gagnon and Marilaine Savard, the first instigators of the Citizens' Committee; also Hélène Rodrigue, Madame M. from Fatima, Monsieur B.-P. B. from Mégantic, Sylvie Girard, Dr. Gérard Chaput, Yves Laflamme, and Richard Labrie. Others were kind enough to offer me their time and explanations, including Jacques Breton, the mayor of Nantes; Daniel Larochelle; Thomas Walsh; and Charles Shearson. Thanks also to Fritz Edler and Jacques Gélineau for their expertise and unwavering support. And, naturally, to my perpetual colleague and accomplice, Daniel Green, with whom this venture began and who shared with me his unparalleled knowledge, the fruit of incalculable hours of work.

Journalist André Noël's masterly preface surely removes any doubt about the need for a commission of inquiry.

Several others who helped and supported me are not mentioned here by name – like the devoted individual who, on July 11, took Daniel Green and me to see Monsieur R. My thanks to him.

ACKNOWLEDGMENTS

My thanks also to Jocelyne Clark and Marie-Ève Pierret, my early supporters.

To Alain Deneault, who encouraged me to write this story.

To Don Wilson, the translator of this English edition, for the quality of his language, his talent for capturing live emotion, and his care in checking fine points, and who masterfully met the challenge of rendering both the emotion expressed and the technical details.

Thanks to Charles Simard at Talonbooks, but also a neighbour of Mégantic, who worked with remarkable devotion and expertise to bring this story to a wider public, so that further tragedies of the kind may perhaps be avoided, and to Catriona Strang and andrea bennett for their meticulous fact-checking and thoughtful copy-editing.

And, of course, Alain and Anaïs, Maximilian, Michaël, my unshakeable base.

My thanks to all.

DON WILSON was born and educated in Ireland, taking degrees in Modern Languages and French Literature at Trinity College Dublin. He has taught at universities in the West Indies, the UK, and at the University of Waterloo, where he spent most of his career. He has twice been long-listed for the Best Translated Book Award in the U.S. and has been a finalist for the French-American Foundation Translation Prize, and for the Governor General's Literary Awards.

ANNE-MARIE SAINT-CERNY has been a social and environmental activist in various NGOs for over thirty-five years. Videographer, essayist, and novelist, her book-length piece of investigative journalism *Mégantic, Une tragédie annoncée* (Éditions Écosociété, 2018) was in its original French edition the winner of the 2018 prix Pierre-Vadeboncœur, a finalist for the 2018 Governor General's Literary Awards for Non-Fiction, and was listed for the 2019 Prix des libraires.

Saint-Cerny participated in the launch of the NGO Fondation Rivières, where she served as vice-president and then general manager, opposing private dams, the harnessing of the Rupert and Romaine Rivers, and campaigning for the preservation of vital watercourses.

Since 2008, as general manager of the Société pour vaincre la pollution (SVP), she has been involved in several investigations on instances of ecological contamination by large corporations, notably the Lac-Mégantic rail disaster and several Canadian mining projects. In 2018, she co-founded Québec's Association des victimes de l'amiante (AVAQ). She was also present in Lac-Mégantic during the full aftermath of the rail disaster and has supported the actions of victims and local committees since 2013. She was the Green Party's 2015 federal candidate for the riding Hochelaga-Maisonneuve.

THE LAC-MÉGANTIC VICTIMS

So that they may never be forgotten ...

Alyssa Charest Bégnoche, age 4
Bianka Charest Bégnoche, age 9
Talitha Coumi Bégnoche, age 30
Élodie Turcotte, age 18
Frédéric Boutin, age 19
Jo-Annie Lapointe, age 20
Marie-Sémie Alliance, age 22
Marianne Poulin, age 23
Kathy Clusiault, age 25
Andrée-Anne Sévigny, age 26
Maxime Dubois, age 27
David Lacroix-Beaudoin, age 27
Geneviève Breton, age 28
Éric Pépin-Lajeunesse, age 28
Mélissa Roy, age 29
Kevin Roy, age 29
Joanie Turmel, age 29
Mathieu Pelletier, age 29
Jimmy Sirois, age 30
Jean-Guy Veilleux, age 32
Michel Guertin Jr, age 33
Gaétan Lafontaine, age 34
Karine Lafontaine, age 35
Yannick Bouchard, age 36
Marie-Noëlle Faucher, age 36
Karine Champagne, age 36
David Martin, age 36
Stéphane Bolduc, age 37
Natachat Gaudreau, age 41

Guy Bolduc, age 43
Stéphane Lapierre, age 45
Diane Bizier, age 46
Martin Rodrigue, age 48
Lucie Vadnais, age 49
Sylvie Charron, age 50
Yves Boulet, age 51
Jean-Pierre Roy, age 52
Denise Dubois, age 57
Réal Custeau, age 57
Henriette Latulippe, age 61
Roger Paquet, age 61
Marie-France Boulet, age 62
Richard Veilleux, age 63
Jacques Giroux, age 65
Louisette Poirier, age 76
Wilfrid Ratsch, age 77
Éliane Parenteau-Boulanger, age 93

Also ...
Kevin Morin, a young firefighter
Yvon Ricard, a musician

*And others, whose families
preferred that their names be
withheld ...*

© 2018 Anne-Marie Saint-Cerny
© 2018 Écosociété
Foreword © 2018 André Noël
Translation © 2020 W. Donald Wilson

All rights reserved. No part of this book may be reproduced, stored in a retrieval system, or transmitted, in any form or by any means, without the prior written consent of the publisher or a licence from Access Copyright (The Canadian Copyright Licensing Agency). For a copyright licence, visit accesscopyright.ca or call toll-free 1-800-893-5777.

Talonbooks
9259 Shaughnessy Street, Vancouver, British Columbia, Canada V6P 6R4
talonbooks.com

Talonbooks is located on xʷməθkʷəy̓əm, Sḵwx̱wú7mesh, and səl̓ilwətaʔɬ Lands.

First printing: 2020
Typeset in Minion
Printed and bound in Canada on 100% post-consumer recycled paper

Interior and cover design by Typesmith
Cover photo *Tanker Cars* by Shauni via istockphoto.com

Talonbooks acknowledges the financial support of the Canada Council for the Arts, the Government of Canada through the Canada Book Fund, and the Province of British Columbia through the British Columbia Arts Council and the Book Publishing Tax Credit.

This work was originally published in French as *Mégantic: Une tragédie annoncée* by Écosociété, Montréal, Québec, in 2018. We acknowledge the financial support of the Government of Canada through the National Translation Program for Book Publishing, an initiative of the *Roadmap for Canada's Official Languages 2013–2018: Education, Immigration, Communities*, for our translation activities.

Library and Archives Canada Cataloguing in Publication

Title: Mégantic : a deadly mix of oil, rail, and avarice / Anne-Marie Saint-Cerny ; translated by W. Donald Wilson ; with a foreword by André Noël.
Other titles: Mégantic. English
Names: Saint-Cerny, Anne-Marie, 1954– author.
Description: Translation of: Mégantic : une tragédie annoncée. | Includes bibliographical references.
Identifiers: Canadiana 2020022283X | ISBN 9781772012590 (softcover)
Subjects: LCSH: Lac-Mégantic Derailment, Lac-Mégantic, Québec, 2013. | LCSH: Railroad accidents—Québec (Province)—Lac-Mégantic. | LCSH: Disaster victims—Québec (Province)—Lac-Mégantic.
Classification: LCC HE1783.C3 S2513 2020 | DDC 363.12/20971469—dc23

MÉGANTIC

A DEADLY MIX OF OIL, RAIL, AND AVARICE

ANNE-MARIE SAINT-CERNY

Translated by W. Donald Wilson

WITH A FOREWORD BY ANDRÉ NOËL

Talonbooks

LONDON PUBLIC LIBRARY

ADVANCED PRAISE FOR MÉGANTIC

"Required reading."
——Marie-Louise Arsenault, Radio-Canada Première

"In this well-documented book, the reader will discover the concealed motives of a greedy and politically well-protected industry whose quest for profit at any cost retains the smell of burnt flesh and human sacrifice – this is neoliberal capitalism, where collateral damage continues to make innocent victims."
——Coalition des citoyens et organismes engagés pour la sécurité ferroviaire de Lac-Mégantic (Lac-Mégantic coalition of citizens and organizations for railway safety)

"Drawing on eloquent testimonies and solid analyses, Saint-Cerny not only takes a look at the questions that have arisen since this railway disaster, but also goes deep, with infinite respect, by listening and giving voice to the women and men who survived Mégantic."
——CSN (Québec's Confédération des syndicats nationaux)

D0896736